Child
Maltreatment

A Handbook for Mental Health
and Child Care Professionals

Arthur H. Green, M.D.

Associate Clinical Professor of Psychiatry
Downstate Medical Center

Lecturer in Psychiatry
College of Physicians and Surgeons
Columbia University

Director, Columbia-Presbyterian
Family Center
Babies Hospital

NEW YORK • JASON ARONSON • LONDON

ISBN: 0-87668-420-7

Library of Congress Catalog Number: 80-66923

Manufactured in the United States of America.

Child
Maltreatment

Contents

Part III
Treatment and Prevention

Part IV
Other Aspects of Maltreatment

Foreword

Dr. Arthur Green is a distinguished and experienced child psychiatrist and psychoanalyst who has devoted his academic career to understanding and treating the problems of child abuse. He has come to this understanding through an optimal combination of intensive clinical work (with both abused children and their parents) and systematic and objective research. In the present book Dr. Green summarizes the product of this experience, adding a broad and scholarly knowledge of research findings and disciplines ranging from sociology to developmental psychology.

Dr. Green invokes a psychoanalytic model to describe the interaction of current and past experience which leads to child abuse or neglect. However, his explanations are at all times lucid, alive, and jargon-free, so that a reader wedded to learning or systems theory will have little difficulty recognizing and being enlightened by the descriptions of abnormal psychological sequences and mechanisms. One of the most striking achievements of this book is the way in which clinical examples are coupled with dynamic explanation. The skillful match of clinical detail with conceptual generalization eases the process of applying the author's observations to the reader's own clinical experience.

The sections on treatment are broad in scope and oriented to practice. They provide guidance in a wide range of treatment activities, from the purely psychological transactions in therapy with both parents and children to clear descriptions of the legal and administrative procedures that may involve the professional. A particularly useful section provides guidance on the establishment of a comprehensive child abuse unit within a hospital setting.

Professionals from many different disciplines are called upon to assist abused children and their families. Because of its clear style and comprehensive scope, all should be helped by this book.

> David Shaffer, M.D.
> Professor and Chairman
> Department of Child Psychiatry
> Columbia University
> College of Physicians and Surgeons

Acknowledgments

A significant portion of this book is based on child abuse research and multidisciplinary treatment carried out at the Brooklyn Family Center within the Division of Child and Adolescent Psychiatry at the Downstate Medical Center. I am indebted to my coinvestigators in research – Dr. Alice Sandgrund, Mr. Richard Gaines, and Dr. Henry Haberfeld – and the members of our treatment staff, who displayed unusual dedication, sensitivity, and perseverance in their therapeutic contact with maltreated children and their families. The treatment staff included Mr. Ernest Power, Ms. Elizabeth Spiegel, Mrs. Barbara Steinbook, Ms. Elaine Boccemeni, and Ms. Jean Stauffer. Dr. Sandgrund and Mr. Gaines also participated in the treatment program. I am also appreciative of the important contributions of Mr. Power and Ms. Spiegel in their supervision of social work students from the Columbia University School of

Social Work, and of Ms. Arlene Hurwitz, Ms. Barbara Thomas, Ms. Lillian Reid, and Ms. Robin Zablow of the faculty of the College of Nursing, who instructed the senior nursing student volunteers. The social work and nursing students themselves made important contributions to our program. The social work students had major casework responsibilities, and participated in counseling and psychotherapy. The nursing students provided the families with home visiting and parenting education. I would also like to thank the numerous child psychiatry fellows and psychiatric residents for their involvement in the treatment of our families. A final word of appreciation is reserved for Ms. Naomi Fein and Ms. Gloria Hunter for their devotion to our families, devotion which extended far beyond their secretarial and administrative duties.

PART I

Introduction to
the Problem

1

Introduction

The main objective of this book is to provide the reader a dynamic understanding of the many facets of child maltreatment and to outline appropriate strategies for its prevention and treatment based on this knowledge. Child abuse will be defined and demographic data presented to illustrate the scope of the problem. An overview of the legal aspects of child abuse – including, in New York State, mandatory reporting, investigation, and supervision of child-abusing families – will be included. The major etiological factors in child abuse will be described: the characteristics of abusing parents which impede their capacity for child rearing, the contributions of the child to his scapegoating and abuse, and the environmental factors which exacerbate and perpetuate the child abuse syndrome. Crucial psychodynamic issues underlying this type of pathological family interaction will be explored, as well as the impact of abuse on the behavior and psychological functioning of the children. The elaboration of a conceptual model for the child abuse syndrome based on an understanding of its basic components will offer a rationale for the comprehensive treatment of the abused children and their families.

The material in this book is based on the author's extensive clinical and research experience with abused children and their families at the Downstate Medical Center, as well as on the recent literature on child maltreatment.

Definition of Child Abuse and Neglect

The definition of child abuse has been continually expanding in recent years. In a classic paper, "The Battered Child Syndrome," Kempe and his collaborators (1962) described child abuse as the infliction of serious injury upon young children by parents and caretakers. The injuries, which included fractures, subdural hematoma, and multiple soft tissue injuries, often resulted in permanent disability and death. Fontana's concept of the "maltreatment syndrome" (1964) included child abuse at one end of a spectrum of maltreatment which also included emotional deprivation, neglect, and malnutrition. Helfer (1975) recognized the prevalence of minor injuries resulting from abuse and suspected that abuse might be implicated in 10 percent of all childhood accidents treated in emergency rooms. Gil (1974) extended the concept of child abuse to include any action which prevents a child from achieving his physical and psychological potential.

In this book, *child abuse* will refer to the nonaccidental physical injury inflicted on a child by a parent or guardian, and will encompass the total range of physical injury. Child abuse will be differentiated from child neglect, and the term *maltreatment* will be used as a general reference to both abuse and neglect. The terms *child abuse* and *child neglect*, based on the legal definitions stated in the New York State Child Protective Services Act of 1973, will be used as follows:

Definition of child abuse. An "abused child" is a child under sixteen years of age whose parent or other person legally responsible for his care:

1. inflicts or allows to be inflicted upon the child serious physical injury, or
2. creates or allows to be created a substantial risk of serious injury, or
3. commits or allows to be committed against the child an act of sexual abuse as defined in the penal law.

Definition of child neglect. A "neglected child" is a child, under 18 years of age, impaired as a result of the failure of his parent or other person legally responsible for his care to exercise a minimum degree of care:

1. in supplying the child with adequate food, clothing, shelter, education, medical or surgical care, though financially able to do so or offered financial or other reasonable means to do so, or
2. in providing the child with proper supervision or guardianship, or
3. by reasonably inflicting or allowing to be inflicted harm or a substantial risk thereof, including the infliction of excessive corporal punishment, or
4. by using a drug or drugs, or
5. by using alcoholic beverages to the extent that he loses self-control of his actions, or
6. by any other acts of a similarly serious nature requiring the aid of the family court.

A child is also to be considered maltreated when, under 18 years of age, he has been abandoned by his parents (or whoever else is legally responsible for his care).

Detection of Child Abuse

The possibility of child abuse must be considered in every child who presents with an injury. A careful history and physical evaluation of the child are warranted when one suspects physical abuse. The physical examination should include a routine X-ray survey of all children under five and laboratory tests to rule out the possibility of an abnormal bleeding tendency. The child, of course, should be hospitalized during this diagnostic evaluation.

While there is no single physical finding or diagnostic procedure which can confirm the diagnosis of child abuse with absolute certainty, the presence of some of the following signs and symptoms derived from the history taking and physical examination is suggestive of an inflicted injury:

History
1. Unexplained delay in bringing the child for treatment following the injury.
2. History is implausible or contradictory.
3. History is incompatible with the physical findings.
4. There is a history of repeated suspicious injuries.
5. The parent blames the injury on a sibling or a third party.
6. The parent maintains that the injury was self-inflicted.
7. The child had been taken to numerous hospitals for the treatment of injuries (hospital "shopping").
8. The child accuses the parent or caretaker of injuring him.
9. The parent has a history of abuse as a child.
10. The parent has unrealistic and premature expectations of the child.

Physical Findings
1. Pathognomonic "typical" injuries commonly associated with physical punishment, such as bruises on the buttocks and lower back; bruises in the genital area or inner thigh may be inflicted after the child wets or soils, or is resistant to toilet training. Bruises and soft tissue injuries at different stages of healing are signs of repeated physical abuse. Bruises of a special configuration such as hand marks, grab marks, pinch marks, and strap marks usually indicate abuse.
2. Certain types of burns are typically inflicted, i.e., multiple cigarette burns, scalding of hands or feet, burns of perineum and buttocks.

3. Abdominal trauma leading to a ruptured liver or spleen.
4. Subdural hematoma with or without skull fracture.
5. Radiologic signs, such as subperiosteal hemorrhages, epiphyseal separations, metaphyseal fragmentation, periosteal shearing, and periosteal calcifications.

Scope of the Problem

The classic description of "the battered child syndrome" by Kempe and his associates in 1962 stimulated nationwide interest in child abuse, which soon became recognized as a major pediatric problem. Between 1963 and 1965 the passage of laws by all fifty states requiring medical reporting of all suspected cases of child abuse led to the formation of child protective services throughout the country. Abusing parents were subjected to investigation and legal process, and the first psychological studies of abusing parents were finally carried out during this period. Improved reporting procedures have demonstrated the true magnitude of this problem. The child abuse law in New York State became effective on July 1, 1964. During the first twelve-month period, 313 cases of child abuse were reported in New York City with 16 deaths. The latest New York City statistics (1978) indicate that 6,442 were reported with 74 deaths. An additional 19,865 children were reported to be neglected. The twentyfold increase in reported cases of child abuse over a thirteen-year period undoubtedly reflects an improvement in reporting procedures as well as an absolute increase in the incidence of child abuse. Yet, since according to most experts in this field there are 15 to 20 actual cases of child abuse for each one reported, the statistics show only the "tip of the iceberg." A recent article by Light (1973) estimated an annual nationwide incidence of 200,000 to 500,000, with 1,500,000 cases of maltreatment if severe neglect and sexual abuse are included. This figure is approximately equivalent to an estimate by Mr. Douglas Besharov, director of The National Center of Child Abuse and Neglect. Besharov indicated that 1,600,000 cases of child abuse and neglect occur each year with 2,000 to 4,000 deaths (1975).

Maltreatment is currently regarded as the leading cause of death in children and is a major public health problem. The proliferation of child abuse and neglect might bear some relationship to the alarming general increase in violence in our society, an increase reflected in the rising incidence of violent crimes, delinquency, suicide, and lethal accidents.

Traditional Disregard of Children's Rights

Viewed in historical perspective, the recent initiation of child abuse reporting laws and a child protective movement in this country and others represents a significant shift in the balance of rights between the child and his parents. In the ancient civilizations of the Hebrews, Greeks, and Romans, children were expendable and had no rights under prevailing law. For example, under Roman law family relationships were governed by the doctrine of *patria potestas,* which granted the father unlimited power over his wives and unmarried children. The *paterfamilias,* the oldest living male ancestor, possessed the right to kill unwanted, deformed, or rebellious children. Infanticide was widely practiced and children could be sold as property. These ancient concepts of paternal absolutism reflected the importance of the family as an indispensable social and economic unit. Whenever families experienced adverse environmental conditions, children's basic needs were routinely subordinated to the welfare of the larger adult society. Under early English law, infanticide was condoned and children could be sold in times of poverty. The Elizabethan Poor Laws ordained that the children of the poor be separated from their parents and put to work. The Factory Acts legislated during the Industrial Revolution enabled parents to contract their children to workhouses and factories and to collect their wages. Children were cruelly chained to machines and forced to work long hours under inhumane conditions. These English attitudes toward family relationships were exported to America during the period of colonization. In 1628 the colony of Massachusetts adopted the Stubborn Child Act, under which a rebellious son could be put to death. In 1874 the American courts first protected a child from cruel and inhumane treatment. The child, Maryellen, was represented in court by attorneys from the Society for the Prevention of Cruelty to Animals, because there were no agencies representing the interests of children at the time. In this century, the growth of the juvenile courts provided an atmosphere within which the problems of children could be managed outside the criminal courts. Eventually the jurisdiction of these courts was extended into the area of abuse and neglect.

Today in America, parents still retain the right to raise children in the manner they see fit. Parents maintain the rights of care, custody, and control over their children, and it is assumed that parents act in the best interests of their children. Children's rights begin only when parental behavior falls below an acceptable minimum and the child's life or health is seriously threatened. From birth until the age of six, when he enters school, the American child depends upon his parents for the identification and satisfaction of his needs. During these formative years he has no access to society. In several European countries, child health visitors regularly assess the development of preschool children in the home, and are able to provide families with counseling regarding infant and child care. In this country and in others, the predominance of parental rights over those of children has undoubtedly contributed to the long delay in identifying and dealing with the problem of maltreatment.

Medicine's Avoidance of the Problem

Medical investigation of the child abuse syndrome did not occur until the 1940s and 1950s, when diagnostic criteria for physical abuse in children were established through the pioneering efforts of radiologists and pediatricians (Caffey 1946, Silverman 1953, Wooley and Evans 1955). Medicine's belated involvement with child abuse was the reflection of a larger societal avoidance of the problem. Despite compelling medical evidence, physicians were reluctant to believe that parents were capable of inflicting serious injury on their children. We might well ponder the reasons for this turning away. As physicians and parents we feel angry and outraged as we empathize with the innocent, helpless, abused children. At the same time, however, our more repressed and largely unconscious identification with the abusing parents causes us considerable guilt, as most of us have occasionally experienced the urge to injure or destroy a child or loved one. When finally confronted with frank and obvious maltreatment, we tend to self-righteously attack the perpetrators, who evoke our own unacceptable emotions.

Intervention

Unfortunately, the capacity of most communities to provide services to maltreating families lagged far behind the rapid increase in reports of abuse and neglect. As a result, protective services caseworkers found themselves overwhelmed with many more cases of maltreatment than they could adequately handle. In addition, they had no resources to provide these families meaningful rehabilitation. It was easier for them to place large numbers of maltreated children in foster homes or institutions in order to guarantee their safety, without fully appreciating the negative impact on both parents and children. In addition to providing an expedient solution to harassed workers with bulging caseloads, the termination of parental rights represented the expression of society's underlying anger and outrage toward the abusers. Perhaps no other group has mobilized such strong emotions in the professionals who deal with them: anger and revulsion toward the parents, pity and sadness for the children. Aroused, the news media depicted these newly discovered child abusers as cold-blooded sadists and murderers who deserved criminal punishment rather than compassionate intervention. Many of the new child advocates proceeded with missionary zeal in their attempts to undo centuries of parental absolutism and restore the rights of maltreated children. But in the process of rescuing the children, the needs of the parents were compromised. The balance of rights shifted significantly away from the parents and toward the children. The immediate impact of this policy seemed positive. After centuries of victimization, children's rights could finally be enforced by law. Maltreated children could be placed in a safe and nurturant environment where they could grow up normally, the abusers would be rightfully punished, and the child advocates could enjoy their sense of accomplishment. However, these rescue fantasies became tarnished with the passage of time. The maltreated children often adjusted poorly to foster care and institutionalization, and many required multiple placements. The natural parents, depressed and bereft of services, proceeded to replace the "lost" children with new offspring. Psychological studies of maltreating parents revealed that many were desperately lonely, isolated individuals who had been victimized during their own childhood and struck out at their children during times of crisis and despair. Most of them responded positively to supportive types of intervention designed to strengthen their parenting. It had become evident that successful intervention in the case of child maltreatment must be unbiased, evenhanded, and geared toward safeguarding the rights of both parent and child. Overidentification with one at the expense of the other will only distort the true perception of the complex parent-child interaction taking place and will interfere with rational decision making.

Reporting Laws

During the 1970s the first child abuse and neglect programs were developed in various parts of the country to provide identification of child abuse and neglect and therapeutic intervention with maltreating families (Holmes 1977). These programs have been based in hospitals, nonprofit agencies, public social service agencies, and communities. On January 31, 1974, the Child Abuse Prevention and Treatment Act (P.L. 95-247) was signed into law, establishing a National Center on Child Abuse and Neglect within the Children's Bureau of the Office of Child Development. This center has been involved in public education, awarding grants to states for the improvement of their child protective services, and giving demonstration and research grants designed to improve the identification, prevention, and treatment of child abuse and neglect.

Psychiatry's Role in Child Abuse

This heightened preoccupation with child maltreatment on national and local levels attracted the attention of professionals from widely divergent backgrounds. Contributions to the field of child maltreatment have come from pediatrics, psychiatry, psychology, social work, sociology, nursing, education, law, and law enforcement. This multidisciplinary involvement has been essential in case finding, investigation, medical treatment, protective intervention, and long-term planning with the families. However, it has also become a source of confusion because of the differing roles, frames of reference, and traditions of each specialty. Unfortunately, the involvement of psychiatrists in the area of child abuse has lagged behind the contributions of other professionals, such as pediatricians, social workers, and nurses. Not until the late 1960s did psychiatrists (Galdston 1965, Steele and Pollock 1968, Silver 1968) begin to contribute to the already sizeable literature on child maltreatment. Treatment programs for maltreating families, whether hospital, agency, or community based, were rarely located in a psychiatric facility or directed by psychiatrists. Many of these programs have experienced difficulty in inducing psychiatrists in their communities to accept consultations and referrals with maltreated children or their parents. Child abuse research sponsored by the National Center has largely been carried out by nonpsychiatrists.

This rather puzzling lack of interest by psychiatrists and other mental health specialists in the area of child abuse and neglect, although complex in origin, can be readily explained. Child abuse was initially conceptualized as a medical and legal problem. The original emphasis on medical detection, medical treatment, protection of the child, and punishment of the perpetrators was not conducive to psychiatric intervention. Abusing parents elicited feelings of anger and revulsion and were usually felt to be untreatable because of their hostility, impulsivity, and lack of trust. "Treatment" often consists of criminal prosecution leading to termination of parental rights. The low incidence of psychosis among abusing parents cited by early investigators (Kempe et al. 1962, Steele and Pollock 1968) was often used as evidence for the lack of psychiatric disturbance. The abusing and neglecting parents often required a wide variety of outreach and basic social services, such as homemakers, housing, day care, and financial assistance on an emergency basis which seemed more urgent than psychological interventions. Their energies were absorbed by issues of day to day survival, with little remaining to invest in psychological interventions which seemed irrelevant. This over-representation of poor disorganized families among those reported for maltreatment remained an anathema to "middle-class" clinicians trained to treat "middle-class" motivated and psychologically sophisticated patients.

Abusing parents rarely seek help on their own. They are usually referred by protective service agencies or the courts. In some cases psychiatric treatment is made a condition of probation. Most abusing parents lack insight and motivation, and are unwilling to accept a "psychiatric" label. They frequently miss appointments which interfere with the treatment process and immobilizes staff. Psychiatrists are also accustomed to operating under conditions of confidentiality and working in isolation with their patients. The probability of having to testify in court seems incompatible with this ideal. They have difficulty in sharing their authority and decision-making role with other individuals and agencies who have the ultimate responsibility for the patient's fate. When psychiatrists have intervened, their therapeutic efforts often proved unsuccessful because of their failure to adapt traditional outpatient psychiatric techniques to the special needs of this difficult population. This lack of success has been used by some to rationalize psychiatry's posture of aloofness and pessimism, thus creating a self-fulfilling prophecy. In multidisciplinary treatment programs, such as those at the University of Colorado Medical Center, the Children's Hospital Medical Center in Boston, the New York Foundling Hospital, and the Downstate Medical Center in Brooklyn, intervention by mental health professionals with abusing and neglecting families has met with considerable success.

While psychiatric intervention with maltreating parents has been limited to a handful of centers throughout the country, treatment facilities for abused and neglected children have yet to be developed. Despite the striking cognitive, developmental, neurological, and emotional impairment observed in these children, there has been an appalling absence of programs offering them psychotherapy or psychoeducational rehabilitation.

Since the study of child maltreatment is in its infancy, the development of effective methods of prevention and intervention depends heavily upon the accumulation of new knowledge about causes of maltreatment and the exact nature of the complex patterns of family and caretaker-child interaction which culminate in physical and sexual abuse, neglect, and failure to thrive of children. This requires multidisciplinary involvement in clinical investigation and research by professionals concerned with parenting, family process, and child care. This book will deal with the impact of recent research findings on current techniques for the prevention and treatment of child abuse and neglect, with one chapter devoted to the latest research in this field. Many of these studies were supported by the National Center for Child Abuse and Neglect.

The author hopes that this book will stimulate mental-health and child-care professionals to respond to the urgent challenges posed by the rising incidence of maltreatment and family violence. Their greater participation in the study, treatment, and prevention of child abuse and neglect should have a beneficial impact on the current and future generations of parents and children.

2

Normal Parenting and Attachment Behavior

The attachment of the mother to her infant is a strong, specific affectional bond that enables the mother to fondle, nurture, comfort, and protect her infant. The actual process of attachment is not completely understood, but may begin with the planning and confirmation of the pregnancy, continue with the perception of the fetus as a separate individual, and culminate in visual and tactile contact with the neonate which proceeds to caretaking and nurturant activity. Earlier influences on maternal behavior, however, are exerted during infancy and childhood through the child-rearing practices of the mother's parents or caretakers. Attitudes and fantasies about babies and child rearing can be traced from one developmental stage to the next as the little girl matures.

After the birth of the baby, the mother-infant attachment or bonding is accompanied by a reciprocal attachment by the infant to its mother by such maneuvers as clinging, smiling, following, crying, and looking (Bowlby 1958).

Preparation for motherhood involves a complex interplay among biological, psychological, cultural, and environmental factors. Freud's theories of infantile sexuality, psychoanalytic object-relations theory (Jacobson 1964, Mahler 1968, Kernberg 1976), and Benedek's studies of mothering and motherliness (1949, 1970) provide a framework for understanding the psychology of maternal behavior. The impact of the various stages of development on the evolution of maternal behavior will be outlined.

Preoedipal Period

The earliest influences on maternal behavior are exerted during infancy and childhood. Early experiences of being nurtured and having dependency needs gratified during the symbiotic relationship with one's own mother generate confidence and "basic trust" in the infant. The infant associates feelings of gratification with mother and mothering. The quality of the infant's relationship with her mother will influence the first self-object representations and their closely linked affects. If gratification predominates, the resulting memory traces of a "good" mother/"good" self dyad will facilitate the baby girl's positive identification with her mother and the development of new object relationships. On the other hand, if the earliest childhood experiences have been largely traumatic and frustrating, early perceptions of a "bad" mother/"bad" self-image might form the nucleus for negative identifications with mother and mothering. The little girl's primary identification with her mother, her corresponding self-image, and the prevailing affective state will have an important impact on the way she will behave with her own child in the next generation.

Phallic and Oedipal Phases

The phallic and oedipal phases of psychosexual development are the next important periods in the preparation for motherhood. Between the ages of three and seven little girls display an increased interest and awareness of their genitals and become curious about anatomical differences between the sexes. Masturbation is commonly observed. Some girls experience rather intense "penis envy," which results in anger toward their mothers. They turn toward their fathers for affection, and display fantasies of "marrying daddy" and having his baby. At this time, little girls are often intensely involved in "mothering" play with their "doll babies." Normally girls renounce their wish for exclusive possession of their fathers because they fear retaliation and abandonment by their mothers. The oedipal period for girls terminates with the consolidation of female gender identity based upon identification with the mother. Pathological resolution of the oedipal conflict may result in difficulties in subsequent sexual identity, sexual behavior, and maternal capacity. For example, oedipal fixations might result in impairment of adult heterosexual behavior because of the unconscious link between sexuality and incestuous impulses toward the father. Identification with the mother will be impaired if she is viewed as destructive and castrating. Unresolved penis envy might result in the devaluation of a female infant, or a seductive, narcissistic involvement with a baby boy.

Latency

The latency period (ages seven to ten) is characterized by a relative diminution of sexual impulses, with a corresponding rapid growth of ego defenses and intellectual functions. Sexual fantasies are subjected to repression and sublimation through the influence of a rapidly developing superego, but are expressed indirectly through spontaneous play with dolls and preoccupation with romantic stories and daydreams. Maternal behavior, based upon an identification with one's own mother, may be revealed more directly in playing with dolls, pets, and young siblings.

Puberty and Adolescence

During puberty and adolescence the girl's identification with her mother is enhanced by maturational and hormonal changes which provide her with the potential for actual child rearing and motherhood. The hormonal influence of the menstrual cycle on the development of motherliness has been described by Benedek (1973). High progesterone levels during the lutein phase of the cycle are thought to be associated with introversion and the intensification of receptive and retentive thoughts and fantasies, representing a psychological preparation for pregnancy, in contrast to the more assertive, object-directed influence of estrogens during the initial phase of the cycle prior to ovulation. Many emotionally deprived teenage girls act out their fantasies of having a baby by becoming pregnant. They vicariously identify with the baby's need for love and nurturance, and often manage to reinvolve their own mothers in caring for their babies and themselves.

Pregnancy

During pregnancy, the high levels of progesterone secretion further intensify receptive and retentive tendencies. Pregnancy is also characterized by increased psychological dependency, a heightened narcissism, and a tendency toward regression. During the first trimester, the woman's major task is the acceptance of her pregnancy. According to Bibring (1961), at first the mother identifies the growing fetus as an integral part of herself. Her perception of the fetus changes after the onset of quickening, the sensation of fetal movements helping her regard the fetus as a separate individual. She begins to develop feelings of attachment, which may be expressed by the active preparation for the baby's arrival. Planning the baby's room and the purchase of baby clothing and a crib indicate some degree of acceptance of the baby and the caretaking role by the mother. Bibring et al. (1961) regard pregnancy as a normal maturational crisis which is resolved when the mother gradually gives up her narcissistic separate object. Brazelton (1973) views the numerous anxieties and psychological upheavals during pregnancy as a means of enhancing her attachment to the baby. Kennell et al. (1970) regard the presence of mourning in mothers following the death of their newborns as evidence of this prenatal attachment. The mother's current relationships with spouse and family, as well as the stability of her immediate environment, also have an important impact on the attachment process during the pregnancy. Disruptive influences such as marital friction, death or separation from important love objects, or moving to another geographical area may weaken the attachment process by causing the mother to feel isolated, unsupported, and incapable of caring for the baby.

Childbirth

The precise impact of childbirth on maternal attachment has yet to be determined. However, some of the traditional obstetrical practices may have a detrimental effect upon the establishment of the mother-infant bond. For example, the depressant impact of anesthesia on maternal and infant responsivity, and the mother's isolation from her spouse and family during labor and delivery, would seem to interfere with the natural course of attachment. Klaus and Kennel (1976) described certain advantages, for both mother and neonate, of home births attended by midwives. The mother remains in control as an active participant. She appears to be in a state of ecstasy immediately after birth, and breastfeeding starts within five to six minutes, beginning with prolonged licking by the infant. The mother's exuberance is shared by the other family members and observers, who become more attached to the infant than the members of the family not witnessing the birth. Natural childbirth in a hospital setting may similarly improve mother to infant attachment. The same authors describe natural childbirth in Guatemala, where a supportive woman stays with the expectant mother during labor and birth. These mothers experience less crying and shorter labors than unattended mothers, and are able to leave the hospital after one or two days to take over full care of their babies.

Postpartum Period

After delivery the interruption of the mother-fetus symbiosis is experienced by the mother as a loss of part of herself and contributes to the typical depressive affect widely observed during the postpartum period. The mother's immediate psychological task consists of transferring her "self-love," which encompassed the fetus, to the baby as a separate individual. This shift is accompanied by a transformation of passive, receptive tendencies into active, giving impulses. Satisfaction of the mother's dependency needs facilitates her capacity for nurturing the infant. She is therefore extremely dependent on her immediate environment. The lack of spouse or family support, or the unresponsiveness of the infant, will tend to perpetuate the usually transitory postpartum depressive state, which in turn might increase the mother's doubts about her ability to care for her new infant. Maternal attachment is also facilitated at this time by the production of the hormone prolactin during lactation, and by the mother's identification with the nurturing behavior of her own mother.

Kennell et al. (1974) and Klaus and Kennell (1970) stressed the importance of the early postpartum period for the development of attachment behavior. They postulated the presence of a maternal sensitive period immediately after childbirth during which complex interactions between mother and infant foster a strong mother-infant bonding. Their theory is based upon observations in animals and humans which demonstrate abnormalities in maternal behavior following a period of separation shortly after delivery. In sheep and goats, separation of the mother from her offspring causes her to butt the infants away and refuse to allow nursing when they are reunited. In humans, Klaus and Kennell observed that minor problems in the neonate which resulted in separation from the mother disturbed the latter's attachment behavior. They felt that these disturbances could last throughout childhood. They carried out a study comparing attachment behavior in normal mother-infant pairs provided with "early and extended contact" and with regular hospital contact. The "extended-contact" mothers were given their babies for one hour after delivery and for five extra hours during the next three postpartum days, while the control mothers followed the usual hospital routine which permitted them to feed and handle the baby every four hours. The extended contact mothers exhibited greater resistance to separation, more soothing, fondling, and eye contact, and more affectionate behavior toward their babies at one month and one year. At two years, the extended contact mothers used more descriptive language, asked more questions, and issued fewer commands than the controls. At five years of age, the extended contact children manifested significantly higher IQs and language performance. Leifer et al. (1972) observed that mothers who were allowed visual contact with their full-term infants during the two or three day postpartum hospitalization spent more time smiling at and holding their babies at four weeks than mothers of prematures who had been separated from their infants for three to twelve weeks following birth.

The documentation of improvement of maternal behavior during the rooming-in experience (McBryde 1951, Greenberg et al. 1973) is additional evidence for the importance of the early postpartum period for the mother-infant bond.

A number of researchers have explored the mechanisms by which the rapidly developing mother-infant bonding is accomplished during the postpartum period. Klaus and Kennell (1966) describe the reciprocal interaction between mother and infant which include simultaneously occurring behaviors which complement each other and bind the pair together.

Touch. Several observers (Rubin 1963, Klaus et al. 1970, and Lang 1972) have described a characteristic touching pattern used by mothers during their initial contact with their newborns, beginning with fingertip touching and proceeding to massaging, stroking, and palm contact. As the touching progressed, palm contact exceeded fingertip contact, with increasingly more touching of the infant's trunk than his extremities.

Eye-to-eye contact. Klaus et al. (1970) reported that 73 percent of the mothers in their study demonstrated a strong interest in waking the infant to see his eyes open. These mothers also showed an increase in the time spent in the en face position from the first to the fifth minute. The infant is capable of seeing at birth, and responds more readily to the human face than to inanimate objects. The infant's gaze seems to elicit maternal responses. A good example of how the visual interaction between mother and infant facilitates their mutual attachment is the infant's smiling response. During the second month, the infant will smile at the mother's face, or at any visual gestalt consisting of two eyes and a mouth shown en face. The infant's smile in response to his mother's face usually elicits a smiling response on her part.

Voice contact. The neonate attends to a female voice in preference to a male voice because of its higher pitch. Many mothers instinctively accommodate to the infant's selective auditory perception by speaking to it in a higher pitched voice than is used in ordinary conversation. In turn, the infant's cry apparently causes an increased amount of blood flow to the mother's breast, which facilitates nursing (Lind et al. 1973).

Entrainment. Observations by Condon and Sander (1974) revealed that the neonate's motor behavior is synchronized with the speech behavior of the adults in his environment. As the infant moves in rhythm to his mother's voice, this feedback stimulates the mother to continue her verbalization.

Hormonal stimulation. Serum prolactin levels of the mother increase after nursing and physical contact with the infant, which in turn stimulates milk secretion in the breasts. The infant's sucking at the mother's breast also causes the release of maternal oxytoxin which fosters uterine contractions and diminishes bleeding.

Maternal organizing function. The mother's establishment of a predictable schedule of caretaking based upon the rhythmic fluctuations in the infant's state and physiological requirements helps the infant reestablish the biorhythmicity which had been interrupted by the birth process. The mother who is sensitively attuned to her infant's needs can facilitate the development of regular sleep-wakefullness cycles and feeding patterns, reducing tension and discomfort. Normally there is a progressive increase in synchrony between mother and neonate during the first week, expressed by the increased time the infant is in the alert state while his mother is holding him. The unique responsiveness of the "alert" infant to the mother's eye contact, touch, and vocalization acts as a positive reinforcer for continued maternal attachment behavior, and enhances the mother's confidence and self-esteem. The poorly attached mother, on the other hand, is less sensitive to the changing states of her infant, and will be less effective in responding to him in an appropriate manner. Misreading the infant's cues may add to his distress and interfere with the development of physiological homeostasis. The irritable infant will, in turn, intensify the mother's ambivalence and self-doubt concerning her competency. A vicious cycle might ensue, in which a derailment occurs in the dialogue between mother and infant, leading to further asynchrony and impaired attachment.

Paternal Behavior

In our culture, the study of parenting and infant care has been largely limited to the interaction between mother and child. The lack of observations and research on the attachment between the infant and his father has reinforced the stereotype that fathers are essentially peripheral and unimportant in the process of raising infants and young children. Our need for a greater understanding of paternal behavior is obvious, since fathers or father surrogates account for approximately half of the reported cases of child abuse in the United States. Some recent studies have attempted to explore the father-infant attachment process.

Greenberg and Morris (1974) described the impact of the newborn on the father. They use the term *engrossment* to identify the father's strong absorption and preoccupation with the neonate. They observed the father's typical perception of the newborn as "perfect," with resulting feelings of elation and increased self-esteem.

Parke (1974) studied the behavior of fathers with their infants alone and in the triadic situation with the mother present. He was unable to find significant differences between fathers and mothers when they played with their infants alone.

When both parents were present, the fathers played a more active role. They held their infants nearly twice as much as the mother, and touched and spoke to them more frequently, though the mothers smiled at their infants more often than the fathers. These findings were demonstrated in both middle-class and lower-class families. Parke suggested that fathers should have extensive contact with their infants in the hospital during the formation of parent-infant bonding and be encouraged to participate more actively in baby care.

Additional research involving father-infant attachment and the fathering process in normal and pathological circumstances would be most useful to child-care professionals.

The following section will explore the etiology of patho-logical mother-infant attachment, and the major components of the child-abuse syndrome: the characteristics of the abusing parents, the children who become their victims, the environ-mental context in which the abuse takes place, and the develop-mental factors associated with the onset of abuse. The last chapter in this section will focus on the other common forms of maltreatment: neglect, sexual abuse, and failure to thrive.

PART II

The Abusing Family

3

Pathological Mother-Infant Attachment

Relationship Between Maltreatment and Disorders of Parent-Infant Bonding

Retrospective studies of abused, neglected, and failure to thrive children and their families revealed that the mothers often failed to exhibit the usual signs of attachment to these children when they were neonates. This bonding failure was associated with physical and emotional disturbances in the mother, a stressful environment during pregnancy and in the postpartum period, and certain abnormalities in the neonates, which often caused them to be separated from their mothers.

Maternal Deviancy

In many cases of maltreatment seen in our program, abnormalities in maternal attachment had been present during pregnancy and in the postpartum period. The maltreating mothers frequently felt overly stressed and undersupported and were fearful of not being able to provide their newborn with adequate care. Mothers who had been abused or severely deprived during their own childhod seemed reluctant to establish a bond with their infants because they feared traumatizing them in a similar manner. Their strong identification with violent parental models, and impending loss of impulse control, often led to a defensive withdrawal from their infants, endowed in turn with the negative characteristics of a despised spouse or parent. The psychological functioning of these mothers was brittle and they seemed to be on the brink of decompensating. Many of them manifested the postpartum depression described in mothers of maltreated and failure to thrive infants by other investigators (Ounsted 1974, Barbero et al. 1963, Leonard et al. 1966, Evans et al. 1972). Others demonstrated more paranoid responses. Several exhibited borderline or subnormal intelligence, which further undermined their maternal competency.

Severe Stress During Pregnancy and the Postpartum Period

All of the maltreating mothers in our program had experienced emotional trauma and environmental crises of severe proportions, which, in combination with the usual stresses of pregnancy and motherhood, impeded attachment behavior and maternal functioning. Typical stressful events included physical abuse or abandonment by a spouse, loss of emotional support by spouse or family, death of a close friend or relative, financial crises, and physical illness. The stresses seemed to exceed the mother's capacity to deal with them. The final impact of these crises left the mothers isolated, unsupported, unloved, and enraged. Since their own needs for nurturance were grossly unsatisfied, they had little or no love to give their infants. They often expected their babies to provide them with love and to confirm their motherliness by responding in a "perfect" manner.

Abnormalities in the Infant

A considerable proportion of the maltreated children seen in our program had demonstrated some physical or behavioral abnormality during infancy. Some of them were premature. Others were colicky and unresponsive, or cried excessively, or exhibited digestive disorders such as vomiting and diarrhea. Perinatal trauma was observed occasionally, associated with twin births, difficult labor, or maternal complications such as bleeding or infection. Similar abnormalities were described in maltreated infants by Ounsted (1974) and Lynch (1975). The high incidence of prematurity and low birth weight in abused children was reported by Klein and Stern (1971), Klaus and Kennel (1976), Lynch and Roberts (1977), and Herrenkohl and Herrenkohl (1979).

In our experience, abnormal infants interfere with maternal attachment in the following manner. First, they require special care, imposing an extra child-rearing burden on the parents. These infants often respond poorly and fail to exhibit reciprocal attachment behavior to effective mothers, thus creating or intensifying a sense of maternal inadequacy. Less adequate or "abuse-prone" mothers tend to interpret poor responsiveness as a willful gesture of defiance. The sick, deviant, malformed, or premature infant also may be regarded as a "defective" product by these mothers, which confirms their sense of inadequacy. They often withdraw from these infants in anticipation of their death or deformity, or to protect them from their anger. In cases of prematurity, the mother has less time available to prepare for childbirth and physical separation from the infant, which also might inhibit the bonding process.

Neonatal Separation and Maltreatment

Separation of the mother and neonate was a fairly common occurrence in cases of maltreatment which took place during infancy. Our case studies, however, could not confirm the primary importance of this separation during the "maternal sensitive period" in the genesis of bonding failure, as advocated by Klaus (1970) and Kennell (1974). In our mothers the maternal attachment process had been severely compromised before childbirth, because of traumatic events experienced during the pregnancy which, in turn, evoked early memories of having been abused and neglected in childhood. In many of these cases the postpartum separations and impaired attachment seemed to be the result of a previously determined maternal psychopathology and ambivalence, rather than the cause of the weakened attachment. The traumatized mothers often withdrew from their neonates, or placed them in the care of others, in order to protect them from their potential neglect or violence. Even when the postpartum separation was medically indicated because of premature birth, it only created an additional obstacle to the bonding process, which had already been disrupted. Thus it would appear that the separation of mother and neonate during the postpartum period is only one of the numerous factors which combine to disrupt the normal process of mother-infant bonding.

The following case vignettes demonstrate how the mothers' failures to effect a normal attachment with their infants during pregnancy and in the postpartum period were associated with various types of maltreatment. In each case the bonding failure had different antecedents and resulted in different types of maternal dysfunction.

Case 1. Kay H., a thirty-four-year-old mother of five children, came to our program because of uncontrollable resentment toward Victor, her twelve-year-old son. Victor, the second oldest of her children, had been scapegoated and neglected by Kay since birth. He was Kay's first child by her husband, Mr. H., who she subsequently divorced after a turbulent relationship in which she was frequently beaten up during their violent arguments. Victor was born prematurely after a seven-month gestation. Kay went into labor after Mr. H. forced her to have intercourse. She resented the pregnancy because the marriage had begun to deteriorate, but Mr. H. insisted on having a child. She tried to abort the fetus early in the pregnancy by pushing on her stomach. She "cringed" when Victor was placed on her abdomen immediately after the delivery and told the nurse to remove him. She recalled that Victor looked like a skeleton. Kay only visited Victor in the premature nursery once or twice a week, and with considerable guilt she confessed that she hoped he would die. Victor was a sickly infant. Besides his slow development, he contracted a persistent diarrhea which resulted in loss of weight. At five months he weighed only five pounds. Kay perceived Victor as being different from other children. He seemed unresponsive and cranky when she attempted to pick him up and cuddle him. He began to remind her of her husband more and more. She left him alone except for feedings, and only brought him out of his room when Mr. H. came home from work. She was further irritated by Victor's slow acquisition of speech and motor skills. He walked after he was two and spoke at age four. Although toilet trained by two and a half, he remained enuretic until he was eleven.

Kay experienced a traumatic childhood herself. She was the fourth of five children. She went to live with an older married sister at the age of five after her mother was hospitalized for psychotic behavior and didn't see her mother again for five years. Her sister turned out to be promiscuous and tried to get her sexually involved with numerous men that she brought to the apartment. Kay ran away from the sister's home at the age of fourteen after the sister's husband tried to rape her. After spending a year in a residential center for girls, she lived with different older sisters and began to do factory work. She became pregnant at nineteen by a man she had dated for a year, and expected him to marry her. When he refused, Kay left him and met Mr. H., who agreed to marry her in order to "give the baby a name" and spare her the shame of having an out-of-wedlock child. However, Mr. H. almost immediately began to taunt and humiliate Kay about the pregnancy and engaged in physical cruelty which persisted until the couple separated six years later, after having Victor and three daughters of their own. Mr. H.'s violence extended to Victor and his older brother, whom he frequently beat. Kay's awareness of Victor's mistreatment by Mr. H., in addition to her own neglect, causes her great concern, but she feels unable to alter her persistent rejection of the child.

Case 2. Mary R., a twenty-eight-year-old married woman, was admitted to the psychiatric hospital one month after the birth of her first baby. She had become increasingly withdrawn, tearful, and lethargic since the baby's birth, and feared that she would hurt the baby by dropping or hitting it. According to her husband, she had been unable to feed or care for the baby, delegating these responsibilities to him. Mary appeared to be quite limited intellectually, and initial psychological testing revealed an IQ of 60. During Mary's hospitalization, Mr. R. abused the infant, which caused it to be placed in a foster home. Upon hearing the news, Mary became elated and her depression lifted quite dramatically. After her discharge from the hospital, she was followed as an outpatient at our clinic. Whenever Mr. R. expressed an interest in regaining custody of the baby, Mary would become extremely anxious and withdraw in her room.

Mary's early childhood was chaotic and turbulent due to her mother's chronic schizophrenic illness, for which she required numerous hospitalizations. Mary spent time in several foster homes during her mother's absences. She only completed the fourth grade in school, and attended a school for the mentally retarded as a teenager. Mary has been married to Mr. R., a postal employee, for seven years. The pregnancy was accidental, but Mary seemed to adjust at the beginning. When questioned about her anxieties about caring for her infant, Mary commented, "How can I take care of my baby, my mother didn't take care of me after I was born because she had a breakdown then." She closely identified with her disturbed, inadequate mother, who lacked child-rearing skills. This negative maternal identification, compounded by Mary's low intelligence, poor adaptive skills, and acute depressive reaction, made her incapable of infant care. Mary's failure to form an attachment to her infant seemed to be a protective and adaptive maneuver considering her severe limitations.

Case 3. Doris, a thirty-four-year-old unmarried woman, experienced pervasive anxiety in caring for her infant son Albert. Albert was healthy at birth, and weighed six and a half pounds. As soon as Doris took him home, he began to lose weight. After a bout of vomiting at the age of six weeks, Doris showed Albert to a neighbor, who recommended that she take him to the hospital because of his malnourished appearance. He was immediately admitted to the pediatric unit because of his dehydration, cyanosis, and malnourishment. Doris then revealed to the pediatrician that she really didn't know how to take care of Albert. When he refused the bottle, she gave him water or ordinary milk instead. She finally dispensed with the formula entirely. Albert was placed in foster care after his hospital recovery.

Doris's pregnancy, birth, delivery, and immediate postpartum condition all seemed to be within normal limits. The pregnancy, however, was unplanned, and marred by a deterioration in the relationship between Doris and her boyfriend Tim, who was the father. Tim was opposed to the pregnancy, and wanted Doris to have an abortion. When she insisted on having the baby, he refused to provide her with any financial support. After many arguments and physical altercations about Tim's lack of support, Doris forced him to leave the apartment. Doris's own family also turned away from her, largely because of their disapproval of Tim and the fact that the baby was conceived out of wedlock.

Doris was the middle child and only daughter in a family of seven children. She always felt like an "outcast" in comparison to her six brothers. She felt rejected and exploited by her mother, whom she had to care for because of a chronic kidney ailment, and rejected by her stepfather. Her mother died three years before the pregnancy with Albert. Doris reacted with depression and a suicide attempt. Doris has been married previously to a man who financially exploited and physically abused her. This marriage ended in divorce, and contributed further to her alienation from her family.

Doris is currently ambivalent toward Albert. She visits the baby regularly at the foster-care agency, and talks about him in a proud and fond manner. Yet she is quite awkward when she handles him and is afraid that she might damage him in some way. She suspects the foster parents of mistreating him whenever he exhibits slight discomfort or a minor physical problem. She acknowledges that some of her difficulties handling Albert might be related to a displacement of her rage toward Tim. At present, Doris is receiving supportive psychotherapy in order to help her work through some of the many problems associated with her impaired capacity to care for her infant.

Case 4. Cathy, a nineteen-year-old unmarried mother, requested help from our program after she had been charged with beating her four-year-old son James with a ping-pong paddle. The child sustained severe bruises and lacerations on the face and back, and was placed in foster care. James had only been living with Cathy and her mother for several months when the abuse took place. She found him increasingly difficult to manage because he often refused to obey her. She also had been depressed as a result of an infection and complications following a recent abortion.

Cathy became pregnant with James at the age of fourteen. She wanted to have an abortion, but her mother insisted that she go through with the pregnancy and keep the child. Cathy confided that the baby "didn't seem real" to her. She tried to take care of the baby with her mother's assistance but felt overwhelmed and gave James to her maternal grandmother when he was three months old. During this time, Cathy's boyfriend, who was the father, refused to support James, and had been physically abusive to her. When James was two and a half years old, Cathy resumed responsibility for his care. Once again she found him too difficult and demanding and after a short time, when he contracted pneumonia, she gave him to her boyfriend's mother. She terminated this arrangement after complaining about the inadequate care James was receiving from this woman. The abusive incident occurred several months later. When James was an infant, Cathy was severely traumatized by her boyfriend, who shot her in the leg following an argument. She felt that the scarring of her leg would spoil her ambition for a modeling career. A severe depression ensued, which exacerbated her excessive drinking.

Cathy felt unhappy and scapegoated by her mother during her childhood. Her mother spent most of her time with Cathy's two older sisters, and rarely responded to her. After Cathy was expelled from school for drinking at the age of twelve, her mother tried to send her to a training school. She finally was admitted to a psychiatric hospital. At this time, Cathy was told by her aunt that her mother "didn't care if she died."

4

The Parents

Characteristics of Abusing Parents

A multitude of behavioral characteristics and psychopathology have been attributed to parents and other adults who engage in child abuse. They have been described as impulsive (Elmer 1963), immature (Cohen et al. 1966), rigid and domineering (Merrill 1962), dependent and narcissistic (Pollock and Steele 1972), chronically aggressive (Merrill 1962), isolated from family and friends (Steele and Pollock 1968), and experiencing difficulties (Kempe et al. 1962). One observer noted that abusive mothers were "masculine while their husbands were passive" (Galdston 1965).

More penetrating impressions of the personalities and underlying psychopathology of abusing parents have been elicited during their psychiatric treatment and while interacting with other children. Steele (1970) described specific key psychodynamics contributing to the parental dysfunction encountered in child abuse. He stressed the importance of the parent's closely linked identifications with a harsh, rejecting mother and with a "bad" childhood self-image, which are perpetuated in the current relationship with the abused child. Abusive parents submit their children to traumatic experiences similar to those they had endured during childhood. Steele observed the use of such defense mechanisms as denial, projection, identification with the aggressor, and role reversal. The last, a maneuver by which the abusing parent turns toward the child for an inordinate amount of dependency gratification, has been noted by other investigators (Morris and Gould 1963, Simons et al. 1966) as well. Galdston (1971) studied the parents of abused preschool children who attended a therapeutic day-care center. He emphasized the importance of unresolved sexual guilt associated with the conception of the child who is subsequently abused. Feinstein and his associates (1964) explored in group therapy the behavior of women with infanticidal impulses. These women displayed deep resentment toward their parents for failing to satisfy their dependency needs. They frequently demonstrated a hatred of men which could be traced to intense sibling rivalry with their brothers. Many of these women had witnessed or been subjected to excessive parental violence. They manifested phobic and depressive symptoms in addition to their fears about harming their children.

The wide variety of behavior and personality traits observed in abusing parents suggests that a specific "abusive" personality does not exist. Rather, individuals with a certain psychological makeup operating in combination with the burden of a painfully perceived childhood and immediate environmental stress might be likely to abuse the offspring who most readily elicits the unhappy childhood imagery of the past.

The greatest area of agreement in the field of child abuse has pertained to the history and background of abusive parents themselves. These individuals usually experienced abuse, deprivation, rejection, and inadequate mothering and were subjected to unrealistic expectations and premature demands by their parents during childhood.

A study of sixty abused children and their families[1] carried out at the Downstate Medical Center by Green, Gaines, and Sandgrund (1974a) yielded the following description of abusing females:

The mothers or maternal caretakers of the abused children frequently reported difficulties with their parents. These relationships were marred by criticism, rejection, and physical punishment. They also described current marital discord and stressed the emotional unavailability and physical brutality of their spouses. They complained of an inability to secure help with the burdens of child rearing, a consequence of their alienation from their spouses and families. Their failure to find support from the environment facilitated turning toward their children for dependency gratification. Their long-term experience of criticism and punishment reinforced their feelings of having been burdensome children and promoted their identification with a hostile, rejecting parental figure.

These women characteristically reported the abused children as aggressive and unmanageable at home and in school. The abused children usually required more attention than their siblings. The mother's perception of the abused child as the most aggressive and demanding of her offspring contributed to the child's scapegoating.

The abusing fathers[2] described similar experiences of deprivation, neglect, and physical abuse during their childhood, and complained about their current relationships with spouse and children. They typically accused their mates of an inability to manage the household and discipline the children. They also complained about the spouse's "spoiling" of the children and would not tolerate the crying and helplessness of infants or

1. Almost all of the families resided in inner-city ghetto areas and represented the lowest socioeconomic group with a majority receiving public assistance. The ethnic composition was primarily black and Hispanic.

2. For the purpose of this book, the term *father* will often include father surrogates, such as stepfathers and boyfriends of the mother, who assume paternal roles in the family.

displays of regressive behavior by older children, such as prolonged crying, clinging, bedwetting, soiling, etc. They viewed
their physical abuse of the children as a necessary part of child
rearing which "all children" experience. They perceived the
abused children as either more "babyish" or more defiant
than the nonabused siblings. In each case these scapegoated
children demanded the most attention.

Typical personality characteristics shared by both male and
female abusers were:

1. They rely on the child to gratify dependency needs that
are unsatisfied in their relationships with their spouses and
families.

2. They manifest impaired impulse control based on childhood experience with harsh punishment and identification with
violent adult models.

3. They are handicapped by a poor self-concept. They feel
worthless and devalued, which reflects the rejection and criticism accorded them by adults during their own childhood.

4. They display disturbances in identity formation. Identifications are shifting and unstable and are dominated by hostile
introjects derived from the internalization of "bad" self- and
object-representations of early childhood.

5. They respond to assaults on their fragile self-esteem with
compensatory adaptation. Because of their need to maintain a
positive facade they must desperately protect themselves from
the awareness of underlying feelings of worthlessness by the
frequent use of such defense mechanisms as projection and
externalization.

6. The projection of negative parental attributes onto the
child causes him to be misperceived and used as a scapegoat in
order to bear the brunt of the parents' aggression.

Psychodynamics

The psychodynamics in a given case of child abuse are
largely determined by the "abuse-prone" personality traits of
the parent while he or she interacts with a "difficult" child in an
unsupportive, nongratifying environment. The relationship

between the abusing parent and the child is distorted by the cumulative impact of the parent's own traumatic experiences as a child reared in a punitive, unloving environment. Individuals who abuse their children cannot envision any parent-child relationship as a mutually gratifying experience, since the task of parenting mobilizes identifications with the parent-aggressor, child-victim dyad of the past. The key psychodynamic elements in child abuse are role reversal, excessive use of denial and projection as defenses, rapidly shifting identifications including pathological identification with the child, and displacement of aggression from frustrating objects onto the child.

Role reversal occurs when the unfulfilled abusing parent seeks dependency gratification, which is unavailable from his spouse and family, from his "parentified" child, based on an identification with the "child-victim." The child's inability to gratify the parent causes him to be unconsciously perceived as the rejecting mother. This intensifies the parent's feeling of rejection and worthlessness, threatening his narcissistic equilibrium. These painful feelings are denied and projected onto the child, who then becomes the recipient of the parent's self-directed aggression. He accomplishes this by a shift toward identification with his own aggressive parent, thus terminating the role reversal. By beating the child, the abuser assuages his punitive superego and attempts to actively master the traumatic experiences passively endured as a child. The scapegoating process continues as the child also becomes the target for aggression displaced from various despised and frustrating objects in the parent's current and past life, such as a rejecting mate or lover, a hated sibling rival, or a depriving parent substitute. These objects are unconsciously linked to the original "parent-aggressor."

The choice of a particular child for scapegoating might depend upon such accidental factors as time of birth, physical appearance, temperament, and/or sex, in addition to actual physical or psychological deviancy. It ultimately is based upon the child's capacity to evoke the negatively perceived characteristics of the parents or of significant others.

Case 1. Sonia, a six-year-old Puerto Rican girl, was severely beaten by her mother when she was four, resulting in a fractured femur. Sonia was the daughter of Ms. G.'s first husband, who, after frequent quarreling, drinking, and "running around," left her when Sonia was one year old. Ms. G. subsequently entered into a common law relationship with a man who fathered her two young boys.

Ms. G. initially married in order to escape from her brutal godparents, who had raised her since the age of eighteen months when her mother had abandoned her. They had been extremely punitive and restrictive. Ms. G. remembered one occasion in which her godfather had broken a flowerpot over her head. Ms. G.'s marriage was arranged by the godparents. She went to work in a factory and was virtually ignored by her husband. She soon became pregnant but did not want a child since her husband spent no time with her. He deserted her the first time when she was six weeks pregnant, and she moved in with her sister-in-law to have the baby. She hoped for a boy, stating, "I don't like girls. Boys are more interesting."

In addition to displacing her rage toward her ex-husband and godparents onto Sonia, Ms. G. obviously identified with her little girl and brutalized her in the same manner she had experienced with her godparents. She described the following feelings toward Sonia: "Since she was born, I let out all the anger and frustration that I had in myself on her. Whenever she came to me, I sent her away with a beating." It is worth noting that Ms. G.'s relationship with her male children is better.

Nonabusive mothers whose children have been battered by husbands or boyfriends exhibit a slight variation in the psychodynamic pattern. The interaction between mother and child begins in a similar fashion as the mother endows the child with the attributes of her own rejecting parents. However, the resulting "bad" childhood self-image derived from her parents is partly maintained and partly transferred to the child, while the internalized "parent-aggressor" is projected onto the abusive mate. The mother retains her identification with the "child-victim" rather than with the "parent-aggressor."

These women submit to the physical cruelty of their mates as a masochistic repetition of their childhood victimization by rejecting, aggressive parents. The pain-dependent attachment to the spouse serves as a defense against their hostility toward the child. This is confirmed by the tenacity with which these women cling to brutal and humiliating relationships, and by their tendency to assume the abusive role if the spouse leaves.

Case 2. Andy N., a seven-year-old youngster, had been repeatedly beaten by his father, Mr. N., with a belt buckle and pool cue for the past three years. The case was referred to the Bureau of Child Welfare when welts and scars on Andy's back and stomach were noticed in school. Andy's mother, Miss J., had also been subjected to violent assaults by Mr. N., her common law husband. On the morning of the interview, Miss J. suffered broken ribs after being struck with an iron bar by Mr. N. He had also stabbed her in the leg several months previously.

Miss J. was also a victim of violence during her childhood. Her alcoholic father beat up her mother and left home when Miss J. was ten years old. She described her mother as an angry woman who whipped her with a belt. Her mother and stepfather forced her to leave home when she became pregnant with Andy at the age of sixteen. When Andy was one month old, he was placed with his maternal aunt while his mother found a job and moved in with her grandmother. Miss J. currently complains about Andy's lying and stealing, and admits to beating him with a belt.

Special Characteristics of Abusing Fathers

Although fathers share equal responsibility with mothers for child abuse, psychological investigation of male child abusers has been conspicuously absent from the battered child literature. Recent review articles (Spinetta and Rigler 1972, Lystad 1975) and annotated bibliographies (National Institute of Mental Health 1972, 1974) fail to list a single publication dealing primarily with this population. Most psychological studies of abusing parents fail to clearly differentiate the personalities and psychodynamics of abusing mothers and fathers (Kempe et al. 1962, Cohen et al. 1966, Zalba 1966, Johnson and Morse 1968, Steele 1970, Terr 1970, Galdston 1971, Spinetta and Rigler 1972) or are primarily based on case histories of abusing mothers (Feinstein et al. 1964, Steele and Pollock 1968, Melnick and Harley 1969, Elmer 1971, Green et al. 1974a). The only specific characteristics attributed to abusing fathers have been their passivity and tendency to reverse domestic roles with their wives because of lack of employment (Merrill 1962, Galdston 1965).

The study of male child abusers has been neglected for several reasons. First, they are physically less available for study. Many fathers or father surrogates are only in the home sporadically, while others are forced to leave by court order; daytime employment makes them less available for interviews. Secondly, their motivation to seek help is less urgent due to their more peripheral involvement with child rearing and the greater ease with which they can delegate domestic responsibilities to their spouse. This is reinforced by societal attitudes which still minimize the participation of fathers in bringing up their children. Finally, few professionals possess the patience and determination required to overcome these obstacles, especially since these violent abusing males are often unpleasant and frightening to deal with. It is easier to refer them to the police or the courts for final disposition.

Therapeutic intervention has been traditionally aimed at strengthening maternal functioning through supportive casework or psychotherapy, mothers group therapy, crisis intervention, and the use of parent aides. The mother's child-rearing tasks are reduced by the deployment of homemakers and day care facilities. It is of crucial importance to develop an intervention strategy also geared to the specific needs and problems of the fathers, since the basic responsibility for abuse is shared by both parental figures in an intact family. It is necessary to explore the personalities and the psychodynamics of the abusing father so that they can be rationally included in the treatment process.

In recent studies (Green et al. 1974b, Sandgrund et al. 1974) of sixty abused children and their parents at the Downstate Medical Center, twenty-six (43 percent) were abused by their father or father surrogate, and eight (14 percent) were jointly abused by their mother and father. Information regarding the abusing fathers or father surrogates was initially obtained from extensive case records from the Bureau of Child Welfare and Family Court and through interviews and psychiatric treatment of the abused children and their mothers because of the general unavailability of these men. More direct contact with the abusing fathers was subsequently effected during their participation in the Downstate Medical Center's Treatment Program for Abused Children and Their Families, which yielded valuable data concerning abusive personality traits and psychodynamics specifically related to their roles as fathers and husbands.

Psychodynamic Issues: Child-Abusing Fathers

In addition to the role reversal, excessive use of denial and projection, pathological identifications, and displacement of aggression onto the child, which are shared by abusing parents of both sexes, abusing fathers exhibit specific personality traits and psychodynamics which reflect differences in sex, family roles, and environmental influences (Green 1979).

Unresolved Sibling Rivalry Based
Upon Maternal Deprivation

As described previously, these men experienced such major frustration during childhood as physical abuse, neglect, and parental abandonment, which prevented the satisfaction of basic needs for nurturance and human contact. They were left with a residue of rage, depression, and mistrust.

The father regards the child as a rival for the attention of his spouse due to the lack of previous satisfaction of his own dependency longings. The competitive rivalry with the child for the mother's love is a repetition of the father's unresolved sibling rivalry during his childhood. His jealousy of the child usually manifests itself during the first years of life when the child requires the greatest amount of nurturing and attention. The father frequently assaults his wife in addition to the child. Beating the wife often occurs when she threatens to leave or when she tries to protect herself and the children from her husband's aggression. The beatings are designed to further intimidate the spouse and reinforce her passive-submissive behavior. In expressing his rage toward the mother–child dyad, he reenacts his frustration and anger at exclusion from maternal contact by rivals during his own childhood. His jealousy and possessiveness of his spouse often extends to her involvement with friends and activities outside of the family.

Case 1. Mr. T., a chronic alcoholic, experienced strong feelings of anger and resentment if his ten-month-old infant cried when he returned home from work. He could not tolerate his wife's feeding and bathing the baby in his presence, especially when he was "hungry and tired," and he frequently struck the baby and his wife if the baby cried. Mrs. T. realized that getting the baby fed and put to sleep before her husband returned was the best way of preventing its physical abuse. Mrs. T.'s preoccupation with the crying infant evoked Mr. T.'s childhood memories of having been deprived of food and love by uncaring foster parents whose preoccupation with their natural children prevented his cries for nurturance from being satisfied.

A closely related pattern of child abuse based on the theme of sibling rivalry is observed in stepfathers who abuse their stepchildren.

Case 2. Mr. P. subjected his eleven-year-old stepson, Don, to severe beatings which resulted in multiple contusions and lacerations and required hospitalization. Don had been living with his maternal grandparents in the south while his mother worked in New York City. She met Mr. P. in New York and married him after a brief courtship. Don, then seven, came to live with them. Since his arrival Don has been a source of constant friction between his mother and stepfather. The latter

complained that Don was a financial burden and any affectionate interaction between mother and son provoked Mr. P.'s
anger. He accused his wife of spoiling Don and failing to curb
his "meanness." When she would intervene to protect Don
from the beatings, Mr. P. threatened to leave unless the boy
was sent back to the grandparents.

Another observation suggesting the importance of maternal
deprivation in the genesis of child abuse by males is that these
men often select girlfriends or mates primarily for their apparent mothering qualities. These women often have children
from a previous union with a history of abuse and/or abandonment by the man. The fathers identify with the tragic plight of
these victims who evoke memories of their own childhood
deprivation and maltreatment. This generates rescue fantasies
which represent an unconscious attempt to repeat and master
the fathers' traumatic family experiences. These ambitious
plans are doomed to failure if the child is "difficult" and the
spouse's own need for nurturance rivals his own. At this point
the would-be rescuer identifies with his violent parents and
actively repeats the abuse that he had passively experienced.

Case 3. Mr. K. was referred to the treatment program
because he had repeatedly abused his five-year-old stepson
Jack, because of his aggressive and hyperactive behavior.
Mr. K. met Jack's mother when he was seventeen, when Jack,
who was an infant, his two-year-old sister, and his mother had
been abandoned by his abusive, alcoholic father. Mr. K. began
to go out with her and developed a strong attachment to Jack.
He soon left his mother's house and moved in with this family,
actively protecting them from the father, who periodically tried
to assault them. Mr. K. identified strongly with them. His own
alcoholic, violent father had beaten him and his mother, and
left the family when he was four. He then lived with grandparents who favored his older and younger brothers. Mr. K.
identified with Jack as the "black sheep" of the family. He
eventually married Jack's mother, adopted Jack and his sister,

and fathered three more children. He began to beat Jack when he became a demanding, hyperactive toddler, and Mrs. K. became increasingly depressed, withdrawn, and ineffective as a mother. At age five Jack had to be hospitalized for sadistic, destructive behavior which included fire setting.

Spouse Abuse

The child-abusing father typically beats his spouse in addition to the child(ren) because of his anger at feeling excluded from their special relationship, due to his unresolved sibling rivalry. Conversely, it is quite rare for an abusive mother to assault her husband. Spouse abuse is more common in cultures in which women have been traditionally the most exploited, i.e., Latin, Carribean, Southern black, the poor, etc. These cultures often consider the sexual and physical intimidation of women by men to be a sign of "masculinity." In many of these families, spouse abuse, with or without child abuse, has been passed on from generation to generation.

Child abuse by the father is often provoked by the sudden and unexpected physical or material burden of child care due to the accidental or intentional unavailability of his spouse. This usually coincides with her withdrawal of emotional support as well. The abuse often takes place while the father is reluctantly caring for the children. At times, the spouse's passive manipulation in this type of abuse is obvious.

Case illustration. Mr. M., a hospital maintenance worker, often abused the two oldest of his four daughters when they were left in his care by his chronically alcoholic and psychotic wife, who periodically withdrew from her husband, children, and housekeeping responsibilities. Mr. M. was obliged to assume these responsibilities in her absence. Mrs. M. admitted: "I knew Bill would stop beating them if I took care of the children, cleaned the house, and gave him sex, but this is my way of punishing him."

Vocational Failure

The male's level of self-esteem is more dependent than the female's on vocational and financial status. This is especially true of members of inner-city minority groups, in which women are expected to keep house and raise the children. The actual or threatened loss of a job can be devastating to a man, especially if he is a father and breadwinner for the family. For many of these fathers, as well as those who have been chronically unemployed, the assertion of power and control over their spouses and children often represents the only source of mastery in daily lives characterized by passivity, chronic failure, and/or impotence.

These men anticipate that their children will compensate for their narcissistic injury and provide them with dependency gratification by being skillful, clever and strong, and by responding to them with adulation and respect. The children are often beaten when they fail to respond in this way. The abuse, however, instills in the child fear and avoidance of the father and propels the child toward others for gratification and safety. The father responds with a sense of betrayal, attacks the child, and a vicious cycle ensues.

Case illustration. Mr. A. was threatened with the loss of his job as a security guard because of poor attendance and difficulties with supervisors. He began to beat his wife for neglecting the home and was abusive toward his boys, four and six years old, because of their failure to keep their room clean and perform household chores. He also became irate when his boys feared confiding in him. Instead, they enjoyed the company of men in the street who provided them with candy and money. Mr. A. was especially sensitive about the reaction of the neighbors, who might conclude that the boys were not provided for at home. He feared losing his prestige as a father and authority figure in the home. With the help of psychotherapy, he gradually learned that his constant criticism and punishment of his sons caused the very behavior he found intolerable.

Abuse of Alcohol

The child and spouse abuse committed by fathers is often accompanied by excessive drinking. In the Downstate study, 50 percent of the reports of abuse by fathers indicated that they were drinking heavily or were intoxicated during their assaultive behavior. The vulnerability of these men to alcoholism is consistent with their psychodynamics. Alcohol is perceived as the ultimate source of the dependency gratification which cannot be obtained from spouse and family, and it temporarily obliterates feelings of inadequacy, depression, and low self-esteem. It also enhances the potential for abuse by undermining inhibitions and brittle defenses against pent-up rage and aggression. Narcotics addiction and use of hard drugs were infrequent in this sample of abusing fathers.

The unresolved issues of maternal deprivation and sibling rivalry and the frequent evidence of alcohol abuse support the conclusion that the basic conflicts of abusing fathers rest on a preoedipal level. This confirms the impressions of Steele and Pollock (1968); however it differs from the observations of Galdston (1971), who stresses the primary importance of parental oedipal guilt and oedipal conflict in the maltreatment of children.

Other Differences Between Abusing Fathers and Mothers

Abusing fathers are unable to acknowledge their feelings of deprivation and dependent longings for their spouse. Expression of these feelings is further discouraged by society's intolerance of male "weakness and passivity." The father's wishes for nurturance are more easily satisfied in the socially acceptable ritual of drinking, which permits the fulfillment of regressive oral fantasies while absolving him from any responsibility for the act. Since her spouse and family are incapable of providing nurturance and satisfaction, the abusing mother seeks gratification primarily from her children. These mothers can express their dependency yearnings more easily than the fathers, but they are seldom fulfilled.

Another contrast between abusing mothers and fathers is observed in their reactions to their spouse's participation in child-rearing activities. Abusing fathers react with jealousy and resentment to their spouses' contact with the children. Abusing mothers, on the other hand, welcome their spouses' all too infrequent involvement with the children. Abusing mothers exhibit envy of their children's attachment to the father only after the relationship with the spouse has terminated and he is no longer living at home.

Differences may also be observed in the quality of role reversal perceived by abusing mothers and fathers. The abusing mother cherishes the child's premature independence as a source of physical and emotional support not forthcoming from spouse or family. The abusing father expects premature performances from his children so they will be able to relinquish their claims on his spouse.

In cases of child abuse by males, the mothers participate by overtly or covertly encouraging their spouses to attack the child. Some mothers may consciously provoke a spouse to commit child abuse by deliberately engaging in behavior designed to frustrate and anger him. These women also masochistically submit to the cruelty and physical abuse of their mates in order to reenact their own childhood victimization by rejecting, hostile parents. The wife's pain-dependent relationship to the spouse binds her hostility toward the child, which is expressed vicariously during the spouse's assault. This is the reason why these women cling to their brutal partners, and tend to assume the role of the abuser if the spouse leaves.

In addition to focusing on the fathers' abuse proneness, intervention with abusing fathers must be supplemented by techniques designed to strengthen the child-rearing capacity of the family and to improve the child's functioning. The use of crisis-oriented comprehensive family services such as homemaking assistance, parent aides, hot lines, day-care and outpatient pediatric and psychiatric treatment facilities for the child can be pivotal in maintaining the stability of these families while the father is being helped.

Relationship Between Child Abuse and Spouse Abuse

Our observation that child abusing fathers frequently batter their spouses suggests that there might be close relationship between child abuse and spouse abuse. Other investigators (Smith et al. 1973, Scott 1978) have also described this tendency. Abusive fathers share many of the traits of the assaultive husbands described in the literature on spouse abuse, such as paranoid symptomatology and pathological jealousy (Hilberman and Munson 1977-1978), alcohol abuse (Gayford 1975, Scott 1974), and social and vocational inadequacy (Gayford 1975). The fact that many of the assaultive husbands proceeded to batter their children (Gayford 1975, Hilberman and Munson 1977-1978) indicates that spouse battering by violence-prone males could be a precursor to child abuse.

The low self-esteem, masochistic traits, dependency, and fear of abandonment exhibited by the battered spouses in our program have also been described in the "battered wife" literature (Geller 1976, Steinmetz 1978, Walker 1977-1978, Rounsaville 1978). The battered spouses in our sample frequently reported having been physically abused during their childhood. They typically chose a violent mate modeled after their own abusive parent (usually the father). This association between childhood abuse and subsequent victimization by a spouse has been reported in the literature on spouse abuse (Gayford 1975, Hilberman and Munson 1977-1978). The exposure of some female children to family violence might facilitate the later development of masochistic object relationships. Yet some of our battered spouses abused their children as well. Gayford (1975) reported that thirty-seven of one-hundred battered women admitted abusing their children. The common observation that many abusing mothers who were victims of childhood violence adopt primarily aggressive identifications and do not choose abusive mates, suggests that multiple factors impinge on the ultimate management of aggression in girls who have been chronically maltreated.

A careful study of the child-rearing practices of battered wives and their abusive husbands and the mental health of their children seems warranted. In addition to being at risk for abuse, children in spouse-battering families are traumatized by witnessing the chronic violence between their parents, which they eventually regard as an expectable ingredient of family life. Hilberman and Munson (1977-1978) noted that one-third of two-hundred and nine children of sixty battered wives displayed evidence of somatic, psychological, and behavioral dysfunction.

In summary, wife-battering and child abuse seem to be closely related. They often occur simultaneously in a given family. In other families, wife-battering might represent an initial stage of violence which is ultimately extended to the children. Aggression between spouses is often a reenactment of the mistreatment they experienced as children, indicating the transmission of violence from generation to generation. Timely therapeutic intervention with families involved in spouse abuse is necessary to prevent the traumatization of the children.

5

The Children

The severity and wide range of psychological impairments attributed to abused children clearly warranted further clinical investigation and research in this area.

Previous Observations of Abused Children

Recent efforts to document the psychological damaje sustained by abused children have uncovered a variety of developmental and behavioral difficulties, but these have yet to be integrated into a comprehensive psychodynamic understanding of the abused child in the context of his traumatic family environment.

Elmer (1965) studied the effects of abuse by comparing abused and nonabused children who had been hospitalized for multiple bone injuries. The abused children showed a higher incidence of mental retardation and speech difficulties. Martin (1972) reported a study in which one-third of a sample of abused children were mentally retarded, 43 percent were neurologically damaged, and 38 percent exhibited delayed language development. Morse, Sahler, and Friedman (1970) discovered mental deficiency in 70 percent of a group of children whose injuries resulted from abuse or neglect. Green (1968) documented a high incidence of self-mutilation in schizophrenic children who had been physically abused. Martin and Beezely (1976) observed the following personality characteristics in a group of fifty abused children: impaired capacity for pleasure, low self-esteem, school learning problems, withdrawal, oppositionalism, hypervigilance, compulsivity, and pseudomature behavior.

Behavioral observations of abused children have found them to be stubborn, unresponsive, negativistic, depressed (Johnson and Morse 1968), fearful, apathetic, and unappealing, with a blunting of their appetite for food and human contact (Galdston 1965), and likely to provoke physical attack from others.

Kempe (1976) observed delays in speech, motor, and social development in a group of thirteen preschool abused children. During psychological testing, they demonstrated excessive preoccupation with the examiner's approval or disapproval. In relating to adults, they were anxious and fearful, and expected punishment or criticism. These children often demonstrated an impaired capacity to play or make use of toys. Galdston (1971) described purposeless, unpredictable, and unpremeditated violent behavior in a group of abused preschool age boys at a special day-care treatment center. Abused girls of this age group were less aggressive, but demonstrated more withdrawal and reliance on autoerotic activities. Both boys and girls exhibited bodily awkwardness and poor motor coordination.

Abused infants have recently become a focus for clinical observations. Kempe (1976) noted that abused infants below six months of age were frequently irritable with a high-pitched irritable cry. These infants also exhibited difficulties with feeding and were hard to satisfy, and began to demonstrate delays in motor and social development. Kempe also described impaired social responsiveness in these infants which became noticeable between six and twelve months of age. They failed to demonstrate the usual anxiety upon separation from their parents or when they were confronted with strangers. They also exhibited "frozen watchfulness" consisting of intense scanning of the environment accompanied by motor passivity and immobility. Gaensbauer et al. (1979) documented disturbances in affective communication in a group of abused infants. They exhibited social and affective withdrawal, diminished capacity for pleasure, a proneness toward negative affects such as distress, sadness, and anger, and an unpredictability and shallowness in affective expression. They also demonstrated a weakened attachment to their mothers and caregivers.

Unfortunately, the reliability of these observations must be questioned because of the failure to include nontraumatized normal control groups. However, a recent controlled study by George and Main (1979) revealed similar impairment in social and affective behavior in abused infants and toddlers. These investigators observed that abused infants and toddlers from one to three years of age physically assaulted their peers in a day-care setting twice as often as the nonabused controls. They also harassed their caregivers verbally and nonverbally, and were the only children who assaulted or threatened to assault them. The abused children were less likely to approach their caregivers in response to friendly overtures. When they did so, they were more like to approach to the side, to the rear, or by turning about and backstepping.

These observations and studies of abused infants and toddlers suggest that their attachment to their mothers and caregivers is noticeably compromised. The fearfulness, irritability, and distress experienced with their parents appear to be readily generalized and reenacted with subsequent caretakers. This is consistent with clinical observations which describe the pronounced difficulties of abused children in relating to foster parents, day-care personnel, and schoolteachers.

Several of these earlier observations stimulated the author's interest in exploring the psychological and emotional sequelae of abuse in sixty school-aged battered children at the Downstate Medical Center (Green et al. 1974b). Thirty normal and thirty neglected, nonabused children comparable in age, sex, and socioeconomic level served as controls. Psychiatric evaluation and psychological testing of these children documented the cognitive impairment and psychological disturbances described by others. The abused and neglected children exhibited significantly lower mean IQ scores than the normal controls. Twenty-five percent of the abused children were found to be mentally retarded with IQs of less than 70. These children also demonstrated severe deficits in a wide variety of ego functions, such as impulse control, defensive functioning, reality testing, object relations, thought processes, body image, and overall ego competency. The abused children also exhibited a rather typical pattern of depressive affect with low self-esteem, which was often accompanied by self-destructive behavior. These abnormalities were often attributable to the disruptive impact of the physical and emotional trauma of deviant and neglectful parenting on the normal development of the child's cognitive and adaptive ego functions, though in some cases the defects of the child preceded and precipitated the maltreatment (Sandgrund et al. 1974).

Most of the abused children required intensive psychotherapeutic and psychoeducational intervention to overcome severe behavioral and educational difficulties. This led to the development of a pilot treatment program for abused children and their families under the auspices of the Division of Child and Adolescent Psychiatry. Approximately twenty abused children were involved in outpatient individual psychotherapy during the past three years. The treatment of the children was complemented by various modes of therapeutic involvement with the parents, such as counseling, crisis intervention, and home contact by visiting nurses. The children ranged in age from five to twelve, and most were seen twice weekly for at least one year. A major purpose of the treatment program was the in-depth exploration of the psychopathology and psychodynamics typical of abused children, and their genetic relationship to a hostile environment. Another aim was the development of specialized therapeutic techniques designed to reverse the psychopathology of the child and to prevent further maltreatment. To the author's knowledge, this is the only specialized program involved in the intensive psychiatric study and treatment of abused children.

Components of the Child-Abuse Syndrome

A more profound understanding of the psychological functioning of abused children was obtained from material derived from the psychotherapy of the children and their parents. This permitted the exploration of the abusive interaction between each child and his family within the context of their physical and psychological environment. Child abuse was regarded as a complex experience consisting of several components rather than as a single variable. The following elements were identified:

1. An acute physical and psychological assault results in a traumatic overwhelming of the child's ego, and subseqently in a fear of annihilation and/or abandonment.

2. This assault is superimposed upon a harsh and punitive child-rearing environment which conveys anger and hostility toward the child.

3. The abused child is usually scapegoated. The scapegoating process consists of the projection of negative parental attitudes onto the child.

4. The abuse is frequently inflicted against a background of poverty, family disorganization, and the interruption of maternal care, resulting in early experiences of object loss and emotional deprivation. This is often a consequence of a step-wise family immigration from rural areas, whereby the parents arrive in the ghetto without the children, who usually remain behind with grandparents. The children are then sent to the city to rejoin their parents when they have found employment and housing. These overly stressed parents often find child care burdensome in their new and unsupportive environment.

5. Central nervous system impairment is often directly or indirectly associated with child abuse.

The relative contribution of each of these factors to the child's psychopathology will vary according to the nature and severity of the abusive episode and the quality of the parent-child interaction. The actual physical assault bearing the threat of destruction and/or abandonment, may be perceived as an overwhelming trauma by the child, corresponding to a "shock" trauma (Kris 1956), while the underlying harsh and punitive parenting, scapegoating, inadequacy of maternal care, and eventual neurological damage might constitute a "strain" or "cumulative" trauma (Khan 1963).

Psychopathology of Abused Children

These immediate and long-term adverse experiences leave a characteristic impact on the cognitive apparatus, ego functions, object relationships, identifications, and libidinal organization of the abused children. Some of the more typical traits and symptoms are: a basic suspiciousness and mistrust of adults; low frustration tolerance with impulsivity; a need for immediate gratification and a need to exploit, manipulate and control objects; expression through motor activity rather than by verbalization and the use of symbols; hyperaggression; and provocativeness. These children are preoccupied with violent fantasies depicting scenes of physical attack, spanking, assault, and retaliation. Such fantasies, elicited spontaneously in play with dolls and puppets, are thinly disguised elaborations of the original abuse.

Developmental lags are often present in the area of speech and language. Unevenness of development is often observed in which deficits are accompanied by precocious achievement in other areas, such as advanced motor abilities, a capacity to perform certain household duties prematurely, and an overall "street wiseness." Unfortunately, these advanced achievements are motivated by fear, rather than by pleasure and mastery. Beneath the facade of "pseudoindependence" is a helpless and depressed child, hungry for, but fearful of, contact, convinced of his "badness" and "worthlessness," feelings appropriate to the maltreatment accorded him. These core feelings of depression, helplessness, and self-reproach are usually defended against and camouflaged by aggressive activities and fantasies designed to convey strength and power, which are influenced by identification with violent parental modes (identification with the aggressor). Repeated experiences of abuse and scapegoating reinforce the child's "bad" self-image. The ensuing pent-up rage toward the abusing parent further contributes to the child's sense of guilt and "badness." This anger, which cannot be expressed directly, is usually displaced toward siblings, peers, and other adults such as teachers and other authorities, or is turned against the self in the form of suicidal behavior or self-mutilation, or is projected onto external objects. The risk of assaultive or suicidal behavior increases when the abused child reaches adolescence. This expression of externally or internally directed aggression represents a repetition of the original violence experienced at the hands of the abusive parent.

These maladaptive behaviors provoke further rejection and punishment, leading to a vicious cycle in which the original traumatic situation is continually repeated but never mastered. This prevents the child from experiencing gratifying object ties and precludes the achievement of normal development. Specific disturbances in ego functions, behavior, and character structure, with their pathological sequelae, may be described in the following manner.

Overall Impairment in Ego Functioning

When viewed globally, the abused children exhibited an overall impairment in ego functioning associated with intellectual and cognitive deficits. They displayed a higher incidence of delayed development and CNS dysfunction than their nonabused peers. Many were mentally retarded. They were often found to be hyperactive and impulsive with minimal frustration tolerance. Motor activity, rather than verbalization, was the preferred mode of expression. Many of them manifested aberrant speech and language development. Although these children were of latency age, they failed to demonstrate the characteristic progressive ego growth and reorganization. There was an absence of the typical latency defenses which enable the normal child to bind anxiety from internal and external sources and to cope with phase-specific stresses and conflicts. The abused children's preoccupation with external danger and their overstimulated drive activity deprived them of the energy necessary for learning and mastery.

"Traumatic" Reaction with Acute Anxiety State

The frightening physical and psychological assault experienced by these children during an abusive episode exposed them to the threat of annihilation and/or abandonment. Many of the children were overwhelmed by both the quality and quantity of the noxious stimulation, which paralyzed ego functioning and resulted in severe panic. This situation resembled Freud's concept of traumatic neurosis and the breaching of the stimulus barrier (1920). The abused children experienced feelings of helplessness, annihilation, and humiliation, which were often accompanied by a loss of ego boundaries. During anxiety states which occurred prior to or during a beating, or in the anticipation of an attack, these children frequently displayed psychotic behavior due to severe ego regression with temporary suspension of reality testing.

Case 1. Doris, an eleven-year-old girl, had been subjected to harsh beatings by her rigid, fanatically religious mother, who was impatient with Doris's failure to perform chores and errands efficiently. Once Doris tried to run away from her irate mother, who chased her with a strap after she accidentally spilled the contents of a package she was carrying. When her mother finally cornered her in the bedroom, Doris panicked and jumped out of the window. She miraculously survived the fall with only a broken femur.

These children exhibited a striking tendency to continually reenact the traumatic situation. Repetition of the trauma was observed in overt behavior and in symbolic activities such as fantasy, play, and artistic productions. It was also encountered in the therapeutic relationship in which the children acted out the role of the "bad child" and sought punishment from the therapist. This "fixation to the trauma" may be considered a defensive reaction which permits the abused child to actively recreate, master, and control the painful affects and anxiety which otherwise might be instigated by the environment. The maladaptive aspects of this pattern are obvious, potentially leading to further maltreatment and punishment, ultimately resulting in a pain-dependent orientation.

Case 2. Sarah, age six, had been a victim of recurrent physical abuse by her mother since infancy. She sustained a broken femur during a severe beating when she was four when her mother attacked her for letting the bathroom sink overflow. During her initial testing, Sarah responded to the examiner's presentation of a hitting scene in a doll family with the comment: "The mother hits the baby for playing with the water." During a psychiatric interview a short time later, Sarah appeared quite anxious upon returning from the bathroom. She told the psychiatrist that she was afraid he would punish her for spilling water from the sink onto the floor.

Khan's concept of "cumulative trauma" (1963) might apply to the long-term interference with the abused child's development caused by the mother's failure to function as a protective shield.

Pathological Object Relationships

Early and pervasive exposure to parental rejection, assault, and deprivation had an adverse effect on the development of subsequent object relationships. Potential new objects were regarded with fear and apprehension. The abused children were not able to achieve Erikson's stage of basic trust (1950). On the basis of previous experience they expected similar frustration and maltreatment from other adults. Violence and rejection were regarded as the major ingredients of human encounters. These children were involved in a perpetual search for "good" objects to protect them from the "bad" ones.

Case illustration. Robert, age nine, and his two younger brothers had been subjected to frequent beatings by their blind, impulsive mother during her frequent paranoid rages. During his initial visits to the playroom, Robert depicted a female "super" doll with flexed muscles, involved in "kung fu," beating and kicking smaller, male soldiers who often cried pitifully for help. With the consolidation of the relationship with the male therapist, the theme of the doll play gradually changed. A "six-million-dollar" man was created, who strengthened a "three-million-dollar" boy with the addition of "bionic" body parts. This pair was now able to cope with the "five-million-dollar" superwoman with ease.

Psychotherapeutic involvement with abused children has provided us with a good opportunity to study the vicissitudes of their object relationships *in statu nascendi.* The typical abused child initially appeared detached and guarded, and was ingratiating in order to please the therapist and avoid punishment. Once he felt safe, he displayed an enormous object hunger. The therapist was overidealized, and the child attempted to incorporate this "good parent" as a source of dependency gratification and as a means of protection against his "bad" parental objects. However, the inevitable frustrations and limitations in the therapeutic relationship incited the child's rage and disillusionment.

The child's increasing anger and provocative behavior led to his anticipation of punishment by the therapist, who was rapidly transformed into the "bad parent." The child's projection of his own rage onto the therapist helped to consolidate this negative image and increase his fear of retaliation. At this point he adopted the negative self-image of the "bad child," representing an "identification with the aggressor" (his own bad parent), in the face of increasing anxiety and helplessness in the treatment situation. The child then proceeded to reenact with the therapist the relationship with the abusing parent. He sought to achieve mastery and control over anticipated punishment through provocative and testing behavior. The rapidly fluctuating self- and object-identifications of the child were facilitated by the utilization of primitive defensive mechanisms.

Primitive Defense Mechanisms

The abused children relied on an excessive use of primitive defenses, such as denial, projection, introjection, and splitting, in order to cope with threatening external and internalized parental images. They were unable to integrate the loving and hostile aspects of their parents and others. This accounted for the baffling tendency of some of these children to completely support their parent's transparent denials and rationalizations concerning inflicted injuries.

While this need to suppress knowledge of parental wrongdoing was occasionally motivated by fear of additional punishment, it also represented the child's need to protect himself from the awareness of the actual and internalized destructive parent and to safeguard the parent from his own murderous rage. The image of the "bad parent" was subjected to denial and was projected onto some other persons, allowing the child to maintain the fantasy of having a "good parent." At times, the child assumed a negative identification in compliance with parental wishes for a scapegoat, thus acting as a willing prop for the projection of the parent's bad, unacceptable self-image. Splitting mechanisms were observed more frequently in those children who were abused by the parent who provided most of the nurturing. Acknowledgment of the destructiveness and malevolence of the primary caretaker, usually the mother, would have placed their tenuous dependent relationship in jeopardy.

Impaired Impulse Control

The abused children were often cited for aggressive and destructive behavior at home and in school. Bullying, fighting, and assaultive behavior were observed in their contact with peers and siblings. The younger children were frequently restless and hyperactive, while the older children and adolescents were commonly involved in antisocial and delinquent behavior. The origin of this problem was overdetermined. The abused children formed a basic identification with their violent parents, which facilitated the use of "identification with the aggressor" as a major defense against anxiety and feelings of helplessness. Hyperaggressive behavior typically followed incidents of physical abuse. Loss of impulse control was further exacerbated by the presence of CNS dysfunction. Due to inadequate superego models and faulty internalization, these children also lacked the usual superego restraints found in normal children during latency. Impulse control was precarious and inconsistent, achieved largely through externalization and fear of punishment.

Case illustration. Tim R., a seven-year-old boy, was referred for psychiatric treatment because of aggressive and poorly controlled behavior in school. He frequently attacked his classmates and even hit his teacher. He was described by teachers as "disobedient and hyperactive." Tim's mother also complained that he misbehaved at home, indulging in temper tantrums, bedwetting, and fighting with children in the neighborhood. Tim had been placed by his mother with a foster care agency at birth, after she had separated from his father. When Tim was eighteen months old, his mother agreed to take him home after the agency was unable to place him with a foster family. At this time, Tim stayed with a babysitter during the day while his mother worked in an office full time. Miss R. was harsh and punitive with Tim. She admitted hitting him in the face when he failed to comply with her demands and subjecting him to many beatings during toilet training. She currently beat him whenever she received a report from school about his misbehaving.

Violent themes permeated Tim's psychotherapy sessions. He was aggressive and provocative with his therapist, and his play usually described murder and mayhem between "good" and "bad" figures, which represented his struggles against his mother and other adversaries. He consistently attempted to prove his strength and invulnerability to himself and his therapist as a means of protection against his mother and violently perceived adults who were extensions of her. He insisted that he is the "strongest" boy in his class, and attempted to engage the therapist in "karate" and "Kung fu" type combat. He then became anxious, fearing retaliation by the therapist in the form of physical attack or abandonment.

Impaired Self-Concept

The abused children were frequently sad, dejected, and self-deprecatory. Their poor self-concept was an end result of chronic physical and emotional scarring, humiliation, and scapegoating, compounded and reinforced by each new episode of abuse. One may hypothesize that the preverbal infant who is repeatedly assaulted acquires an unpleasurable awareness of "self" consisting of painful sensations and painful affects linked to the primary objects. This painful self-awareness is transformed into a devalued self-concept with the development of cognition and language. These children ultimately regard themselves with the same displeasure and contempt their parents directed toward them. The young children who were repeatedly punished, beaten, and threatened with abandonment assume that it was a consequence of their own behavior, regardless of their actual innocence. This loathsome self-image often created such anxiety and discomfort that it had to be projected or displaced onto others. These negative self-representations were often attributed to a specific doll or puppet in the playroom. At times the poor self-concept was disguised by compensatory fantasies of grandiosity and omnipotence.

Case illustration. Karen, a seven-year-old girl, was referred to the outpatient child-psychiatry clinic because her mother could not tolerate her poor school performance. Her mother continually referred to Karen's stupidity and was certain that the child was retarded. Karen was untidy and dishevelled when she came to her appointments. Her clothes were often torn and stank of urine. Her therapist began to notice evidence of physical injury in the form of a black eye, scratches and bruises. Her mother admitted that her husband had started to assault Karen and the other children. Emergency placement for Karen and her siblings was effected, and she was able to continue her treatment during her stay at a children's shelter. Karen ascribed her injuries to fights at school and to falls, persistently defending her parents. She confessed to being stupid and dumb, and expressed guilt over the break up of her family. She lamented: "If I only had done the laundry, my mother wouldn't have been beaten up by my father and we wouldn't have broken up." She voluntarily assumed the role of the scapegoat. Incidentally, Karen's test results indicated an IQ of 108 with perceptual-motor problems and dyslexia.

Masochistic and Self-Destructive Behavior

Abused children commonly exhibited such overt types of self-destructive behavior as suicide attempts, gestures and threats, and various forms of self-mutilation. These were often accompanied by more subtle forms of pain-dependent activity in the form of provocative, belligerent, and limit-testing behavior which easily elicited beatings and punishment from parents, adults, and peers. Accident proneness was another form of self-destructive activity frequently observed in this population. Forty percent of our research population of abused children manifested direct forms of self-destructive behavior, a significantly higher incidence than in the neglected and normal controls (Green 1978). In the majority of cases, the self-destructive behavior was precipitated by parental beatings or occurred in response to actual or threatened separation from parental figures. This finding is of special importance, since self-destructive behavior is seldom observed among latency and preadolescent children in the general population. Thus, those events occurring in normal latency which seem to have self-preservative functions are interfered with in the abused child.

The overall impairment of ego functions and impulse control in these children increased their tendency to reenact the parental hostility and rejection directed toward them. Self-destructive behavior represented the child's compliance with parental wishes for his destruction and/or disappearance. The child's acting out of parental hostility directed toward him has been described as an important factor in the etiology of adolescent suicidal behavior (Sabbeth 1969). The self-destructive behavior of the abused child may also be viewed as the end result of the transformation of feelings of low self-esteem and self-hatred into action.

Case illustration. Betty, an eight-year-old girl, had been physically abused by her impulsive, schizophrenic mother. Many of the beatings had been triggered by the mother's heavy drinking. Her mother had also been frequently hospitalized for acute psychotic episodes. When Betty was seven, she jumped off a swing in response to the commands of a "woman's voice." Betty engaged in self-deprecatory and self-destructive rumination during her psychotherapy sessions. Some of her typical comments were: "I'm terrible; I can't sit still; I always hurt myself; I fall off my bike and lean against a hot radiator." When she was angry with her therapist, Betty would often bang her arm or head against a hard object, stick herself with a pin, or threaten to jump out of the window.

Difficulties with Separation

The abused children often reacted to actual or threatened separation and object loss with intense anxiety. This was frequently traced to numerous experiences of separation and abandonment by parental figures during infancy and early childhood. Hypothetically, chronic physical abuse might have increased the vulnerability of these children to separation because each beating implies the parent's withdrawal of love and wish to be rid of the child. The abused child's frequent lack of object constancy resulting from cognitive impairment and/or cerebral dysfunction also contributed to the separation problems by interfering with the construction and internalization of the mental representation of the absent object. Acute separation anxiety was often observed in the treatment situation in response to the therapist's vacations and departure from the hospital. The children were commonly unable to leave the playroom unless they were given a tangible object which they could utilize to represent the absent therapist.

Case illustration. Earl, age six, was hospitalized with severe burns and multiple injuries as a result of abuse by his mother and maternal grandmother. Foster placement was arranged following his discharge from the hospital. Earl was referred for psychiatric treatment because of unmanageable behavior in kindergarten. Following his therapist's return from vacation, at the onset of treatment he noted with distress that the toys were not in their usual order and that someone had eaten the candies. He complained that someone else would be playing with the therapist the next day when he wasn't there. Near the end of the session, he began to cut erasers off the pencils and attempted to cut off some of the therapist's hair which he wanted to take home.

Difficulties in School Adjustment

Most of the abused children exhibited major problems in school adjustment. Their limited attention span, frequent hyperactivity, and cognitive impairment resulted in deficient academic performance. At times these children demonstrated specific learning disabilities such as dyslexia, expressive and receptive language disorders, and perceptual-motor dysfunction on the basis of minimal brain dysfunction or maturational lag. Their aggressivity and poor impulse control contributed to behavior problems with peers and teachers. Their parents were frequently called to school because of their disruptive behavior and learning difficulties, and this often led to further abuse. A vicious cycle often ensued, consisting of academic and behavioral problems, parental beatings, and increased disruptiveness in the classroom due to the displacement of anger at the parents onto the teachers. Chronic school difficulties leading to disciplinary action and placement in special classes for the emotionally or intellectually handicapped produced further adverse effects on the abused child's previously damaged self-esteem.

Case illustration. Don, a seven-year-old boy, was referred for psychiatric consultation by his teacher, who described the following behavior in the classroom: "Don has a violent temper in the classroom. Children are afraid to sit next to him because he is constantly threatening and fighting with them. He assaults children if they don't give him money he asks for. He also steals cookie money and pencils from his classmates. He displays foul language and grabs the genitals of the boys and girls. He has temper tantrums in which he throws himself down and rolls around on the floor. He recently urinated on another child in class." Don had been abused by his father, who had been ordered out of the home by the court. Most of the beatings were precipitated by reports from the school about Don's misbehavior.

Central Nervous System Impairment

Although a high incidence of central nervous system dysfunction among abused children has been reported in the literature (Johnson and Morse 1968, Elmer and Gregg 1967, Morse et al. 1970, Martin et al. 1974), the precise etiology of this impairment has been the subject of considerable controversy. With the exception of obvious cases of massive head trauma resulting in skull fractures with subdural hematomas (as originally described by Kempe et al. [1962] in their seminal paper on the "battered child syndrome"), brain damage alone would not appear sufficient to explain CNS impairment. The uncertain impact of child abuse on neurological development has been noted by Martin et al. (1974), who showed that appreciable numbers of abused children with skull fractures and subdural hematomas were neurologically normal, while numerous abused children without head injury exhibited neurological deficits. Because most abused children manifest a variety of soft-tissue injuries as opposed to major skull trauma, it is important to clarify this issue.

Several hypotheses have been offered to account for neurological impairment observed in children not known to have sustained massive head injuries. Caffey (1972) described how vigorous shaking of a child's head could result in petechial hemorrhages in the brain. Neglect (Coleman and Provence 1957), malnutrition (Scrimshaw and Gordon 1968, Birch 1972), and maternal deprivation (Bekwin 1949, Spitz 1945, Bowlby 1951) often accompanying child abuse have all been implicated in impaired neurological development. Some observers (Sandgrund et al. 1974, Milowe and Lourie 1964) have postulated that this impairment may precede and even provoke abuse by rendering these children hyperkinetic and difficult to manage. Most retrospective studies of abuse victims have revealed neurological impairment (Martin et al. 1974, Smith and Hanson 1974, Baron et al. 1970), mental retardation (Elmer and Gregg 1967, Morse et al. 1970, Martin et al. 1974, Smith and Hanson 1974, Birrell and Birrell 1968), and language deficits (Martin et al. 1974, Smith and Hanson 1974). Such problems could severely strain the child-rearing capacities of abuse-prone parents (Green et al. 1974a). Whether neurological impairment precipitates abuse, is one of its effects, or is merely concomitant, remains problematic.

There is considerable evidence that the proportion of premature births among abused children is substantially higher than regional averages (Elmer and Gregg 1967, Martin et al. 1974, Klein and Sern 1971). The prevalence of unrecognized physical handicaps (Ounsted et al. 1974) and congenital anomalies (Birrell and Birrell 1968) is also significant. Several interpretations based on these findings have been suggested concerning the role of the child in the abuse process (Friedrich and Boriskin 1971). The most direct causal inference is that abused children may be less responsible and manageable due to a preexisting deviancy, rendering them vulnerable to scapegoating. These deficits are tolerated poorly by narcissistic parents who respond abusively when their threshold for frustration is breached. Prematurity or difficult infant temperaments may also impede the establishment of maternal-infant bonds. Faranoff et al. (1972) found that mothers who later abuse or neglect their children visited low birth-weight infants less frequently than normal control mothers. Ounsted et al. (1974) observed "high-risk" mother-infant dyads characterized by puerperal depression among the mothers and colicky, irritable children who cried excessively and were prone to sleep difficulties.

Unfortunately, the major weakness in most studies documenting neurological problems associated with child abuse has been the failure to compare them with control children from otherwise similar backgrounds.

A study was carried out at the Downstate Medical Center exploring the relationship between the abusive environment and CNS development (Green et al. 1979). The neurological competency of physically abused children who were not known to have sustained severe head trauma was assessed. Neglect, family disorganization, and emotional deprivation were controlled by including nonabused, neglected, and normal comparison groups. The neurological evaluation of the one-hundred and twenty children (sixty abused, thirty neglected, and thirty normal) followed the psychological and psychiatric studies described above. The children received physical, neurological examinations, including an EEG, and a battery of perceptual-motor tests. On the basis of all available information, the pediatric neurologist assigned each child a global rating of impairment. 52 percent of the abused children received designations of moderate or severe impairment, compared to 38 percent of the neglected children and only 14 percent of the controls.

The higher incidence of neurological impairment among the abused and neglected children was anticipated, but the finding that the abused children were not significantly more damaged than their neglected counterparts was contrary to expectation. The CNS impairment documented in this study indicated relatively subtle neurological dysfunction rather than structural damage. In many instances, these developmental lags and deficits in perception, coordination, and integration of sensory stimuli would not have been detected by the usual neurological examination, but were clearly evident in the careful neurological evaluation and series of perceptual-motor tasks designed explicitly to reveal subtle neurological impairment. Similarities in the nature and prevalence of impairment in the two maltreatment groups, in contrast to the relative intactness of the controls, suggest that the adverse physical and psychological environment associated with maltreatment may be of greater neurological consequence than the physical assault itself. The combination of behavioral and neurological disability in the maltreated child could result from abnormal child rearing, poor prenatal and infant care, nutritional deficiency, inadequate medical care, and abnormal (insufficient or excessive) sensory stimulation. Although the control children were also chosen from families on public assistance, more of these households were intact, with somewhat greater availability of social support systems. The maltreating families appeared to represent the extremes of deprivation and chronic disorganization within their own subculture.

The neurological and developmental sequelae produced by the maltreating environment frequently contributes to the child's vulnerability to abuse by rendering him more difficult to manage. A vicious cycle often emerges, consisting of inadequate or abnormal parenting, neurological and behavioral impairment, physical abuse, further impairment, etc. CNS abnormalities may even occur initially as adaptations to the maltreating environment. Martin (1976) suggests that developmental lags in speech and motor development might represent the abused child's inhibitory response to parental admonitions against spontaneous speech and motor expression.

The results of this study implicate poverty, family disorganization, and related environmental factors prevalent in low socioeconomic status maltreating families in the adverse neurological development of abused and neglected children. Because these children are particularly susceptible to subtle neurological impairment, neurological examination of these children should be specifically devised to detect these manifestations. In order to assess the impact of physical abuse independently, it would be necessary to conduct a similar study in a middle-class context.

Contributions of the Child to
His Abuse and Scapegoating

Several investigators have described the role of the child in precipitating his own abuse (Milowe and Lourie 1964, Green et al. 1964a, Helfer 1976, Ounsted et al. 1974). In our experience the behavior of certain children makes them ᴵ difficult to manage than their siblings, and would even creat greater than average child-rearing burden for very adequat parents. These "vulnerable" children fall into several categories:

1. Infants or young children who respond poorly to nurturing, such as hypertonic, irritable, or colicky infants who are difficult to satisfy and comfort, or hypoactive, sluggish babies who may be perceived as unresponsive and uninvolved. Mothers readily perceive each of these patterns as a rejection and confirmation of their maternal inadequacy.

2. Children with major psychological impairment who would pose a management problem for an average family, including disruptive children with poor impulse control, hyperkinetic children with "minimal" or more pronounced cerebral dysfunction, and learning disabled children who function poorly at school.

3. Physically and developmentally impaired children with prominent defects who are burdensome and difficult to care for. This category includes children who are mentally retarded, suffer from chronic physical illness, or who exhibit congenital anomalies. Narcissistic abuse-prone parents readily perceive these children as current symbols of their own defective self-image.

Case illustration. Ira, an eight-year-old black youngster, was hospitalized at the age of four for multiple welts and bruises after a beating administered by his father. His mother complained about his provocative and disruptive behavior, which included soiling, wetting, and failure to do what he was told. Ira had four younger siblings, ages six, five, and four, and nine months. His mother claimed that he demanded more attention than the infant. The father continued to beat Ira until he left home. Both the mother and her current boyfriend continued to hit the child when he became provocative, attributing his deviancy to willful disobedience.

Ira's developmental history indicated that he was born prematurely during the seventh month of gestation and weighed two pounds at birth. He exhibited a marked delay in his speech

nent. His speech was often incoherent dur-
d at times he failed to comprehend what
Full Scale IQ on the WISC was 54, and
mination yielded signs of unequivocal
t was felt that Ira's receptive and expres-
...pairment represented an aphasic disorder.
... impaired behavior and physical functioning of these vulnerable children are frequently regarded as willfully motivated
rather than as a consequence of their incapacity by abuse-
prone parents, who typically display high levels of expectation
for their offspring. This observation suggests that counseling
of the parents of deviant children might be of value in the
prevention of abuse.

Long-term Effects of Child Abuse

The cumulative impact of physical abuse, harsh and punitive
child rearing, scapegoating, and frequent separation from parents, which has such a devastating effect on the behavior and
psychological adaptation of the abused child, may be expected
to continue to jeopardize his future life adjustment as he passes
through adolescence and adulthood. Pathological identifications with violent parental models, chronic anger, low self-
esteem, and the tendency to perceive others with fear and
distrust will cause a predictable disruption of future personal
relationships and the capacity for love and intimacy. The full
extent of the damage in these areas can only be assessed after
the abused child negotiates adolescence and develops a fairly
consistent lifestyle as he relates to his job, peers, love objects,
and eventually his children. The period of adolescence is often
quite pivotal for victims of abuse, as many of these brutalized
youngsters become assaultive, antisocial, and self-destructive,
at great cost to themselves and to society. Many of their pathological identifications and personality characteristics are solid-
ified toward the end of adolescence, rendering them more
refractory to therapeutic intervention. Many abused girls begin
adolescence with unwanted pregnancies and the premature

burdens of motherhood, which may significantly influence their future lives.

Impact of Adolescence on the Psychopathology of the Abused Child

During the adolescent period the aggressive, impulsive, learning impaired abused child may begin to exhibit the type of impulsive behavior which deviates more grossly from societal norms. These adolescents often drop out of school. The boys frequently become involved in delinquent or antisocial activities. The girls often display chaotic sexual behavior, which may result in premature and unwanted pregnancy. These transformations are catalyzed by certain biological, psychological, and social events during adolescence.

The rapid increase in physical growth and musculature provides increased strength for engaging in assaultive behavior. The incessant pressure of sexual and aggressive drives further upsets the unstable equilibrium between ego controls and impulses, resulting in a surplus of aggression and sexuality which permeates object relationships. The characteristic "acting-out" behavior during the adolescent period further enhances the conversion of sexual and aggressive fantasies into action, which is frequently used as a defense against passivity.

The usual restructuring of superego, ego ideal, and identifications from childhood fails to occur in these adolescents after disengagement from their parents. In the normal adolescent, changes in these structures are effected through contact with new peers and adults, who provide models for identification quite different from the parents. In the case of abused adolescents, fixation to the childhood sadomasochistic identifications with abusing parents limits their capacity to experiment with new models. Their compulsion to repeat the original trauma propels them toward violent and aggressive peers and adults. Lower-class status and a subculture characterized by social disorganization, promiscuity and early pregnancy, poverty, and crime create a plentiful supply of poorly controlled antisocial individuals as "stand-ins" for the abusing parents. Thus, the

adolescent process perpetuates the earliest pathological identifications of these children, rather than modifying them.
The following sections describe some of the most important
and frequently observed long-term sequelae of child abuse.

Pathological Object Relationships

Early and pervasive exposure to parental rejection, assault,
and deprivation has an adverse effect on the development of
subsequent object relationships. Potential new objects are
regarded with fear and apprehension. Victims of abuse are
unable to achieve Erikson's (1950) stage of basic trust.
We have witnessed the tendency of abused children to perpetuate the "aggressor-victim" relationship in new encounters
with peers and adults. The tendency to repeat the original traumatic encounters provides them with a means of controlling
the maltreatment they expect from others and also influences
their choice of objects during adolescence and adulthood. For
example, after the onset of puberty, it is common for abused
and deprived girls to engage in premature sexual relationships
which often result in early and unwanted pregnancy. Many
choose sexual partners and boyfriends who physically abuse
and exploit them. Their submission to violent and rejecting
males often represents a repetition of their maltreatment during
childhood. They retain their self-concept as a bad child and a
primary identification with the "victim," which is enhanced if
their mothers had been assaulted by their father or father surrogates. When they become parents, they often assume an
identification with their own violent parents (identifications with
the aggressor) which is exacerbated by projecting their undesirable characteristics onto their children. Women with a childhood history of physical abuse by their fathers are often unable
to separate violence from sexuality, and become involved in
pain-dependent forms of sexual activity. Prostitution is common among women who had been sexually abused as children.

Case illustration. Carrie, a twenty-six-year-old mother of
two, had been victimized during her childhood by a brutal,

sadistic father, who beat her, her mother and her nine siblings with a mule whip. Her father was also a gun collector who shot stray dogs and forced his children to watch them slowly die. At age twelve, Carrie was sent to live with an aunt after her father had sexually abused her. She met her husband, Mr. A., when she was seventeen. She was happy with him until after her daughter was born, when he began to beat her. After a severe beating which resulted in her hospitalization, Carrie left her husband and moved in with her mother. The husband came to the mother's house and threatened Carrie and her daughter with a gun. On one occasion, he abducted her at gunpoint and locked her in the apartment. Mr. A. finally returned to the South, where he was imprisoned after killing two policemen.

When abused boys enter adolescence, they are more likely to relate to objects in an aggressive, hurtful manner. Boys who have been victimized by abusing mothers are likely to release their pent-up rage with girlfriends and spouses. If their fathers were the abusers, they readily utilize them as violent role models in their relationships with their families. When abused boys become parents, they are likely to abuse both their children and spouses.

Pathological Child Rearing

From the vantage point of the child-abuse specialist, it would appear that a history of child abuse, neglect, or exploitation would clearly predispose an individual to become an abusing parent, since the vast majority of abusing parents we deal with have been abused and scapegoated during their childhood. However, we don't come in contact with formerly abused individuals who do not abuse or maltreat their children and we do hear about formerly abused children who become model parents, consciously striving to protect their own children from the very abusive practices which they had experienced. Some of these parents might even veer toward the opposite extreme of overprotection and excessive permissiveness, but this type of outcome would seem to be the exception rather than the rule.

One might speculate that the abused child can only become an adequate parent if he had been able to develop a satisfying relationship with a benign nonpunitive parental figure, such as the nonabusing parent or a relative, who was available as a protective role model. Since one usually parents the same way that one was raised as a child, the individual who was abused, scapegoated, and exploited as a child is likely to inflict these experiences upon his offspring unless some type of therapeutic intervention takes place. Similarly, victims of parental neglect and abandonment repeat this pattern with their children, as maltreatment is transmitted from one generation to the next.

Individuals who have been abused as children cannot envision a parent-child relationship as a mutually gratifying experience. The task of parenting mobilizes identifications with the parent-aggressor/child-victim dyad of the past. If the mother does not receive support and dependency gratification from her spouse or family, she turns to the child for the satisfaction of these needs, and the affirmation of her maternal competency. Most children are incapable of satisfying these demands, thus intensifying feelings of unlovableness and incompetence. These painful feelings are threatening to the mother's precarious narcissistic equilibrium, and are subjected to denial and projection onto the child, who then becomes the scapegoat and target for the mother's self-hatred. This is facilitated by a shift toward an identification with her own aggressive parent. By beating her child, the abuse assuages her punitive superego and attempts to master actively the traumatic experiences passively endured as a child.

The scapegoating process continues as the child also becomes the target for aggression displaced from various frustrating objects in the mother's current and past life, such as a rejecting mate or lover, a hated sibling rival, or a depriving parental figure. These objects are unconsciously linked to the original "parent aggressor." The choice of a particular child for scapegoating might depend upon such accidental factors as time of birth, physical appearance, temperament, sex, in addition to actual physical or psychological deviancy.

Cognitive Impairment

The devastating impact of physical abuse and hostile parenting, superimposed upon a background of neglect and deprivation, on the intellectual and cognitive functioning of abused children has been demonstrated by numerous investigators (Sandgrund et al. 1974, Elmer 1965, Martin 1974, Morse et al. 1970). In a research study of schoolaged maltreated children at the Downstate Medical Center (Sandgrund et al. 1974, Green et al. 1974b) we discovered that 25 percent of the abused and 20 percent of the neglected children were in the mentally retarded range (IQ below 70). Many more of these maltreated children were functioning far below their intellectual potential and had to be placed in special classes for the learning and emotionally disabled. While the intellectual impairment of some of the abused children may have been produced by chronic trauma to the brain it was felt that many of these children provoked abuse because of pre-existent neurological or cognitive deficits.

The cognitively impaired abused children encounter severe learning difficulties as they progress in school. They display a pattern of academic failure and misbehavior in the classroom, which often provokes additional beatings by their parents. This further damages their already diminished self-esteem and increases their sense of failure, leading to major narcissistic injury. As adults, they tend to project these inadequacies onto others, especially their children. Quite understandably, if a child has some actual intellectual or developmental impairment he will be poorly tolerated and easily scapegoated by a parent who experienced similar handicaps as a child. The formerly abused adult with cognitive impairment is poorly equipped to function in society. His low frustration tolerance and inability to plan for the future contribute to the development of a compensatory lifestyle characterized by impulsivity and the need for immediate gratification. The disorders in speech and language displayed by these individuals exacerbate the acting out of conflicts and feelings. Intellectual impairment will interfere with parents' ability to correctly perceive and understand the needs

and behavior of their children. We are not surprised at the finding of Smith et al. (1973) indicating that nearly half of two
hundred and fourteen abusing parents were of borderline or
subnormal intelligence.

Vocational Failure

Former victims of child abuse whose school experiences
were marred by behavior problems, learning disability, and
academic failure are usually unable to complete the usual high-
school curriculum. When they drop out of school, their limited
education and cognitive weakness place them at a great disadvantage in the competition for employment. They are frequently unemployed or find themselves limited to menial jobs,
thus confirming and increasing their sense of inadequacy and
depression. This vocational failure also insures their entrap-
ment in the cycle of poverty and public assistance and increases
their tendency to use their children as a source of narcissistic
gratification. Quite often, they attempt to overcome their barriers through an illusory escape into crime, drugs, or alcohol.
Vocational failure is usually more devastating to males because
of greater societal demands for their performance as wage
earners and family providers. It is striking that vocational
inadequacy, a sequel of child abuse, becomes a common
precipitant of child abuse when these men become fathers.
Formerly abused women with similar limitations can more
readily avoid the stigma of vocational undesirability by confin-
ing themselves to domestic pursuits, but they also encounter
difficulties when they seek or find employment.

In our performance-oriented society, vocational failure typically undermines a male's sense of masculinity. This situation is
compounded if the unemployed father assumes child-rearing
and household responsibilities. Physical abuse by fathers or
father surrogates often takes place in situations in which they
feel overwhelmed by child-rearing duties they feel are more
appropriately handled by their spouses. Their inability to support their families, however, contributes to a vicious cycle in
which their wives often must seek employment out of the
homes, forcing the husbands to assume what they regard as a

homes, forcing the husband to assume what they regard as a passive, feminine role. The father's striking out at spouse and children might represent both a protest against this "role-exchange" and a crude affirmation of his masculinity. Unfortunately, the tyrannical control over spouse and children is often the only source of gratification for many of these fathers, who have been deprived of the economic and psychological rewards of vocational success.

Violence, Crime, and Delinquency

Several observers (Duncan et al. 1958, Satten et al. 1960, Tanay 1969) have proposed a link between child abuse and subsequent violent behavior, which seems to justify the adage "violence breeds violence." This link has been inferred from studies of violent individuals who had been abused during childhood. Alfaro (1977) documented a high incidence of delinquent and criminal activity in an adult population who were reported abused or neglected as children in the previous generation. This correlation between child maltreatment and subsequent violent criminal activity has been confirmed by in-depth psychological explorations of maltreated children referred to the Comprehensive Treatment Program for Abused Children and Their Families at the Downstate Medical Center because of aggressive and antisocial behavior. Data derived from psychoanalytic psychotherapy of these children revealed the mechanisms by which the abused child is gradually transformed into an assaultive, antisocial adolescent and adult.

The abused child, reared under conditions of parental assault, harsh punishment, scapegoating, and deprivation, learns to regard his environment with fear and distrust. He anticipates pain and frustration from parental encounters, rather than comfort and gratification. He gradually generalizes from these negative experiences with primary caretakers and views the outside world as an extension of the sadomasochistic pattern of family life. The "angry parent/bad child" interaction becomes the prototype for subsequent dyadic relationships. The absence of memories of parental love, care, and tenderness robs him of the capacity for optimism, affection, and empathy. Since the object world of the victim of abuse consists mainly of aggressors and victims, aggressive assaultive behavior becomes the natural adaptive response to the threat of annihilation and humiliation from others. Impaired impulse control and frequent existence of brain damage facilitate the translation of aggressive fantasy into action.

Case histories of two abused children will illustrate the relationship between early exposure to abuse and pathological child rearing and the subsequent development of violent, aggressive, and life-threatening behavior. In the absence of active intervention, both of these boys will probably become violent and potentially homicidal adults.

Case 1. Louis, a small, waif-life eleven-year-old Puerto Rican boy, was recently referred for psychiatric treatment after he persuaded his three-year-old half-brother to drink some lye. This child required a resection of his esophagus and managed to survive after being hospitalized for over a year. Louis returned to his mother and her boyfriend when he was nine, after living with his abusive father and stepmother in Puerto Rico since the age of two. He had been subjected during this seven-year period to chronic physical abuse which included beating on the head with a hammer and burns on his body inflicted with a hot iron. Since rejoining his mother, Louis had been extremely rough and aggressive with his two younger half-brothers. He also displayed hyperactive, aggressive behavior in school, frequently hitting and kicking his classmates. Louis conveyed his violent feelings quite dramatically. "Sometimes I hate people because they bother or hit me. Once I hit the teacher in Puerto Rico because she punished me. I hit a kid in school who stole my pencil. I knocked him down the stairs. I hit my little brother when he makes too much noise. When I get nervous, I punch the wall and hit my head against the radiator."

During his initial months of psychotherapy, Louis was extremely hyperactive and could not remain in the playroom for more than twenty minutes. When frustrated, he would bang his fists or head against the wall. One of his favorite activities at home consisted of catching mice and smashing their heads with a hammer. He would then flush them down the toilet. When asked to explain the reasons for this behavior, he pointed to the scars and ridges on his scalp, exclaiming, "This is what my father did to me." Louis could also be charming and ingratiating. He usually related to adults as need-satisfying objects. When frustrated, however, he would become impulsive and violent. Whenever he felt challenged or humiliated, he would try to engage his "adversary" in physical combat. His extreme sibling rivalry was also expressed in therapeutic relationships. He became irate whenever he saw other children entering or leaving his therapist's office and expressed the desire to fight with them.

Case 2. Charles T., a tall, well-built, sixteen-year-old black youngster, was reunited with his mother in New York at the age of fifteen, after spending the majority of his childhood with his maternal aunt and grandfather in the South. Charles was returned to his mother by his aunt after he was placed on probation for shooting his junior high-school teacher with a pellet gun. This incident occurred after he was reprimanded by the teacher in front of the class for picking on a classmate. After this teacher hit him with a ruler, Charles announced that he would return with a gun and take revenge. He carried out the threat and proceeded to shoot the teacher in the leg.

After his return to New York, Charles continued to exhibit difficulties in school. He was abusive to a younger brother and was involved in stealing. Another violent incident occurred when Charles shot a gun into a crowd of hostile white youths who were taunting him and several of his friends because they had entered a white neighborhood after a rock concert. Luckily, no one was hit, and Charles was arrested on the spot. Charles had obtained the gun by stealing it from his friend's father and carried it with him in anticipation of attack. He seemed unperturbed when confronted with the possibility that his use of firearms might have resulted in someone's death or severe injury, blandly responding, "If someone was killed, he deserved it."

Charles's current social adjustment is poor. He associates with children younger than himself because he has trouble competing with his peers. His principal interest and hobby is training dogs. He is fascinated with bull terriers because "they can be trained to kill men." In a recurrent fantasy, his bull terrier carries out his command to kill a menacing German shepherd.

Charles experienced a traumatic early childhood. He was born when his mother, Miss T., was thirteen. She had been living with a female cousin and her husband when Charles was conceived. Miss T. had been physically and sexually abused by the cousin and her husband repeatedly since she was sent to live with them at the age of four when her mother died. Her mother had also beaten her. When Charles was born, Miss T. lived alone in a room and did not have enough money to adequately feed and clothe him. She regarded the baby as "unreal, like a doll." When he cried out of hunger, she beat him "so he would go to sleep. I beat him so long, he'd be crazy," Miss T. confessed. "I hit him with a belt, extension cord, and clothes hanger."

Miss T. is fully aware of Charles's violent potential as an adult. She's afraid he will become a child abuser or murderer. Although he recalls having been beaten by his aunt and some teachers, he has no conscious memory of the physical abuse experienced at the hands of his mother during his first four years of life.

The behavior of these children is typical of abused boys[1] of their age, with whom they share several common features. They were exposed to physical and psychological abuse, neglect, and separation from parents since early childhood, which resulted in substantial psychological and cognitive impairment with poor impulse control and damaged self-esteem. Their identifications with violent, aggressive parents were not modified by positive attachments to loving parental

---

1. Abused girls may display similar aggressive patterns prior to puberty. During adolescence their delinquent activity is more frequently complicated by sexual promiscuity, running away and masochistic behavior.

figures. Identification with the aggressor was used as a primary defense in situations of anxiety provoked by fears of attack, humiliation, and abandonment, which were linked unconsciously to memories of traumatic victimization in early childhood. Their aggressive behavior was an adaptive maneuver designed to master the original trauma by active repetition. It was also used as a device for relieving tension, and as a pathological form of self-esteem regulation, in which depression and helplessness were replaced by aggressive and destructive actions associated with omnipotent fantasies. Their action orientation was accompanied by difficulties in language and symbolization. They manifested little or no guilt during their violent behavior and lacked a capacity to empathize or identify with their victims.

These children regard all human relationships as encounters between aggressors and victims. They are distrustful and uncomfortable in the presence of benign, caring individuals, and usually seek to restore the familiar sadomasochistic interaction by engaging in provocative behavior, thus protecting themselves against possible betrayal and rationalizing their continued defensive use of aggression.

Implications for Treatment

The abused child will perpetuate the original sadomasochistic interaction with his parents in all subsequent relationships unless changes can be effected in his inner world. Therefore therapeutic intervention with his parents or placement outside of the family will, in themselves, be insufficient to prevent the long-term sequelae of abuse. Damage to the abused child's ego functions, cognitive capacity, and self-esteem requires vigorous psychotherapeutic and psychoeducational intervention. Modification of pathological, internalized self- and object-representations can be effected through play therapy and psychotherapy, but it is preferable to begin treatment during childhood. Reversing the pathological character traits and inner world of the abuse victims is more difficult once they are consolidated during the adolescent process.

Nevertheless, comprehensive treatment programs, using such therapeutic modalities as counseling, psychotherapy, group therapy, crisis intervention, and child-rearing assistance, have been able to successfully interrupt the cycle of abuse, scapegoating, and identification with the aggressor operating in the abusive adult. To accomplish this, the individual must be able to understand the link between his current violent patterns and his childhood experience of maltreatment.

Perhaps the most decisive way of interrupting the generational cycle of abuse is through prevention and early intervention with parents at risk for maltreatment. This provision of education about child development and child rearing for young parents and teenagers, access to nurseries and day-care centers for working mothers, and the availability of child-rearing assistance at times of crisis are methods of prevention which have been used successfully in recent years.

6

The Environment

Environmental Factors Associated with Child Abuse

While environmental stress has often been suggested as a prominent etiological factor in child abuse, the precise definition of this relationship has eluded most investigators. One author has attributed child abuse almost exclusively to socioeconomic determinants (Gil 1968, 1970), while most researchers agree that environmental stress serves as a catalyst, in some instances, for an abuse-prone personality.

In addition to Gil, economic pressures were important findings in studies by Elmer (1967), Kempe et al. (1962), Young (1964), Johnson and Morse (1968), and Bennie and Sclare (1969). Contrary evidence can be obtained in Paulson and Blake (1969) and Steele and Pollock (1968) who observed child abuse in economically advantaged populations. These authors and others (Adelson 1961, Allen, Ten Bensel, and Raile 1969, Holter and Friedman 1968, Kempe et al. 1962, Simons et al. 1966, Green 1976, Green et al. 1974a) place far greater emphasis upon personality factors and intrafamily dynamics.

The stress argument has at least in part been predicated on the high percentage of low socioeconomic status, multiple problem families in child abuse registers throughout the country. Gil's 1967 study (1970) revealed that nearly 60 percent of the families involved in abuse incidents had been on welfare during or prior to 1967, and 37.2 percent of the abusive families had been receiving public assistance at the time of the incident. 48.4 percent of the reported families had incomes below $5,000 in 1967, when 25.3 percent of all American families had such low incomes. The American Humane Association's national survey of reported cases of maltreatment in 1977 (1979) indicates that this pattern continues. The median family income of the 1977 families involved in substantiated cases of abuse and neglect was $5,361 or 36 percent of the United States median income of $16,009. The median family income of neglecting families was even lower, $4,633 or 29 percent of the median. Forty-four percent of abusing and neglecting families were receiving some form of welfare.

It is probable that reporting procedures themselves have led to the great emphasis on socioeconomic determinants, because of the disproportionate number of deprived persons being served by municipal agencies. Any controlled study which matches for socioeconomic status is compelled to look beyond such variables as family income for the origin of child abuse. The conclusion that Spinetta and Rigler (1972) reach in their review of the literature is far more likely – that environmental stress is neither necessary nor sufficient for child abuse but that it does, in some instances, interact with other factors, such as parent personality variables and child behaviors, to potentiate child battering.

Environmental stress includes current events that widen the discrepancy between the limited child-rearing capacity of the parents and increased child-rearing pressures. The stress may consist of a diminishing of child-rearing resources, due to a spouse's illness or desertion, or to the unavailability of an earlier caretaker, such as a neighbor or some other family member.

Another environmental stress is the actual or threatened loss of a key relationship that provides the parent with emotional security and dependency gratification. This may occur when the spouse becomes physically or emotionally unavailable or when ties with parents or important relatives are severed due to estrangement, illness, or death. Additional child-rearing pressures, such as the birth of another child, children's illnesses or the temporary care of other children occasioned by illness or death of friends or relatives, create environmental stress that might lead to child abuse.

Case 1. Calvin, a ten-year-old black boy, was referred to the Bureau of Child Welfare by the school guidance counselor because bruises, scars and cuts were observed all over his body. These resulted from beatings inflicted by his father, Mr. A., who was an alcoholic. Mr. A. began to beat Calvin and his two younger children regularly with a knitted ironing cord two years before, after he had assumed full-time child-care responsibility when his wife became incapacitated following a stroke. Mr. A. decided to leave his job and seek public assistance in order to take care of the three children. These arrangements broke down however when the pressures of child care caused an increase in his drinking, accompanied by a progressive loss of impulse control.

Family size has been recognized as another environmental factor related to child abuse. It might be expected that large numbers of children would be stressful for a parent or caretaker. Several observers have documented this relationship.

Young (1964) found that 37 percent of one-hundred and eighty families involved in abuse or neglect had between six and twelve children, while only 20 percent had fewer than three children. Gil (1970) reported that the proportion of families with three or more children is higher among child-abusing families than among the total U.S. population. The proportion of families with four or more children was nearly twice as high in the abusing sample than in the general population. Light (1973) presented a comparison of the family size of child abusers in the United States, New Zealand, and England. The percentage of abusing families with one child was much lower than the national average in each of these countries. On the other hand, two to three times as many abusing families in the United States and New Zealand have four or more children than the national average for all United States and New Zealand families.

A number of investigators have cited the importance of unemployment as a contributing factor to child abuse. Gil (1970) reported that only 52.5 percent of the fathers in his sample were employed throughout the year preceding the abuse incident. Galdston (1965), Young (1964), and Green (1979) also demonstrated a relationship between unemployment and child abuse. In addition to financial problems, the lack of a job poses a threat to the father's self-esteem. In Green's sample of abusing fathers, humiliating and beating their children and spouses provided them with a sense of power and masculinity, which compensated for the impaired self-image related to their vocational inadequacy or unemployment.

Justice and Duncan (1975) described the contribution of work-related pressures to the environmental stress which triggered child abuse. They cited four types of work-related situations: unemployed fathers caring for children at home, working mothers with domestic obligations, overworked husbands who neglect their wives, and traumatic job experiences resulting in undischarged tension. Justice and Justice (1976) were able to document the importance of stress in terms of excessive life changes in child-abusing families by means of the Social Readjustment Rating Scale developed by Holmes and Rahe (1967).

Bronfenbrenner (1974) and Garbarino (1976) suggested that the degree to which socioeconomic forces support or undermine the family as a setting for parent-child relationships is a critical factor in the etiology of child maltreatment.

Garbarino compared socioeconomic and demographic characteristics of fifty-eight counties in New York State with their rates
of reported child abuse and neglect. The study indicated that
the degree to which mothers in a particular county were subjected to socioeconomic stress without adequate support systems was more significantly related to the incidence of
maltreatment than the general economic conditions affecting
the family. High rates of maltreatment typically occurred in
impoverished communities providing inadequate educational
and child-care facilities for working mothers in one-parent
families with few support systems.

Case 2. Sally, a thirteen-year-old girl, lived alone in a single
room with her infant son. She had been evicted from the home
of an older female cousin before the baby was born. Sally had
lived with this cousin since she was four, when her mother
died. The cousin forced Sally to do an inordinate share of the
housework and subjected her to frequent beatings. The
cousin's husband involved her in an ongoing sexual relationship for several years. Sally described how she initially regarded
her infant as a "doll baby," who would make her happy if she
was nice to him. Instead, the infant was cranky and cried con-
tinuously, and failed to calm down after bottle feedings. She
began to hit the baby in desperation in order to quiet him
down, but this only made him cry more. She frequently lacked
money for milk and baby food, and had no one to turn to for
help. The beatings continued until Sally, depressed and overwhelmed by the burden of infant care, finally placed the baby
in the care of an aunt.

The apparent high incidence of abuse among multiproblem
families of lower socioeconomic status can be explained by the
impact of poverty on each of the three major variables associated with child abuse. Lower socioeconomic status contributes to an increase in environmental stress through family
disorganization, problems of employment, inadequate
income, poor housing, and excessively large numbers of
children. Poor inner-city families also provide a background

conducive to the development of abuse-prone personality traits. The traditional use of physical punishment and reliance on authoritarian forms of child rearing and family interaction is transmitted from one generation to the next. Finally, the higher incidence of perinatal trauma in these families contributes to the physical and psychological deviancy which makes children vulnerable to abuse and scapegoating.

The concrete aspects of poverty, i.e., a lack of money, inadequate, overcrowded and unsanitary living conditions, family disorganization, high crime rate, and unsafe neighborhoods, exert a stressful impact on family life and parental functioning, and might trigger the onset of maltreatment. It is likely that a background of poverty is more intimately related to neglect than physical abuse. Many reports of neglect are based upon the failure to provide children with adequate physical care and supervision, which is often difficult to achieve for the typical female-headed, large, inner-city "poverty" family on public welfare, without child-care assistance. Neglect petitions frequently cite the failure of the child to attend school. Overwhelmed, mothers with many children of school age are frequently incapable of knowing the whereabouts of a child once he leaves the house in the morning. The mismanagement of limited welfare funds might contribute to a shortage of money for food or clothing which endangers the health of adults and children alike. The prevalence of rodents and vermin in dilapidated tenements is often used by investigating protective caseworkers to confirm an otherwise equivocal allegation of neglect. Thus many of the substandard living conditions routinely observed in impoverished inner-city ghettos may be considered "neglectful" by middle-class standards.

If we consider the variables of environmental stress, parental personality traits, and characteristics of the child as a complementary series of factors leading to abuse and neglect, we might hypothesize that the combinations of these factors will change as we ascend the socioeconomic ladder. For example, middle-class abusers would be likely to demonstrate more abuse-prone personality traits which might be more easily provoked by a relatively milder stressful condition than a poverty class population of abusing parents. Middle-class parents are also less likely to be cited for neglect, as they possess the material resources to provide for the basic physical requirements of their children and the capacity to employ substitute caretakers. The aberrant child-rearing practices of these parents might more frequently fall into the category of "emotional" abuse or neglect, which includes more subtle symptoms of maltreatment, such as emotional detachment and indifference, ridiculing and humiliation short of physical abuse, infantilization and overprotection, etc. The inability of middle- and upper-class parents to adequately care for their children on the basis of abuse-prone personality traits derived from their own pathological childhood experiences may be compensated for by delegating primary parenting responsibility to nursemaids, governesses, and boarding schools.

Institutional Abuse

Children placed in an institutional or agency setting may be subjected to individual acts of abuse or neglect at the hands of caretakers, or may encounter institutional practices which are detrimental to their physical or emotional development.

The phenomenon of institutional abuse of children has attracted considerable attention since the widely publicized 1970 investigation of the Willowbrook School, which uncovered widespread abuse and neglect of the mentally retarded residents. Since then, maltreatment has been reported in various public and private child-care facilities, including psychiatric hospitals, training schools, reformatories, day-care centers, residential treatment facilities, group homes and foster homes.

Aside from physical and sexual abuse and neglect by individual staff members, children have experienced inadequate overall physical and psychological care due to substandard institutional practices, such as improper medication, overcrowding, inadequate staffing, poor nutrition, improper use of restraints, and prolonged incarceration.

In recognition of the importance of this form of maltreatment, New York State has empowered its protective service organization to investigate cases of institutional abuse. The State Bureau of Licensing also requires that all state facilities rendering child care establish a special review committee to investigate all suspected incidents of maltreatment. Similar instances of maltreatment also occur in private facilities for children. Fraiberg (1977) cites the growth of a new child-care "industry" providing substitute mothering for babies and preschool children. This "industry" consists of day-care centers, short-term child-care and baby-sitting services, drop-in centers, and mother helpers, many of which are unlicensed and unsupervised. Fraiberg seriously challenges our society's encouragement of mothers of infants and preschoolers to work outside of the home, while relying on "institutionalized" child-care facilities to provide substitute parenting.

7

Developmental Factors
Associated with
the Onset of Child Abuse

Although the etiology of child abuse might be determined by the interaction among key factors such as parental abuse-proneness, characteristics of the child, and environmental stress which triggers the abuse, this does not fully explain the exact timing of the onset of abuse. This may occur at any age in a given child, from the neonatal period through adolescence. However, each stage of the child's development imposes unique child-rearing tasks upon the parents. Abuse-prone individuals who might demonstrate adequate parenting at certain stages seem overwhelmed and incapable of handling the child at a different age. Each developmental stage of the child constitutes a phase-specific stressor to the parent, based upon its capacity to evoke unresolved parental conflicts. Once abuse and scapegoating become an integral child-rearing practice during a given developmental period, maltreatment usually continues throughout subsequent stages unless intervention takes place. The various stages of development will be presented with regard to the specific child-rearing tasks that each imposes on the caretaker, and the typical conflicts generated in both parents and child.

Infancy (Birth to Twelve Months)

Most parents who abuse their infants during the first year demonstrate a serious impairment in the capacity to establish an effective bond with the helpless neonate, who is completely dependent upon the caretaking environment. The infant depends upon his mother for the satisfaction of basic needs involving feeding, physical care, and relief of tension, and the establishment of early patterns of physiological regulation. Physical abuse is only one symptom of a parent's inability to satisfy the needs of an infant. Other examples of parental dysfunction during this stage are withdrawal and neglect, which might result in the infant's failure to thrive, or severe psychological disorders such as postpartum depression or psychotic states. Parents who abuse infants have usually experienced negative feelings toward the child during pregnancy. The mothers often report that the pregnancies were unwanted, or associate them with guilt. Some of them admit to unsuccessful attempts at abortion. Many of them demonstrated a marked aversion to the neonates right after birth. Some of them experienced early separation from their infants because of prematurity or neonatal illness. Others, especially teen-age mothers, were prevented from assuming a major caretaking role by their own parents. Most mothers who abuse their infants demonstrate a serious impairment in the initial process of attachment or bonding.

Mothers who abuse their infants have usually experienced severe maternal deprivation during their own childhood. They were often abandoned by their mothers and raised by multiple caretakers. They are unable to tolerate the helplessness and dependency of their infants because this evokes memories of their own unsatisfied cries for nurturance. Their massive denial of the helplessness and immaturity of the infant is expressed by inappropriate child-rearing techniques which force the infant into precocious "independent" activities far beyond his developmental capacities. These mothers initiate rapid weaning and premature toilet training, and often try to force their infants to walk before they are able. These activities are linked to the unconscious fantasy that their infants will grow up rapidly and "take care" of them.

Case illustration. Doris's two-and-a-half-year-old son, Ernie, was admitted to the hospital suffering from malnutrition. X-rays revealed numerous old fractures of the ribs and legs at different stages of healing. Ernie was born two months premature and remained in an incubator for a month. Doris was concerned that Ernie was a "lazy" infant who would be slow in his development. She immediately placed him on solid foods and refused to pick him up when he cried in order not to "spoil" him. Doris and her husband tried to get Ernie to walk when he was six months old by propping him against the wall in a standing position.

Doris already had four children by the age of eighteen. Her early childhood was extremely traumatic. She had been placed with an extremely controlling and physically abusive maternal grandmother shortly after her birth, when her mother left home to come to New York. Doris was raised with a younger sister, who was the grandmother's favorite. Doris had been scapegoated and deprived while she was growing up. She recalls having been frequently beaten by her grandmother for alleged misbehavior which was actually caused by her sister. When she was sent to live with her mother at the age of twelve she was sexually abused by her mother's boyfriend. When she informed her mother, she accused Doris of lying, and failed to intervene. Doris finally ran away to live with an aunt.

Toddlerhood (One to Three Years)

This period is characterized by the child's dramatic thrust toward autonomy during his growing separation and individuation from his mother. The onset of locomotion and the rapid acquisition of speech permit the toddler to exercise his curiosity about his immediate environment. He often behaves in what appears to be an oppositional and obstinate manner in his striving for independence. His exploratory activities, messiness, and "getting into things" are often quite trying for the parents. The toddler's quest for separateness, however, is counterbalanced by his anxiety about separation and abandonment, prompting him to alternately cling to and dart away from his mother. This separation anxiety peaks at seventeen to eighteen months of age during the rapprochement period. The ambivalence and negativism of toddlers is interpreted by some parents as willful disobedience or rejection. Parents who are controlling, rigid, and inflexible, and who have unresolved conflicts regarding aggression and control from their own childhood, are likely to manifest child-rearing difficulties with the toddler. Some mothers with unresolved separation anxiety are threatened by the growing autonomy of their children. Parents who are rigidly compulsive about cleanliness might react very punitively during toilet training. In general, an individual who was raised by rigid, controlling parents who were especially punitive during the period of toddlerhood will be at risk for abuse and maltreatment during this stage of their own children's development.

Case illustration. Lucille, a three-year-old girl, was placed in a foster home after it was discovered that she had been physically abused by her mother, Doris T., since she was fifteen months old. A medical and radiological examination revealed evidence of old multiple fractures at different stages of healing. Doris admitted beating Lucille because of her "badness" which allegedly began when Lucille was old enough to walk and "break" things. Doris became especially incensed at Lucille's failure to comply with her demands during toilet training, which became a "battleground." Doris beat Lucille whenever she failed to produce a stool when placed on the potty, and when she wet herself, despite the fact that Lucille was only a year and a half at the time. Doris also described getting angry at Lucille whenever she refused to eat what was given to her. Doris regarded Lucille as a "good" baby during her first year because she was quiet, and seemed easily soothed by the bottle, but Doris was unable to tolerate her daughter's normal expression of autonomy during early toddlerhood. She accused Lucille of trying to control her. "She's not the mother, I am," Doris exclaimed. Doris feels that Lucille's problems were caused by her boyfriend's sister, who indulged and spoiled her during a week she was allowed to care for the child. "Lucille came home and expected me to do everything for her, after that," said Doris.

Doris described a bitter and frustrating childhood characterized by feelings of rejection and abandonment by her own mother, who preferred her two sisters. "My mother just had me, but she didn't act like a mother. I had to do everything for her. She never bothered with me but she was nice to my sisters," Doris complained. Doris recalled how her mother beat her for not performing all the household chores imposed upon her. She also was frequently abused by her alcoholic father.

Lucille appears to be the target of much of Doris's rage which was originally directed toward her rejecting, controlling mother and her preferred siblings. This configuration persists in Doris's current perception of Lucille's foster mother as an adversary who is overindulging the child and her "evil ways."

Phallic-Oedipal Period (Three to Six Years)

During this period, the child becomes more acutely aware of sexual differences and establishes his gender identity. Sexuality is more openly expressed in play and fantasy, and masturbation is commonly observed. The oedipal child acts in a seductive manner toward the parent of the opposite sex, and regards the same-sex parent as a hostile competitor who becomes the object of aggressive fantasies. The child then fears retaliation by this parent in the form of castration, rejection, or abandonment. Parents with unresolved oedipal conflicts of their own are likely to strike out at their same-sex child who acts in a seductive but phase appropriate manner with their spouse.

Other parents, with long standing guilt over their own sexuality, cannot accept any of the emerging sexuality of their children. Parents who initiate physical abuse of their children during this stage of their development have usually been exposed during their own oedipal period to traumatic events which interfered with the development of a normal sexuality. Some of them were victims of sexual seduction or incest during childhood. Many of the mothers had been sexually promiscuous and became pregnant in their early teens. Some mothers, at the opposite extreme, were sexually constricted and guilt-ridden, and were unable to accept any sexuality due to its link with unconscious incestuous fantasies. A considerable number of these parents became fanatic devotees of fundamentalist religious groups in order to buttress their sexual repression. They subsequently used their religious doctrine as a rationalization for beating their children for "sinful" sexual activity.

Case illustration. Debby, a seven-year-old girl, had been subjected to recurrent physical abuse by her mother for alleged mutual masturbation with her five-year-old sister, Joan. According to their mother, Ms. Virginia P., the sexual explorations began when Debby was five and her sister was three. Ms. P. habitually examined Debby's panties for stains or some other evidence of masturbation. She would then accuse Debby and punish her with a beating. The physical abuse was accompanied by verbal humiliation and threats of abandonment.

Ms. P.'s childhood had been marred by early abandonment by her mother, and a punitive relationship with her grandmother, who used to beat Ms. P. and her twin sister while they slept. At the age of fourteen, she was placed in a training school, where she had engaged in some homosexual activity. Debby's masturbation and seductive behavior with her younger sister undoubtedly evoked her mother's long-standing guilt over her own homosexual activities and fantasies, which she handled by attacking Debby with the full fury of her punitive superego.

The School-Age Child (Six to Twelve Years)

The growing cognitive and social competency of the school-age child is highly valued by parents who are stressed by the relative helplessness and dependency of the pre-school child. However the child's establishment of extra-familial relationships with peers and other adults in the school setting is often perceived as disloyalty by paranoid, narcissistic, and controlling parents, who expect exclusive and unswerving loyalty from their offspring. The child's capacity to form close ties with others may be unconsciously regarded as a rejection and abandonment by this type of parent, thus giving rise to abuse. Such parents typically restrict the outside activities of their children to a minimum. They keep their children at home after school with the rationalization that playmates in the neighborhood will hurt them, or "get them into trouble," etc. A typical unconscious fantasy accompanying this possessive behavior is the wish that the child provide them with the love and nurturance that they have been deprived of from others.

Another precipitant of abuse of school-age children is impaired school functioning, either academically or behaviorally. Children who are behavior problems or academic failures in school are particularly irritating to parents who have had similar difficulties during their childhood. These children remind them of their own inadequacy, which they cannot tolerate, and they lash out at them for their inability to compensate for the parents' failures. Unfortunately, a vicious cycle ensues: the parental abuse and humiliation further enrage the child, who proceeds to once again displace his anger in the classroom, which provokes further abuse, etc. The child's tendency to identify with his violent parent as a role model also contributes to his misbehavior in school. It is not surprising that many of these abusing individuals were beaten by their parents for similar academic failure and conduct disturbances in school.

Case illustration. Nancy, age nine, came to a community center with bruises and welts which were inflicted by her mother, Mrs. Pearl S., with a belt and an electric cord. Mrs. S.

was in her last month of pregnancy at this time, and had two younger daughters, aged three and one. Pearl admitted abusing Nancy, but felt that the beatings were justified because of the latter's "badness." Pearl recited a long list of complaints about Nancy's provocative behavior toward her, which included staying out late at night, stealing things (including money), and failure to do her "chores," which consisted of taking care of her baby sisters, feeding them, and washing clothes. It was clear that Nancy could not possibly comply with her mother's unrealistic expectations of her. Pearl was also enraged at being called to school because of Nancy's frequent disruptive behavior in the classroom, and she complained about Nancy having "too many" friends.

Pearl experienced many separations from her own mother as a child. She had been hospitalized for five years between the ages of three and eight because of a chronic spinal disorder. Her mother only visited her about once a month. Soon after her return home, her mother sent her to live with a cousin in the South, together with her two brothers. At the age of sixteen she met Mr. T. and soon became pregnant with Nancy. Pearl returned to New York after Nancy was born, and began to work, while Mr. T. remained behind. In New York, Pearl met Mr. C., who fathered her daughter Cora. When he lost his job, their relationship deteriorated. Pearl returned south shortly after Cora's birth, leaving Cora and Nancy, then six years of age, with their maternal grandmother. Pearl resumed her relationship with Mr. T. once again, and he fathered Lila, who was born two years later. Pearl finally left him and returned to New York with Lila to rejoin Cora and Nancy. She met Mr. S. shortly afterwards, and became pregnant by him. Their relationship was superior to her previous involvements. He was stable, supportive, and had steady employment. They married shortly after the birth of Richard.

From Nancy's point of view, her mother's return from the South with a new baby after a two-year absence was quite traumatic. Nancy then had to adjust to her mother's new boyfriend and another pregnancy. Nancy felt a keen sense of abandonment and extreme sibling rivalry, which was intensified when as the oldest daughter she was forced to assume a maternal role with the younger children. Nancy's anger toward her mother for depriving and abandoning her was expressed by her provocative behavior and her stealing money, which was unconsciously equated with love. Her misbehavior in school represented a displacement of some of her resentment toward her mother. Pearl, on the other hand, felt overburdened at the prospect of resuming the caretaking role with Nancy and Cora, in addition to raising the infant Lila. When she became pregnant again, she tried to force Nancy into a "maternal" role (role reversal) instead of providing her with the love and affection she needed so badly. This precipitated the power struggle between them which unfortunately ended in Nancy's physical abuse. On a deeper level, Pearl equates Nancy simultaneously with her own rejecting mother, and with an aspect of her own devalued childhood self-image. In her pattern of abandoning her lovers after they provide her with babies, and leaving her children in her mother's care, Pearl actively repeats with others what she had passively endured as a helpless child.

Puberty and Adolescence
(Twelve to Eighteen Years)

Although the physical abuse of adolescents is fairly common, this phenomenon has been overlooked in the child-abuse literature. Lourie (1977) cites statistics demonstrating that 25 to 30 percent of protective service caseloads across the country are adolescents.

The developmental tasks of adolescence have a far reaching impact on the structure of the family. In the process of separating from parents and achieving a new individuality, and integrating monumental physical and sexual changes into his personality, the constantly fluctuating adolescent poses a threat to the stability of his parents, whose tolerance for change diminishes when they reach middle age. Three crucial developmental issues of adolescence may each give rise to conflicts with the parents.

Separation

The undoing of parental bonds and the increased involvement with peer group may be particularly stressful to narcissistic and dependent parents. Single mothers might be especially reluctant to loosen their ties to adolescent children, upon whom they are abnormally dependent. Beating an adolescent may represent a last ditch effort by the parent to re-create the atmosphere of the preadolescent parent-child relationship. Abuse-prone parents less frequently attack the clinging adolescent who fears separation from his family.

Control

The typical rebellious and defiant behavior of adolescents, which accompanies and facilitates the dissolution of their childhood bonds with their parents, is challenging and trying for most parents. Before a more mature identity is achieved in later adolescence and the parental relationships are restructured, the adolescent exhibits a wide range of egocentric and provocative behaviors which challenge prevailing adult standards. Messiness, long hair, experimentation with drugs and alcohol, participation in gangs, truancy, and involvement in delinquent activities are various ways of achieving emancipation from long-standing parental influence and control. Impulsive, domineering parents might resort to physical abuse during the power struggle with such adolescents. Narcissistic parents, who often cannot bear to relinquish control over their offspring, are understandably threatened when their children reach the threshold of complete independence.

Sexuality

The emergence of adult-like sexuality in adolescents, associated with dramatic physical and hormonal changes, often produces severe conflict within the family. Sexual experimentation and promiscuity are poorly tolerated by both sexually repressed parents and by parents who had indulged in chaotic sexual behavior during their own adolescence. Parents are usually less tolerant of the adolescent sexuality of their daughters. Many parents feel stigmatized by the sexual acting out of their children, and are distressed by the possibility of early, unwanted pregnancy. Mothers who themselves had been pregnant as teenagers are at the greatest risk for abusing their teenage daughters, who readily evoke their own repressed guilt. Teenagers who become pregnant are often subjected to the same rejection, humiliation, and physical abuse that their mothers had experienced.

Case illustration. Following her first menstrual period at the age of twelve, Mary was beaten and humiliated by her mother, Mrs. M. Upon examination of the blood-stained sheets, Mrs. M. suspected that Mary had been sexually involved with a neighbor. Mrs. M.'s continued preoccupation with the potential dangers stemming from Mary's sexual maturity was used as a device to control her daughter and restrict her freedom. This led to a steady deterioration of their relationship. Mary was subjected to beatings, and Mrs. M. also threatened to send her to her father, who was living in England. When Mary became pregnant when she was sixteen, Mrs. M. abused her after she refused to take a cathartic designed to induce an abortion. She ran off with her boyfriend after this incident and proceeded to have the baby.

Mrs. M.'s preoccupation with and intolerance of her daughter's emergent sexuality became more understandable as she described her own early life. She was born out of wedlock, and her mother left her in the care of her maternal grandmother and aunt when she was a year and a half. Her mother resumed caring for her when she was twelve, and old enough to do the housework. Shortly after her menarche, her mother's boyfriend began to make sexual advances toward her. She told her mother about it, but she refused to believe her. When she was fourteen, this man tried to rape her. Her mother responded by sending Mrs. M. to live with another aunt, because she was too dependent on the boyfriend to challenge his behavior. Mrs. M. eventually met Mary's father when she was eighteen.

She had four children by him, but he deserted her just before the date he had promised to marry her.

It is clear that Mrs. M. reacted to Mary's menarche with severe anxiety, as it evoked the guilt-ridden memories of her own unhappy initial confrontations with sexuality, which led to her humiliation and reabandonment by her mother. Through the mechanisms of projective identification, Mrs. M. repeated with Mary the critical and punitive behavior she had experienced at the hands of her mother.

8

Other Forms of Maltreatment: Neglect, Sexual Abuse, and Failure to Thrive

Neglect

Neglect is by far the most common form of maltreatment, reported cases outnumbering those of physical abuse by three to one in New York City in 1978. Despite the fact that neglect is a more prevalent problem than abuse in this country, it has received much less attention from child-care professionals, researchers, and social agencies. Neglect is usually less obvious and less dramatic than physical abuse, and is more difficult to define. According to the New York State Child Protective Services Act of 1973 neglect is legally defined as the failure of the parent or guardian to supply the child with adequate food, clothing, shelter, education, medical care, and supervision. It also includes abandonment of the child and loss of control through the use of alcohol or drugs by a parent or caretaker.

In many cases, neglect appears to be unintentional and closely associated with substandard living conditions in inner-city slum areas. In a broader sense, neglect might refer to the failure to provide the child with adequate parenting to insure the realization of his potential for normal physical and psychological growth and development. Neglectful practices include inadequate parenting, interruption of maternal care, affective and social deprivation, parental detachment, indifference, overstimulation, inappropriate and premature expectations of the child, and failure to understand or anticipate the needs of the child at specific stages of development. Neglect frequently entails "sins of omission," while abuse involves "sins of commission."

Neglecting Parents

Pavenstedt et al. (1967) described basic personality characteristics of neglecting parents encountered in disorganized lower-class families during a community intervention project. Many of these parents were psychotics or alcoholics, and engaged in antisocial activities. They tended to re-create previous patterns of childhood deprivation in their own families, failed to achieve competency as parents, and were unable to provide adult role models for their children. Their own deprivation caused their needs to take precedence over their children's needs, which they often failed to recognize. These parents also manifested poor object relations due to a basic mistrust of others, and failed to achieve a clear self-concept. They were limited in language development and abstract thinking, and therefore were action oriented and impulsive. They often failed to provide their children with adequate stimulation and verbal communication, and rarely played with them. They frequently left their children alone, or with the nearest available child or adult, and neglected their health needs. They also tended to demonstrate impulsive and aggressive behavior in an unpredictable manner.

Giovannoni and Billingsley (1970) compared neglecting mothers with adequate mothers in a controlled study of a poverty-level population. The neglecting mothers were differentiated from the adequate mothers by the following characteristics: they had more children, frequently lacked a husband, experienced a greater amount of current stress, exhibited impairment of relationships with their extended families, and were poorer than their adequate counterparts. The neglecting mothers also demonstrated inadequacy in meeting the dependency needs of very young children. Green (1976) was able to elicit differences among neglecting, abusing, and normal control mothers from a similar poverty background by their responses to a structured interview. The neglecting mothers reported the highest incidence of unplanned pregnancies and the absence of a husband or male companion at home. They also exhibited the highest rates of alcoholism, psychosis, and chronic physical illness.

Polansky et al. (1968) studied child neglect in a rural community. Ten families were observed, with widely varying patterns of neglect ranging from alcoholism and abandonment to chronic low levels of child care and housekeeping. In contrast to neglecting mothers from urban areas, these mothers were overly dependent upon their own mothers or mothers-in-law and often lived in close proximity to them. The rural neglecting mothers exhibited separation anxiety and tended to foster symbiotic relationships with their children. These mothers demonstrated either eruptive acting-out behavior or apathy and futility. Diagnostically, they were placed in the category of "inadequate personality" or "infantile personality" on the basis of prominent preoedipal fixations, poor impulse control, poor capacity for symbolization, and over reliance on the pleasure principle and primary process thinking.

Galdston (1968) differentiated two subtypes of neglecting parents on the basis of their defensive organization. The first type relies upon projection as a major defense and regards the child as the embodiment of their own undesirable attributes. This type is closely related to child abusers, but instead of striking at the children, they distance themselves or delegate the care of the child to someone else. The second type uses denial as a primary defense and fails to see the child as belonging to them. These parents are unable to empathize with their children and have trouble feeding and caring for them.

Impact of Neglect on Child Development

The damaging effects of neglect and maternal deprivation on infants and young children living in institutions have been documented in the pioneering studies of Spitz (1945), Bowlby (1951), Goldfarb (1945), Burlingham and Freud (1944), and many others. These children displayed physical and developmental retardation and cognitive impairment, especially in the area of speech and language, and an impaired ability to form human attachments. The adverse impact of institutionalization was ascribed to the unavailability of a consistent caretaker.

Subsequent studies by Coleman and Provence (1957) and Prugh and Harlow (1962) revealed that similar experiences of deprivation resulting in impaired development could be found in children living in intact homes as a result of insufficient or distorted maternal care. This type of parental dysfunction is frequently encountered among lower socioeconomic groups living in inner-city slums. Terman and Merrill (1937) and Golden et al. (1971) found that the cognitive development of lower-class children fell significantly behind the cognitive performance of middle-class children by the age of three. Marans and Lourie (1967) hypothesized about the impact of aberrant patterns of parenting on children from disadvantaged families. They postulated that multiple mothering caused children to develop difficulties in subsequent object relationships and that the lack of verbalization in the home inhibited the normal acquisition of speech and language and symbol formation. They also felt that these children's withdrawal from the environment was a consequence of inconsistent perceptual stimulation. Malone (1967) described the following sequelae in children from neglectful disorganized families: learning difficulties, diminished initiative and enjoyment in play, limited spoken language, concrete thinking, literalness and inflexibility, use of imitative identifications, nonspecific friendliness, lack of body care and accident proneness, and poor object permanence. Delinquency (Rutter 1972, Bender 1947) and psychopathology (Bowlby 1946) have also been attributed to family disorganization and institutionalization. Green et al. (1974b) reported that school-age neglected children exhibited significant ego impairment in areas of reality testing, object relations, impulse control, and defensive functioning compared to normal controls. The neglected children also manifested more anxiety, depression, and disturbances in body image. Sandgrund et al. (1974) described an impairment of intellectual functioning in the same group of neglected children. Twenty percent of these children were retarded, with IQs below 70. Green et al. (1979) documented significant neurological impairment in these neglected children compared to the normal controls, based upon pediatric neurological examination including EEGs and perceptual motor testing. Thirty-eight percent of the neglected children were found to be moderately or severely impaired, as compared to 14 percent of the controls. The neurological deficits in the neglected children were attributed to poor prenatal and infant care, nutritional deficiency, inadequate medical care, and abnormal (insufficient or excessive) sensory stimulation.

Case 1. The H. family consists of Mr. and Mrs. H. and their seven children at home. Four older children are out of the home. The neglect petition alleges that the preschool children receive no medical care. The apartment is filthy and foul-smelling, and the children's beds are wet, dilapidated, and inadequate for sleeping. Carl, the eleven-year-old, is a severe behavior problem in school, as is his brother Randy, age ten. Both boys come to school in filthy clothing. Carl has severe tantrums and throws furniture around the classroom.

Mr. H. suffers from hypertension and as a result is unable to work steadily at a factory job. The family receives public assistance to augment his income. Mrs. H. only completed the sixth grade in school. She became pregnant when she was fourteen years old. Her first three children were fathered by different men. She subsequently married Mr. H., who is the father of the next eight children. Mr. H. appears to be of borderline intelligence. He is quite withdrawn and barely communicates. He seems to have little awareness of what goes on in the family, and is unaware of the problems of his children. Mrs. H. constantly belittles her husband for not making enough money and not spending time with the children. She is a religious fanatic who goes to church every day and preaches love and nonviolence to her children, yet she is impulsive and a rigid disciplinarian. She had been an aggressive, heavy drinking woman before her religious transformation. She often acts irrationally, and the children seem to be frightened of her. She has a tendency to lose the gist of what she's talking about and has to be constantly refocused. She is easily overwhelmed by her family responsibilities. Upon psychiatric evaluation she received the diagnosis of schizophrenic reaction, chronic undifferentiated type.

Sally, the H.'s six-year-old daughter, was referred for a psychiatric evaluation. She was friendly and spontaneous during the interview. Her speech was marred by a prominent articulation defect. She expressed violent themes in her doll play, for example, running over the mother, father, and baby dolls with a toy train, because they "bother her and cuss her." She indicated that she likes to fight with other children and she readily placed a boy and girl puppet in a sexual embrace. In the middle of the interview, she began to ask the psychiatrist for food and candy, seeming to be dealing with her anxiety by these oral dependent strivings.

On the psychological testing, Sally performed intellectually in the dull normal range. Her Full Scale IQ was 80, Performance IQ 78, and Verbal IQ 85. She did poorly on the block design subtest, suggesting some perceptual-motor difficulty and immaturity. Her performance on the Bender-Gestalt indicated problems with impulsivity. The projective tests revealed a great deal of conflict over dependency needs which she feels are unfulfilled. Sally views her mother as punitive and unloving. The resulting aggressive feelings directed toward the mother engender guilt and conflict. Her awareness of this poorly repressed hostility makes her feel as if she is a bad girl. Some of the hostility is directed inward and some projected onto the external world. Sally's Rorshach indicates anxiety and fear of her aggressive impulses. She manifests loss of control and perceptual distortions in response to situations generating strong affect. At such times her reality testing may be mildly impaired. Her self-concept is quite poor, as characterized by her primitive figure drawings without mouths and with small legs. She also demonstrates an inadequate female identification, associated with her ambivalence toward her mother.

Case 2. The P. family, consisting of Mrs. Martha P., a thirty-four-year-old mother, and her seven children ranging in age from five to fifteen, was referred to the family court on a neglect petition by the attendance teacher of their school district because the children failed to attend school and Mrs. P. was apparently unable to supervise and control them. In addition to truancy, the fifteen-year-old boy participated in a burglary, and the fourteen- and thirteen-year-old girls were involved in glue sniffing. The thirteen-year-old had been previously hospitalized with a diagnosis of childhood schizophrenia. Walter, twelve years old, is the most difficult to manage, according to Mrs. P. He steals, snatches pocketbooks, sniffs glue, wets his bed, is assaultive with his younger siblings, and runs away from home. Mrs. P. was married for ten years until her alcoholic husband, who fathered all but the two youngest children, died of cirrhosis of the liver. The last two children are supported by their father, Mr. H., who visits the family once or twice a week.

Mrs. P. is a small, weary-looking, but neatly dressed woman who appears overwhelmed and chronically depressed. She admits to having little control or impact on her children, who either ignore her or are actively disobedient. They complain about school, and accuse her of not providing them with adequate clothing. Mrs. P. claims that she is doing the best she can within the limitations of her welfare budget. She states that she is often unable to get up in the morning to get the children to school because she stays up late at night waiting for the older children to return home. When exasperated, she threatens to send the children away, or occasionally resorts to physical punishment. Because of his outstanding difficulties, Walter received a physical, psychiatric, and psychological evaluation, which provided the following pertinent data. The physical examination showed Walter to be below the third percentile for height and weight. The neurological exam and EEG were normal. On the psychiatric interview, Walter appeared to be sullen, depressed, and somewhat dishevelled. He claimed to be tired as a result of going to bed late the previous evening. His mood brightened during a game of checkers with the interviewer, but he demonstrated minimal tolerance for the interviewer's questioning. He expressed some pleasure in fighting, and acknowledged that he occasionally gets into trouble. He expressed a distrust of his brothers and sisters, and claimed that they steal his money.

On the psychological testing, Walter recorded a Full Scale IQ of 62 with a Verbal IQ of 66 and a Performance IQ of 65, with a potential for borderline functioning. He performed in an immature and concrete fashion on more structured intellectual tasks. His answers were sparse in content and reflect a tough "streetwise" adaptation. Performance on the Bender-Gestalt revealed impulsivity and possible organicity. Projective tests were rather unrevealing, as he tended to give short answers and frequently rejected material. He is able to hold himself together by means of denial and occasional compulsivity, but when faced with threatening or emotionally stimulating material, he has difficulty integrating and organizing his responses. He regards the world as threatening and feels helpless and impotent. His poor self-image and lack of masculine identification are reflected in his tiny, inadequate figure drawings. He sees social relationships as revolving around aggression. He tends to regress and acts out in stressful situations which threaten him, yet he has trouble dealing with aggressive material and either represses or projects these impulses. He also expresses insecurity and uncertainty around gratification or oral needs. For example, on the CAT, he told a story about a big rooster stealing from some chicks.

Walter's retarded physical and cognitive development and emotional immaturity may be viewed as the result of the cumulative impact of object loss, inconsistent and ineffectual parenting, family disorganization, and emotional deprivation, conditions all too common in our inner-city ghettos.

Case 3. Miss M., the twenty-eight-year-old mother of six children, was charged with neglect following an investigation of the family after the murder of her oldest child. This ten-year-old girl had been strangled by a man who had lured her into his apartment with a promise of food. The detective who visited the M. apartment found the five remaining M. children, ranging in age from nine to three, alone, filthy, and poorly dressed. The apartment was dirty and broken down, the kitchen lacked a refrigerator, and the beds lacked blankets and linens. Further investigation revealed that Deborah and Tom, her nine-year-old brother, had been frequently seen by neighbors on the street at 3:00 A.M. begging for food and money. Tom is retarded and epileptic and receives special schooling. The Family Court remanded the children to a maternal great aunt because of Miss M.'s inability to feed, clothe, or supervise them.

Miss M. was born in Arkansas and was sent to live with her maternal grandmother in New York when she was a baby. She dropped out of school in the tenth grade. She became pregnant with Deborah when she was sixteen. Her six children were fathered by four different men, none of whom had a protracted relationship with her. According to the maternal aunt, Miss M. seemed incapable of caring for the children. Since her recent involvement with a boyfriend, she had frequently left the children unattended and appeared to be unconcerned about them. Miss M. currently lives across the street from her aunt's apartment, but rarely comes over to visit the children. She apparently has no interest in regaining custody of the children.

Stanley M., the six-year-old, was referred for evaluation by his great aunt because of her concern about his tendency to mouth and swallow inedible objects such as crayons and pencils. In the psychiatric interview, Stanley demonstrated considerable hyperactivity and a limited attention span. He was preoccupied with his sister's death, and the man who "threw her out of the window." He spoke about being terrified of monsters at night which he handled by hiding under the covers and covering his ears. He exhibited a rather blatant denial of discomfort concerning his mother's absence and the fact that he didn't know his father. His speech disorganized into gibberish under pressure. On psychological testing, Stanley scored 79 on the Full Scale IQ, with a Verbal IQ of 76 and a Performance IQ of 86. He exhibited minimal frustration tolerance during the testing. The Bender-Gestalt revealed immaturity and impulsivity. Aggressive and violent themes intruded on projective testing, with frequent projection of oral aggression. Maternal figures were seen as bad and threatening, but anger toward them was denied. Male figures were idealized and regarded as powerful. Relationships between men and women were highly sexualized. Stanley exhibited frequent denial of his weakness and vulnerability.

In retrospect, it appeared that Stanley's chronically impaired ego functioning, a consequence of neglectful and inadequate parenting, left him insufficiently prepared to cope with the traumatic impact of his sister's violent death.

Intervention

The relatively greater impact of environmental factors in the etiology of neglect, compared to other forms of maltreatment, requires the adoption of an intervention strategy specifically geared toward reducing environmental stress and strengthening parental functioning. The major therapeutic focus should be in the home. Since neglecting families are usually overwhelmed by poverty, family disorganization, and large numbers of children, a vigorous deployment of essential social services to insure adequate food, clothing, shelter, and medical care is warranted. An outreach program should be established which will provide neglecting families with education in parenting, household management, and child-rearing assistance.

This may be provided by homemakers, paraprofessionals, and visiting nurses. Neglecting mothers often require special training to increase the level of stimulation for their children. Direct observation of mother-child interaction in the home may be used as a valuable therapeutic modality. Day-care programs for infants and preschool children may be utilized as a vehicle for reducing the burdens of child care, and as a training site for the improvement of parent-child interaction. Supportive carework, individual and group psychotherapy, and counseling are also useful to neglecting parents to combat their apathy and depression. Family planning and coordination of medical care should also be given a high priority.

Because of their widespread cognitive and emotional difficulties, neglected children of school age often require psychotherapy and psychoeducational assistance and can benefit from a supportive, need-gratifying relationship with a benign, predictable adult. Neglected children often require placement in special classes because of their academic and behavioral difficulties. They can benefit from after-school programs, sport groups, and youth organizations. Therapists working with neglected children must maintain active liaison with members of the therapeutic team involved with the parents, and with schools, community organizations, and social agencies.

In conclusion, neglecting families require the same type of crisis-oriented multidisciplinary team intervention and provision of comprehensive family services recommended for child-abusing families.

Sexual Abuse: Description and Incidence

Sexual abuse is cited as a type of child abuse in the New York State Child Protective Services Act of 1973. The American Humane Association (1972) estimates that there are 200,000 to 300,000 cases of female child molestation in the United States annually, with at least 5,000 cases of father-daughter incest. However the true incidence of sexual abuse is probably much higher, because it is harder to identify than physical abuse. The injuries are mostly psychological, and unlike physical abuse, the children are often willing participants in the sexual contact. Swanson (1968) reported that 76 percent of sexually abused children knew the offender, and in 60 percent of the cases the abuse took place on multiple occasions. According to Jaffe (1975) only 15 percent of two-hundred and ninety-one cases of sexual abuse involved physical injury. As is the case with physical abuse, a spectrum of sexual abuse exists ranging from inappropriate physical contact with fondling and general sexual overstimulation through excessive nudity, which represent exaggerations of the norm, to frank sexual activity initiated by parents or other family members. The most typical sexual contact between adults and children consists of fondling or intercourse between a female preadolescent or adolescent and her father or stepfather. This type of sexual activity may continue for years without being reported. Children of all ages, ranging from infancy through adolescence, may be sexually exploited and made to submit to genital, anal, or oral sexual contact.

Sexual abuse resembles physical abuse in several ways. First, it entails a loss of impulse control on the part of the adult. Secondly, it is an expression of "role reversal" in which the child is used to gratify a need of the parent. Finally, it occurs within the context of a pathological pattern of family interaction. For example, when a young girl has a sexual relationship with her father, the mother usually actively or passively condones the behavior. Men frequently turn toward their daughters for sexual and emotional fulfillment which they can no longer obtain from their wives. In many cases, a mother will consciously or unconsciously encourage her daughter to replace her as a sexual partner for her husband. In another type of family constellation, a mother will seduce her son to compensate for an unavailable or absent husband. The nature of the contact may range from sleeping in the same bed without actual genital contact to frank incestual intercourse. Children are also exposed to homosexual contact with their parents, or they might be encouraged to witness parental sexual activity under the guise of "modern sexual enlightenment." Swanson (1968) found that one-third of the incidents of sexual abuse were precipitated by drinking while Peters (1976) indicated that half of such cases were alcohol related.

In many instances, children are sexually abused by their siblings, aunts, uncles, or stepparents, or by adults unrelated or unknown to them. In a retrospective survey, Gagnon (1965) found that 26 percent of twelve-hundred college-age females reported a sexual experience with an adult prior to age thirteen, with only 6 percent of these incidents reported to authorities. This suggests that the true incidence of sexual abuse is probably much higher than the statistics would indicate.

Giarretto (1976) describes a relatively high socioeconomic status of families referred to the Child Sexual Abuse Treatment Program in Santa Clara County, California. The average annual income of these families was $13,413 and the mean educational level was 12.5 years. If these statistics were representative of sexually abusing families throughout the country, it would suggest that poverty and family disorganization are more important etiological factors in physical abuse than in sexual abuse. This might also indicate the greater importance of parental personality factors in the genesis of sexual abuse.

Personality Factors in Sexually Abusive Adults

The bulk of the literature on sexual abuse concerns incestuous fathers. Weinberg (1955) described the following categories: 1. An introversive personality with minimal extrafamilial social contact. 2. A psychopathic personality who practices indiscriminate sexuality and is unable to form tender attachments with spouse and family. 3. A pedophilic personality who is psychosexually and socially immature and who seduces other children as well as his own.

Mohr (1962) described the tendency of the last type to retreat from the fear and discomfort of peer relationships to less threatening contact with children. They rarely attempt intercourse and prefer body contact, fondling, and oral contact. Heterosexual pedophiles are attracted to both boys and girls.

Summit (1978) discussed additional types of incest which were determined by the personality of the offender. These included misogynous incest, imperious incest, child rape, and perverse incest. In misogynous incest, fear and hatred of women predominate. These men present a history of conflict with their mothers and become involved in violent behavior with women, such as rape and wifebeating. They regard their daughters as possessions, and tyrannize them with sexual and physical abuse. In imperious incest, the fathers endow themselves with a domestic grandiosity, a caricature of the male chauvinist role, which compensates for a lack of achievement in other areas. The child rapist is characterized as a chronically antisocial violent person who needs to frighten and overpower his victims in order to feel sexually adequate. Participants in perverse incest involve children in the acting out of forbidden sexual fantasies which are frequently polymorphously perverse in nature, often involving multiple partners. Fathers who physically abuse their children share the angry and tyrannical feelings toward spouse and children attributed to the misogynous fathers, and display some of the grandiosity of the imperious sexual abusers.

Descriptions of mothers involved in incestuous behavior leading to intercourse with their children are quite rare. Wahl (1960) reported two cases of consummated maternal incest. One of the mothers was a chronic alcoholic. However, overtly seductive behavior short of coitus by mothers toward their sons has been frequently encountered and well documented. This type of behavior ranges from parading nude in front of their sons or sleeping in bed with them to genital fondling and masturbation. Incestuous mothers would appear to be much more psychiatrically impaired than incestuous fathers, which might be a reflection of the stronger taboo against mother-son incest. Mothers have a greater opportunity than fathers to sublimate incestuous impulses in such child-care activities as nursing, bathing, changing, and toileting.

Effects of Sexual Abuse on Children

There have been varying opinions about the impact of sexual abuse on the child victim. Several clinicians have asserted that incest and sexual abuse may be psychologically harmless (Bender and Blau 1937, Yorukoglu and Kemph 1966, Rascovsky and Rascovsky 1950). The majority of the observers, however, have reported a variety of physical, psychosomatic, and psychological symptoms resulting from sexual abuse. The exact nature of the child's response depends upon several factors, such as the relationship to the perpetrator, the type of sexual activity, the child's degree of compliance, the use of force, the presence of physical injury, the age of the child and his stage of development, and his pretraumatic level of psychological functioning. The family's reaction to the incident will also influence the child's response.

Sexually abused children frequently exhibit regressive symptoms and behavior, such as thumbsucking, nailbiting, enuresis, and encopresis, following the incident(s). Sleep difficulties with nightmares have also been observed, as have increased fearfulness and phobias. Girls who were sexually abused by a male may demonstrate marked mistrust and anxiety in the presence of males. Psychosomatic symptoms may appear in the form of vomiting, abdominal pains, or headaches.

Older children are more likely to manifest guilt and depression. At times, the guilt might be more in response to the consequences of the sexual incident on the members of the family rather than to the actual abusive episode. Older children and adolescents might demonstrate behavioral and academic difficulties in school, delinquency, conversion symptoms, or panic states, the latter frequently accompanying a homosexual seduction or assault on an older boy. Older children might express feelings of being dirty and worthless. Adolescent girls frequently display promiscuous sexuality of a masochistic nature, which might reflect unconscious fantasies perpetuating the sexual union with the father.

Sexual abuse of children may result in physical sequelae such as genital injury, pregnancy, or venereal disease.

Sgroi (1977) observed that gonorrheal infections in children are usually indicators of sexual assault.

The long-term effects of sexual assault and incest are difficult to ascertain because of the lack of carefully controlled longitudinal studies. However, studies of adults who had been sexually abused during childhood are quite revealing. Giarretto (1976) cited evidence indicating that female drug addicts, prostitutes, and women with pronounced sexual difficulties were exposed to a high incidence of sexual abuse and incest during childhood. Rosenfeld et al. (1977) discovered frequent evidence of frigidity, promiscuity, and depressions in adults who reported having had childhood sexual experiences. Furthermore, they noted that many of the sexually abusing parents had been subjected to sexual abuse during their childhood. Thus it appears that childhood exposure to sexual abuse might impair the individual's sexual and parental functioning in the next generation, in the same way that experiencing physical abuse as a child will exacerbate the development of a child-abusing personality in adulthood.

Evaluation and Treatment

Because of the enormous stigma attached to sexual abuse and incest, all professionals involved in medical and psychological evaluations must respect the family's initial denials and reluctance to participate out of guilt and shame. These resistances are even more pronounced if the offender is a family member. Therefore the initial contacts must be supportive and tactful, and the staff must be able to control its negative feelings toward the abuser, while at the same time guaranteeing the child's safety. If the abusing adult refuses to participate in the treatment program, and remains in the home, the child should be referred for temporary placement.

The sexually abused child should receive a complete medical and psychiatric evaluation following the incident. The physical examination should be conducted with utmost sensitivity, since a gynecological examination may be quite traumatic in itself. The procedures should be explained so that they are not perceived as a punishment for the fantasied transgression. The child should also have the opportunity to ventilate feelings about the incident(s) with a therapist in order to reduce the traumatic impact. Younger children should be allowed to reenact these experiences in the playroom, using dolls, puppets, and drawings to facilitate their mastery over the trauma. They also must be helped to understand what happened to them in a manner commensurate with their level of development. Supportive psychotherapy or counseling might be sufficient to help the child with the acute sequelae of the abuse if the traumatic impact of the sexual assault gradually subsides over time, and age-appropriate defensive functioning ensues. With some children, prolonged impairment of functioning, with guilt, persistent neurotic symptoms, low self-esteem, learning inhibitions, and behavior problems, requires longer-term psychotherapy. Some children might require additional treatment when they reach adolescence or adulthood because of impaired sexual functioning attributable to the earlier trauma.

Like physical abuse, sexual abuse of a child by a family member is a sign of pathological family relationships. Therefore treatment of the child must be accompanied by a psychiatric evaluation of the whole family. Cooperation by the family is usually necessary to insure the child's involvement in treatment; otherwise, parental resistance will be transmitted through the child as the latter is confronted with a loyalty conflict. Individual counseling or psychotherapy of both parents is recommended because of the compliance of the nonabusing spouse. Giarretto (1976) recommends individual counseling for daughter, mother, and father, followed by mother-daughter and father-daughter counseling and family counseling, for typical cases of father-daughter incest. There should be close cooperation between the treatment staff and the probation officers of the juvenile court. If possible, the sexually abusing parent or surrogate should be given the opportunity to participate in a treatment program as an alternative to a jail sentence. Criminal prosecution should be used as a last resort, when all efforts toward rehabilitation and maintaining the intactness of the family have been exhausted. In cases where it was necessary to remove the child from the home, efforts should be made to insure the child's return as quickly as possible. If sexual abuse is complicated by neglect, family disorganization, or economic stress, the provision of appropriate social services should be included in the treatment plan.

Case 1. Kate B., a thirteen-year-old black girl of middle-class background, was referred for psychiatric evaluation after her parents discovered that she had been involved in a sexual relationship with her twenty-eight-year-old cousin, Robert, who was living with the family. Mr. B. became irate when he found out about the relationship, and forced Robert to leave the house. Mrs. B., on the other hand, seemed relatively unconcerned. She believed that Kate's contact with Robert was not unusual, although she felt that they shouldn't "carry on" in the house. Mrs. B. prided herself on being sexually enlightened, and boasted that she began having intercourse at the age of eleven. She had several part-time jobs, and was rarely at home. Mr. B. operated a beauty salon, and attended college in the evenings. According to Kate, she rarely saw her parents, and the house was disorganized and in a state of disrepair. Kate became depressed after the affair was terminated. She claimed that Robert was her best friend, and that she had no one else to confide in. Mr. B. had prohibited her from going out with boys. It was clear that Kate's sexual liaison with her cousin was sanctioned by her mother, and that it was largely motivated by loneliness and the need for companionship, which her parents were unable to provide. It also became apparent through family interviews that Kate's blatant sexual activity at home was the only way she could get her parents' attention. They only seemed to respond to her in a crisis.

Case 2. Nancy G., a twelve-year-old black girl, was referred for medical and psychiatric evaluation after she informed her mother that she had been involved in a sexual relationship with the mother's boyfriend, Mr. E., for a period of four months. The G. household consisted of Mrs. G., Nancy's Jamaican-born mother, who was a former schoolteacher, Mr. E., and four younger children ranging in age from seven years to four months, fathered by Mr. E. Nancy's father was Mr. G., who had formerly been Mrs. G.'s husband. Mr. E. initiated the sexual relationship with Nancy at the time of the birth of the youngest child, which also coincided with the deterioration of his relationship with Mrs. G. She complained about his physical and mental cruelty, accused him of having several girlfriends, and stated that he was physically abusive toward her. On one occasion, he had to be restrained from throwing her out of a window. Mrs. G. also complained about Mr. E.'s pattern of getting her pregnant and failing to keep his promise to marry her. She claimed that she was initially happy with Mr. E., whom she met after the termination of her brief marriage. However, arguments ensued when he insisted that she become pregnant and give up her teaching career.

Nancy saw a psychiatrist when she was eleven because of academic problems at school and stealing money from her mother. She also fought frequently with her half-siblings. She viewed her mother as overly critical, demanding, and ungiving. She felt overburdened with household responsibilities and was rarely permitted to socialize with her friends.

Psychiatric intervention with the family revealed that Mr. E. was severely depressed, and that he and Mrs. G. were unable to communicate. Instead, they used Nancy as the vehicle for their rage toward one another. Mr. E.'s seduction of Nancy clearly represented a humiliation of Mrs. G., while the latter's scapegoating of Nancy was a displacement of her anger toward Mr. E. In addition, Nancy symbolized Mrs. G.'s own unacceptable traits, which slowly unfolded during the therapeutic process. For example, she recalled childhood feelings of disgust and self-loathing which stemmed from rejection by her father because she had been his darkest skinned child.

Failure to Thrive Syndrome

The term *failure to thrive* describes infants and children who fall below the third percentile in weight and height without demonstrable organic etiology. They usually gain weight rapidly when provided with an adequate diet during hospitalization. Spitz (1945) first reported that infants living in institutions failed to thrive and exhibited emotional and cognitive impairment as well. This syndrome was attributed to the absence of mothering, and lack of stimulation in the institutional environment. Subsequently, similar sequelae were observed in neglected and deprived infants who were being cared for by their mothers.

Characteristics of Mothers

When mothers of failure-to-thrive infants were studied, they exhibited a significant degree of psychopathology. Barbero et al. (1963) found them to be depressed and helpless, with low self-esteem, and environmentally stressed. Elmer (1960) and Leonard et al. (1966) made similar observations, the latter also citing alcoholism as a pathogenic factor. Fischoff (1971) reported that failure-to-thrive mothers demonstrated severe personality disorders. Evans et al. (1972) studied forty families with failure-to-thrive infants. They divided the mothers into three groups. The first group was extremely depressed, had sustained a recent object loss, and had a good prognosis. The second group was depressed but exhibited chronic losses and had very deprived living conditions. The third group was angry, hostile, and abusive, and perceived their children as "bad." The last two groups had been poorly mothered themselves. Talbot et al. (1947) hypothesized that failure to thrive resulted from a failure of mother-child bonding. The failure-to-thrive syndrome has been reported across all social classes and in families that are usually intact (Glasser et al. 1968). Unfortunately, these investigations were based on cases reported without control groups, so their generalizability is limited.

Leonard et al. (1966) described their series of failure-to-thrive mothers as women who were unwilling or unable to provide adequate nurturance because of a lack of support from spouse and family, and as a result of inadequate mothering when they were children. Kotelchuk and Newberger (1977) also demonstrated that failure-to-thrive mothers were significantly more isolated than control mothers and received less support from their families and neighborhood.

In a controlled study, Pollitt et al. (1975) observed that mothers of failure-to-thrive children demonstrated less verbal and physical contact with their children than mothers of normal controls, were less affectionate, and more prone to use physical punishment. The most consistently observed traits of failure-to-thrive mothers include depression, punitive behavior, unsupportiveness, and an impaired capacity for nurturance.

Observations of the Children

Leonard et al. (1966) described the following characteristics in failure-to-thrive infants: minimal smiling and vocalization; lack of cuddliness; superficial personal and social relationships; and an absence of separation and stranger anxiety. Bullard et al. (1967) observed feeding difficulties, delayed development, vomiting and/or diarrhea, and impaired fine and gross motor development. Over half of the children exhibited continued growth failure, emotional disorder, and mental retardation upon follow-up examination. Riley et al. (1968) also demonstrated the persistence of growth inhibition in eighty-three failure-to-thrive children over a two-year period. Glaser et al. (1968) described frequent school failure and mental retardation in failure-to-thrive children when they reached school age. Fischoff (1973) described various forms of autoerotic behavior in these infants, such as rocking, headbanging, nodding spasms, sucking of fingers or fist, and rhythmic hand movements. In a controlled study, Pollitt and Eichler (1976) reported that failure-to-thrive children manifested a significantly higher prevalence of developmental disturbances in eating, sleeping, and elimination than the healthy controls. They also demonstrated a reduced caloric intake.

Barbero (1975) described bizarre eye behaviors in failure-to-thrive infants. They displayed a wide-eyed gaze and tended to scan their environment. They avoided eye contact by looking or turning away, or by actively covering their face and eyes with a hand. Barbero also noted that these infants tended to exhibit extremes of spacticity and rigidity on the one hand, or a decreased muscle tone on the other. They also seemed immobile.

Wolff and Money (1973) described abnormal sleep patterns in failure-to-thrive children. Periods of sleep disturbance were associated with retarded growth and a reduced secretion of human growth hormone. The sleep disorder and hormonal deficiency were reversible when the environment of the children was improved. Gordon (1979) studied the interaction of eight failure-to-thrive infants with their mothers. These infants ranged in age from twelve to nineteen months. Compared with controls who had been hospitalized because of acute medical illness, the failure-to-thrive children demonstrated significantly less distress during separation from their mothers and less crying and fretting during their mother's absence. The authors concluded that these infants were unable to communicate their distress and therefore unable to elicit nurturant responses from their caregivers. They suggested that the underresponsiveness of these infants might be a more important etiological factor than alleged maternal deficiency in the genesis of this syndrome.

Hufton and Oates (1977) carried out a long-term follow-up study of twenty-one failure-to-thrive children, reviewing them at an average of six years and four months after their initial hospitalization. Five of the children remained below the tenth percentile in weight. Most of the children displayed numerous behavioral and educational difficulties. Ten of the children were classified as abnormal personalities on the basis of anti-social or neurotic traits by a questionnaire completed by their teachers. Sixteen of eighteen mothers who completed a similar questionnaire described these children as "abnormal." The mothers reported a high incidence of lying, temper tantrums, speech problems, enuresis, and overactivity in these children. Educational testing revealed that two-thirds of the children were one or two years behind their age level in reading. On the WISC, one-third of the children had verbal scores significantly lower than their performance scores. The families of these children were characterized by marital instability, economic difficulties, and a high incidence of depression in the mothers.

The authors also observed that most of the children were the youngest in a large family, and it was suggested that the extra child was more than the mother's already overburdened resources could manage. Hufton and Oates recommended the initiation of supportive intervention with failure-to-thrive mothers during the infants' hospitalization which would focus on feeding and infant care. This program would be continued in the home by visiting community social workers, in order to prevent long-term sequelae in these children.

Etiological Considerations

Since the feeding experience is one of the most crucial and affect-laden elements of the mother-infant relationship, aberrant maternal behavior can adversely affect the infant's feeding patterns. Conversely, the infant who fails to ingest sufficient nutriments because of an intrinsic physical or physiological abnormality will have a negative impact on the mother's quality of nurturance and infant care, and her sense of maternal competency.

Despite the documentation of maternal inadequacy and psychopathology in mothers of failure-to-thrive infants, and immediate and long-term physical, developmental, and psychological sequelae of the children, a clear cut etiology for this syndrome has yet to be demonstrated. Although it might be presumed that a disorder in the earliest mother-infant relationship pertaining to feeding is of crucial importance, it is difficult to separate cause and effect. It has been demonstrated that deprived infants (Whitten et al. 1969) and monkeys (Kerr et al. 1969) gain weight when they are provided with adequate nourishment despite the persistence of a depriving environment. As in the case of child abuse, numerous etiological factors probably underlie the failure-to-thrive syndrome. Maternal contributions might consist of inadequate nurturance as a child, the presence of specific unresolved oral conflicts, and social isolation and a perceived lack of support in infant care from spouse and family. The mother might be initially insensitive to the infant's nutritional requirements, resulting in forced feeding or underfeeding. The infant might contribute his own constitutional vulnerability, consisting of a deficient sucking reflex or increased gastrointestinal sensitivity. It is striking that these infants display a general decrease in appetitive behavior in addition to their avoidance of food. As the feeding disturbance becomes chronic and the infant becomes malnourished and socially unresponsive, an additional stress is imposed upon the mother. The poorly thriving baby reaffirms the mother's sense of inadequacy and adds to her negative feelings toward the child, which may have been present originally. Additional environmental stresses which might impinge on the family, such as marital friction, financial crises, and increased child-rearing burdens generated by the siblings of the failure-to-thrive infant, will further contribute to the disequilibrium between mother and infant.

Treatment should be provided for the baby and the parents. Most failure-to-thrive children improve during hospitalization, usually increasing their intake and enjoyment of food and gaining weight. In most hospitals, the baby is assigned to one special nurse who provides most of the feeding. Hospitalization of the child also provides the treatment staff (pediatrician, nurse, social worker, etc.) with an opportunity to develop a supportive relationship with the parents, especially the mother. Once the infant begins to thrive, it is possible to interrupt the vicious cycle of maternal insufficiency, infantile growth failure, and maternal frustration and inadequacy. Several investigators (Evans et al. 1972, Leonard et al. 1966, and Fischoff (1973) have described the resistance of many of these families to therapeutic intervention. The parents' feelings of guilt and inadequacy are often mobilized by the infant's improvement in a hospital setting in contrast to its failure to respond to the parents at home. Therefore the therapeutic intervention with the infant and his family should not be terminated upon discharge from the hospital when the baby's nutritional status improves. The families should be provided with the appropriate supports (social services, child-care education, visiting nurse contact, psychiatric consultation, etc.) to strengthen parental functioning. If necessary, the family should be referred to protective services for monitoring. When the parents are extremely resistant, and the infant fails to maintain improvement after he returns home, foster-care placement might be required.

It is evident that further controlled studies and clinical research will be necessary to understand the precise impact of subtle alterations in the mother-infant relationship on the infant's physical growth and development. Long-term followup studies of the physical and psychological development of failure-to-thrive children would be of great importance. Our current information regarding the failure-to-thrive syndrome warrants its inclusion in the category of "maltreatment," since it appears to be a consequence of parental dysfunction similar to the syndromes of child abuse and neglect. Personality factors and childhood experiences of mothers of failure-to-thrive children are quite similar to the characteristics of abuse-prone and neglectful mothers. It may be hypothesized that the crucial ingredients of this syndrome, as in child abuse, are the "high-risk" mother, vulnerable infant, and stressful environment However, these children seem to lose their appetite for all object relationships, as well as for food, while the typical abused child strives to maintain object ties at any cost. It would not be surprising, then, if future studies demonstrated more pervasive long-term psychological impairment in these children than in those subjected to other forms of maltreatment.

PART III

Treatment and Prevention

9

Treatment:
General Considerations

Unfortunately, efforts toward the rehabilitation of abusing families have not kept pace with the recent nationwide increase in the reporting and public awareness of child abuse. Social scientists have deplored the inability of states and cities to supply services and treatment for the great influx of maltreating families (DeFrancis 1972, Oviatt 1972, Nagi 1975). The impact of punitive societal attitudes toward abusing parents is still reflected in the investigation and management of newly reported cases. In many states cases of abuse are reported to law enforcement officials rather than to protective service agencies. The initial contact with abusing families emphasizes investigation and confirmation of the alleged incident, which is usually incompatible with the development of a therapeutic strategy. Placement of the children in foster homes and institutions has become the major mode of intervention, owing to the relative scarcity of social and psychiatric services for abusing families and the difficulties experienced in involving abusing parents in traditional counseling and psychotherapy. Abusing parents are still too frequently presumed to be unmotivated for help and therefore beyond rehabilitation.

Some progress has been made recently toward the development of child-abuse treatment programs through the pioneering efforts of a group of pediatricians, psychiatrists, and social workers at the University of Colorado Medical Center at Denver, Colorado. The Denver group was the first to systematically describe the clinical dimensions and psychology of child abuse and base innovative treatment techniques on this body of knowledge. This group collaborated in the publication of three basic texts on child abuse which were edited by Helfer and Kempe (1968, 1972, 1976), and stimulated the development of comprehensive treatment facilities for maltreated children and their families in other parts of the country.

The growing evidence that child maltreatment was associated with severe parental dysfunction and psychiatric disorder, combined with the favorable publicity received by the Denver model, resulted in a steady increase in referrals to psychiatrists for consultation and treatment of abusing parents. However many psychiatrists simply accepted the referrals as they came along, and dispensed whatever treatment was available at their particular clinic or institution, without taking the special needs of this population into consideration. The traditional psychiatric out-patient setting failed to solve the problems of the abusing parent, because of the reasons outlined in chapter 1, which contributed to the therapeutic nihilism of psychiatrists and discouraged further referrals from child protective services.

Most psychiatric clinics are not equipped to provide the type of outreach and crisis intervention required by these patients. Strengthening of parental functioning and family life through regular home visits by nurses, homemakers, and the therapist himself is beyond the scope of the average mental health facility. But specialized multidisciplinary treatment facilities for abusing families like the University of Colorado Medical Center have reported considerable success. Helfer (1975) and Pollock and Steele (1972) estimated that about 70 to 80 percent of abusing and neglecting families respond satisfactorily to therapeutic intervention. Multidisciplinary child-abuse consultation teams are now being established in various parts of the country to improve the diagnosis and management of cases of abuse and maltreatment. Child-abuse treatment centers established in certain hospital and community settings have provided rehabilitation and social services to strengthen abusing and neglecting families in crisis. This author experienced similar success in the rehabilitation of abusing parents at the Downstate Medical Center's comprehensive treatment program. The success of these programs can be ascribed to their use of a wide variety of crisis oriented therapeutic modalities, including home intervention, which will be outlined in detail. Unfortunately, these specialized programs are so few in number that the vast majority of maltreating families do not receive treatment services during or after the investigation by protective services. In New York City 26,307 cases of child abuse and neglect were reported in 1978, yet only three relatively small treatment programs are in existence.

While effective psychiatric intervention with maltreating parents has been limited to a handful of programs throughout the country, treatment facilities for abused and neglected children are almost nonexistent. Despite the developmental deviation, severely impaired psychological and cognitive functioning, depression, low self-esteem and impulsivity described in these children as a consequence of a traumatic child-rearing environment (Martin 1976, Green 1978a), there has been an appalling absence of programs offering them psychotherapy or psychoeducational rehabilitation. A crucial ingredient of the treatment process is the modification of the pathological identification and inner world of the abused child. If this is not accomplished, the child perpetuates his struggle with internalized "bad parents" with new objects in his environment. In the author's opinion (Green 1978b) amelioration of the abused child's traumatic home environment, which must precede individual treatment of the child, is often not sufficient to reverse his ego impairment and maladaptive personality changes. Failure to provide the abused child with psychological rehabilitation after his physical wounds have healed has serious consequences. These untreated abused children are a constant drain on the resources of our communities, due to their vulnerability to mental illness, vocational and educational failure, proneness toward violence and criminality, and their tendency to repeat abusive patterns with their own children in the following generation. The child-abuse treatment program at the Downstate Medical Center reported significant improvement in the children after one year provided the parents were involved in some aspect of the program (Green 1978b). Crisis nurseries and day-care programs have also been utilized successfully with preschool maltreated children.

Any plan for the prevention or treatment of child abuse must be designed to create a safe environment for the child and to modify the potentiating factors underlying abuse. Therefore, an effective treatment program must deal specifically with the parental abuse-proneness, the characteristics of the child which make him vulnerable for scapegoating, and the environmental stresses which trigger the abusive interaction.

Perhaps no other major social and health problem has attracted attention from so many different and widely divergent professional and volunteer groups. Most treatment programs, therefore, are of a multidisciplinary nature, with participants from social work, child protective services, the law, law enforcement, nursing, pediatrics, psychiatry, child psychiatry, and psychology. The program's operational base may originate from social agencies, hospitals, protective service units, community organizations, mental health centers, and volunteer groups. This type of intervention will vary according to the backgrounds of the participants, their experience, and their frames of reference. Each treatment modality has its adherents and detractors, and it is clear that the rehabilitation of child-abusing families is in a preliminary stage. Most treatment programs provide counseling and social services to maltreating parents; fewer programs treat the children directly. The following five chapters will describe in detail the process by which the parents and children can be helped, and the various types of organizations which can effectively deliver therapeutic services. Chapter 14 deals with broader ramifications of placement of maltreated children outside of their homes. This type of intervention, although still necessary on occasion, has been deployed too often and too indiscriminately. Chapter 15 presents ideas on the prevention of maltreatment.

10

Helping the Parents

The major objectives of an ideal treatment program are to provide both parent and child with a broad, comprehensive, and relevant spectrum of services, so that the family constellation may be strengthened and maintained where possible. The program elements should be designed to modify the three important etiological factors underlying the maltreatment process.

Protecting the children and preventing further abuse receive immediate priority. This should be followed by a concerted attempt to modify the personality traits of the abusing parent which interfere with his capacity for parenting. Therapeutic intervention with the parents may proceed with the children remaining at home, or during their temporary placement if indicated. The primary objectives of the therapeutic contact with abuse-prone or abusing parents are:

1. Helping the parent establish a trusting, supportive, and gratifying relationship with the therapist and with other adults.

2. Helping the parent improve his chronically devalued self-image.

3. Enabling the parent to receive satisfaction from his own accomplishments and from contacts with others, so he will no longer depend on his children to bolster his self-esteem.

4. Providing the parent with a positive child-rearing model for identification.

5. Helping the parent develop nonabusive disciplinary and child-rearing techniques.

6. Enabling the parent to derive pleasure from the child, and increasing the parent's capacity to "give" (love, warmth, attention, etc.) to the child, so that the role reversal will be eliminated.

7. Providing the parent with basic information about child rearing and child development. Special counseling will be made available to parents of vulnerable children with physical, emotional, and intellectual impairment.

8. Helping the parent to understand the relationship between the painful experiences of his own childhood and his current misperception of the child.

The traditional outpatient psychiatric treatment process must be greatly modified if these goals are to be attained. A multidisciplinary comprehensive treatment program with a strong outreach component is the most appropriate type of intervention for these families. The facility may be hospital or community based, and should provide most of the following services: psychiatric evaluation, individual counseling and psychotherapy, group psychotherapy, family therapy, crisis intervention, home visiting, social services, twenty-four-hour hot line, education in child rearing and child care, legal assistance, medical treatment, and vocational assistance and rehabilitation. The abused children and their siblings should be provided with medical care, psychiatric and developmental evaluation, play therapy and psychotherapy, and psycho-educational assistance if necessary. Both parents and children would benefit from the availability of a crisis nursery for the short-term care of abused infants and preschoolers.

The crucial ingredient of any treatment program is the involvement of the parent in a corrective emotional experience with an accepting, gratifying, and uncritical adult. The helping person need not be a psychiatrist or physician. Social workers, nurses, psychologists, and mature volunteers who have parented successfully may be trained to help maltreating parents.

The therapist must be active, supportive, and flexible, and must eventually provide the type of dependency gratification which these parents were previously unable to obtain. "Giving" to the parent may be expressed in the form of providing child-rearing advice, being available on an emergency basis, making visits to the home, securing necessary medical services for the family, establishing liaison with the schools and with the numerous social agencies as an advocate of the parent. Group therapy has been extremely helpful to abusive mothers as a means of ventilation and support, and as a bridge to social involvement. Some abusing parents prefer to participate in self-help groups, such as Parent's Anonymous, where there is no contact with professionals or public agencies.

A comprehensive treatment program should also be designed to reduce the environmental stresses most likely to trigger episodes of child abuse. Assistance with direct child care by means of babysitters, day-care facilities, homemakers or visiting nurses, the availability of a twenty-four-hour emergency hotline, and the provision of indispensable material resources such as food, clothing, and shelter, would reduce the discrepancy between the limited parental capacity and the increased child-rearing burdens of abusing families.

Special Problems in the Treatment of Abusing Parents

The treatment of child-abusing parents poses special difficulties beyond those usually associated with a psychologically unsophisticated, primarily lower-class, multiproblem population. The following characteristics of the abusing parents

dealt with before a therapeutic relationship can be
.shed.

1. These parents are often unmotivated to seek help, or
even overtly hostile to the suggestion that they might experience emotional difficulties. They typically lack insight, and
deny and project their problems onto other people or situations. Confronting them about these tactics would be counterproductive. It is more effective to accept their projections and
empathize with their frustrations in dealing with significant persons and situations. One might initially focus on the "difficult
child" or on material issues such as financial and housing problems, where intervention might be less threatening and even
considered helpful.

2. Their suspiciousness and basic mistrust of authorities interfere with the formation of a therapeutic alliance. This results
from their lifelong experience of humiliation and criticism at the
hands of their parents and subsequent authority figures.

3. The fragile self-esteem of these parents impairs their
capacity to accept help and counseling from the therapeutic
team. Constructive suggestions concerning child rearing and
home management might be rebuffed if they are construed as
criticism. The parents require continual reassurance and support, especially during the initial stages of treatment. Their
basic dependency needs must be gratified before "demands"
can be placed on them.

4. The abusive parents are masochistic and provocative,
and they exhibit a stubborn tendency to turn the treatment
situation into a repetition of their frustrating and humiliating
interaction with their parents and spouses. The treatment staff
must be trained to handle this provocative behavior without
counterreacting.

5. The impact of ongoing investigative and punitive procedures by protective services or the court inhibits the establishment of a confidential and trusting relationship with the therapist. The problem of confidentiality may be eased by divorcing
the investigation and court-related activities from the treatment
process. Psychiatric evaluations and recommendations required
by the court should be performed independently by their own
personnel.

The following obstacles to treatment are primarily determined by personal attitudes and feelings elicited in therapists by abusive parents and the act of child abuse itself.

1. The phenomenon of negative countertransference involves the natural tendency of the therapist to instinctively condemn and dislike a parent who would cruelly assault and humiliate a helpless infant or child. The parent's primary therapist, as well as the whole treatment staff, must learn to control feelings of anger and self-righteous indignation toward the parent. The expression of such attitudes obviously precludes the development of a therapeutic alliance.

2. The therapist tends to act out the role of a "good parent" who rescues the child from his brutal family. These rescue fantasies are often accompanied by efforts to prematurely transform the abusing mothers and fathers into model parents. Abusing parents are unable to tolerate this competitive and patronizing attitude, which evokes deep-seated feelings of inadequacy experienced during confrontations with their own parents.

3. The marked degree of parental ambivalence toward therapeutic involvement, characterized by rapidly alternating periods of infantile demands for dependency gratification and hostile withdrawal, imposes a great deal of frustration on the therapist. These parents also frequently arrive late or miss their appointments, and seem unappreciative of the therapist's investment of time and energy. Their apparent lack of cooperation and commitment to the treatment process is a threat to the narcissistic gratification of the therapist.

These formidable obstacles to the development of a viable therapeutic relationship with abusing parents initially caused many workers in the field to doubt the value of therapeutic intervention in modifying their behavior. For many, placement of abused children in foster homes and institutions seemed to be the safer and more expedient solution, despite its great expense and obvious limitations. However, many of those who continued to work with abusing parents realized that their failure to adapt to the traditional outpatient model of psychiatric social service intervention could be remedied by major modifications of the usual techniques. A multidisciplinary "team" approach with a shift in focus from the outpatient clinical setting to the home has proved effective. The delivery of comprehensive services, including crisis-oriented home visits, telephone hot lines, parent groups, homemaking assistance, visiting nurse intervention, and day-care facilities for infants and small children, reduces adverse environmental pressures and fosters a strengthening and stabilization of crisis-ridden families. This comprehensive intervention has helped overcome the obstacles to therapeutic involvement and facilitate positive changes in the child-rearing patterns of abusing parents.

Case Illustrations

The following case histories demonstrate some of the many facets of the therapeutic process and various types of intervention which can be successfully utilized to modify abusive behavior.

Case 1. The T. family became involved with our treatment program when Jack T. sought help in controlling his impulses to hit Jacky, his ten-month-old son. Mr. T., a forty-year-old, intermittently employed housepainter, was referred to us by his counselor at an alcoholism treatment center. He could not tolerate Jacky's crying, which he felt was designed to manipulate him. His request for help was perceived with a sense of urgency, since he had previously abused two young daughters several years ago. Both of these children sustained multiple fractures and were subsequently placed in foster homes and eventually adopted. The T.'s first child died as a result of crib death, but may have also been abused. Jacky was apparently conceived to relieve the T.'s emptiness and depression caused by the loss of the three older children. This represented their final attempt to succeed as parents, since Mrs. T. requested a tubal ligation after Jacky was born. Rose T., Jack's thirty-six-year-old wife, presented herself as a depressed, confused woman who appeared much older than she was. She was obviously ineffective in caring for Jacky and managing the household, and often delegated these responsibilities to her husband. She was sad and embittered about the loss of her older children, for which she blamed Mr. T. After several joint interviews with both parents and the child, it was clear that Jack was the dominant parent who usually held and tried to comfort Jacky, while Rose passively blended into the background. When she became more assertive with the baby at our urging, her husband would often criticize her.

It soon became clear to us that Jack's impulses to hit his son were experienced mainly when he returned home for dinner, hungry and tired. At this time, he became enraged if Jacky was not quietly sleeping. If Jacky was being fed by Mrs. T. or if he was crying or fussing, Jack experienced mounting resentment. After a short period in individual psychotherapy, Jack recognized that he felt neglected and jealous of his son when the latter was being cared for by Mrs. T. Jack recalled painful memories about his early childhood as a foundling and a foster child. He remembered being hungry and lonely. He was always the last to be fed, as the natural children of the foster parents "came first." Jack also could identify with Jacky's cries of hunger, since he had suffered from malnutrition in one of his foster homes. He realized how these experiences left him ill-prepared to function as a devoted parent.

The treatment plan for the T. family consisted of helping Jack utilize his newly gained insight concerning the relationship between his childhood deprivation and abandonment and his anger toward Jacky to understand and control his abusive impulses. The therapist also helped Jack to deal with his vocational problems by exploring some of his paranoid attitudes toward his boss, and assisting him in obtaining a new chauffeur's license to replace one which had been revoked for drunken driving. As Jack was able to get more painting jobs, his self-esteem rose and he became less "rivalrous" with his infant son. Jack was also encouraged to continue to control his drinking through participation in Alcoholics Anonymous.

Rose learned to become more active in caring for Jacky, but this required a considerable amount of education in child rearing and child development, which was accomplished through her relationship with a visiting student nurse. As Rose began to intervene more appropriately with Jacky, his greater responsiveness to her parenting provided her with a sense of effectiveness which she had never experienced before. Her greater involvement with Jacky relieved Jack of the extra child-rearing burdens which had previously triggered his violent temper. Both Jack and Rose attend the parents' group.

The T.'s have been in our program for about four years. A striking development took place during their contact with us. Jack managed to locate and establish a relationship with his natural mother, whom he had never seen before. Other positive changes include Jack's recent plans to obtain painting jobs on a free-lance basis. Although Jack's drinking still remains a problem, he has completely refrained from hitting Jacky, who is now almost five. Jack occasionally strikes his wife when intoxicated, so that his potential for violence is still a factor which makes continued supervision of this family essential.

Case 2. Miss Jane C., a thirty-five-year-old blind unmarried black woman, was referred to the treatment program after her discharge from Kings County Hospital, where she was treated for paranoid psychosis. She sought help because she feared that she would beat her three sons, ages nine, six, and five. She experienced the greatest difficulty with Raymond, her nine year old, because of his school problems and his alleged unwillingness to physically assist her when traveling. In addition to her blindness, she suffers from sarcoidosis and hypertension.

Jane had to be hospitalized after she became delusional about Raymond attempting to harm her. She accused him of not helping her with household chores and refusing to assist her in walking from place to place. She imagined that he was going to push her in front of a car or throw her down the stairs in retaliation for the beatings she had inflicted upon him.

Jane was born in South Carolina, the second of ten siblings. She attended school through the sixth grade. Jane recalled a sad childhood marred by chronic illness. She suffered from respiratory problems, painful joints, and poor eyesight. She felt she was a burden to her parents, who failed to provide her with medical care and did not get her glasses when her vision was failing. She still bears scars from many beatings by her mother, who struck her with sticks, belts, and even a fireplace iron. Jane's mother also kept her away from school when she was twelve in order to work in a restaurant. Jane is currently estranged from her mother, who she feels is no longer interested in her.

Jane came to New York at the age of eighteen to work as a domestic, but within two years she had lost her vision after an operation for glaucoma and cataracts.

She began a relationship with Mr. H., the man who subsequently fathered Raymond, when she was twenty-four. He continued living with his wife and five children. The relationship continued for four years, until after the birth of Carl, her second son. Soon afterwards Jane met Mr. S., who fathered her youngest son, Samuel. Mr. S. maintains only sporadic contact with Jane because of his frequent traveling as a racetrack employee. Jane admitted her anger about the last two pregnancies. She tried to abort each time by starving herself and drinking excessively.

The deployment of a visiting student nurse uncovered valuable information about the patterns of interaction in the C. household. It was apparent that Raymond was being used by his mother as a "seeing-eye" companion. Jane expected him to return home immediately after school to help her with shopping and cooking. He was also obliged to accompany her to various medical and psychiatric appointments at the hospital, frequently causing him to miss school and peer-group activities. It was clear that Jane was placing excessive demands on Raymond to act like a parent at the expense of his own psychological growth and development. This parasite like relationship with Raymond represented an extreme example of "role reversal," in which the parent inappropriately uses the child to gratify her own dependency needs.

The student nurse also described Jane's problems with Carl, age six, who seemed restless, hyperactive, and confused. Carl would often touch his mother's breast or genitals, and attempted to do the same with the nurse. Jane was noticeably more depressed when Mr. S. was out of town or not in touch with her. During these times she would often drink, and was likely to beat the children for not gratifying her. Her relationship with her homemaker was observed during the home visits. The homemaker seemed quite patronizing and critical of Jane, finding fault with her for being sloppy in the house, and for not controlling her children properly. It became clear that Jane related to the homemaker as to her own critical mother. The following strategy for therapeutic intervention was carried out. The student nurse, J., developed a supportive, nonjudgmental relationship with Jane and also performed such concrete services as taking her blood pressure, checking her medication, and helping to coordinate her numerous medical appointments. Jane began to confide in J. and would call her at home during times of stress. Jane was assigned to a senior social worker on a regular basis and to a psychiatrist for the supervision of her medication, while J. continued the home visits. Some major therapeutic issues evolved during the first few months of casework. First, Jane failed to make appropriate demands on her boyfriend who was actually able to spend more time with her and the children when she requested it. Secondly, Jane's excessive dependency on Raymond was explored. Jane realized that she demanded of her son the kind of care that she never received from her own family as a child. The worker helped Jane understand and respect Raymond's need for autonomy and independence. Ultimately, suggestions were made concerning Jane's procrastination and resistance to involvement in her own rehabilitation. She had started to learn braille and secretarial skills, only to drop them during her last two pregnancies. The worker attempted to remotivate Jane to continue these projects as a means of achieving some independence. With the worker's support, Jane was able to replace the first homemaker with someone less critical and more empathic. In addition, Jane received counseling about the special problems and needs of her children. J.'s home observations led to psychiatric evaluations of the three children. Raymond was found to be hyperactive and impulsive, with learning difficulties, and was referred to a resident child psychiatrist for psychotherapy and medication. J. and the homemaker described Carl's bizarre behavior, which included frequent tantrums, headbanging, uncontrolled genital play, and attempts to poke his younger brother with knives and scissors. Carl often got up at night to turn on the gas. His speech was repetitive and often echolalic. He was observed on the child psychiatry inpatient unit where he displayed provocative, sexually aggressive behavior and had difficulty relating to his peers. He was felt to be psychotic with central nervous system impairment and residential treatment was recommended. Jane, however, was unable to tolerate the separation, so plans were made for Carl to attend a special school and receive supportive psychiatric treatment on an outpatient basis. Sam, age five, was impulsive and somewhat hyperactive, but was the least disturbed of the children. He was referred to a male social worker for psychotherapy with an emphasis on socialization and corrective object relationship. Jane was persuaded to join the parents' group, after having resisted for some time. She feared being criticized and ridiculed, as she had in the past by her family and peers. Instead, she received acceptance, support, and encouragement from other parents with similar difficulties, establishing positive contact with peers for the first time. We hoped that these gratifying experiences would act as a bridge to the establishment of social contacts in her community.

In review, the establishment of a supportive, noncritical relationship with the student nurse and social worker satisfied some of Jane's needs for approval, dependency, and social contact. These professionals also served as a "hot-line" by being available to Jane in times of crises. These relationships relieved some of the burden placed on the children to gratify the mother's needs (role reversal). The therapeutic relationships were also designed to mobilize Jane's initiative and independence, improve her self-esteem, and enhance her capacity for experiencing pleasure in personal relationships and in her own achievements.

Counseling and child-rearing advice concerning the special problems and needs of her children counteracted Jane's

paranoid stance toward them. She realized for the first time
that their behavior was not always volitional, under their control, and designed to hurt her. She recognized that they were
in difficulty and needed special treatment. She began to
understand that in beating her children, she was repeating the
brutality that her mother had directed toward her. She was
introduced to forms of discipline other than physical punishment, and gradually realized that beatings only made the
children more aggressive. The involvement of the children in
therapeutic relationships, and the presence of a visiting nurse
in the home, reduced their fear of annihilation and/or abandonment at the hands of their mother. In a way, the children's
extensive contact with the treatment team in the hospital setting promoted an "institutional transference." The visits to the
various hospital clinics and the contact with professionals were
regarded as positive experiences which acted as a buffer
against the chaotic and uncertain conditions at home.

   Case 3. Mr. Don H., a security guard, had periodically
abused his wife and his four- and six-year-old sons, especially
while he was drinking. He became angry when the boys misbehaved at home or in school, and when they engaged in
"babyish" behavior, which consisted of bedwetting and kissing
their mother. This clearly evoked Don's own "bad" childhood
self-image, as bedwetting and behavior problems were typical
of his early difficulties. Don accused his wife, Edna, of spoiling
the boys, especially during her attempts to protect them from
his beatings. He was also angered when the boys sought out
other men in the neighborhood to supply them with money or
candy. Don feared that this would prove that he was unable to
gratify them, and that the neighbors would conclude that he
wasn't a good father. Don complained to his therapist about
Edna's lack of responsiveness, failure to keep the house
orderly, and inability to discipline the children. Edna's treatment with her own therapist revealed that her passivity and
detachment were a product of her chronic depression and
were related to her anger toward Don for drinking and "running around" with other women. He excluded her from his

social life for long periods of time. She retaliated by not talking to him and refusing to sleep with him, which in turn provoked him to seek out other women. Edna's withdrawal elicited Don's childhood memories of maternal deprivation and of the death of his mother, who had been a prostitute.

Exploration of the unsatisfactory marital patterns took place during several joint therapy sessions attended by both spouses and their respective therapists. Don was encouraged to share most of his pleasurable activities with his wife, but he complained that she kept things from him. With great difficulty, Edna confessed that whenever she approached Don with a problem or complaint, he threatened to beat her. Don was able to acknowledge the counterproductive impact of his intimidation of his wife and sons, and became aware of his role in their alienation from him. Edna's renewed efforts to confide in her husband met with more success. As she became more available to him, the time and energy he had spent on the "street" were shifted back into the home. As Edna assumed more responsibility for the discipline of the children, and provided more structure in the home, Don's relationship with the children improved and less of the interaction included provocations and punishment. This couple, who had been on the verge of separation, managed to effect a more satisfying relationship and greater ease of communication. The increased capacity of each spouse to satisfy one another's yearnings for dependency eliminated the need for role reversal and abuse by the father and passive-aggressive withdrawal by the mother. Don's increasing awareness of the link between the regressive and provocative behavior of his boys and his own angry protest as a deprived child was crucial in altering his patterns of abuse. A gradual understanding and acceptance of his turbulent childhood permitted him to identify with his sons and develop a capacity for empathy.

The H.s' six-year-old boy also received psychiatric intervention because of violent, aggressive behavior in school. During his brief psychotherapy, he was helped to contain and control his impulses by "working through" his anger toward his abusive father in the playroom. A gradual internalization of controls and formation of superego components were fostered through identification with the therapist and the introduction of "latency" defenses. The simultaneous intervention with parents and child in the H. family made it possible to interrupt the vicious cycle of child abuse, childhood aggression, and further physical punishment.

Case 4. Mrs. Lily N., a twenty-one-year-old Puerto Rican mother of three, was referred to the program by a local child protective agency after she had failed to follow through with her court-ordered treatment. Her three children, Eddy, three, Julia, one and a half, and Juan, six months, had been placed in foster care a year previously following Eddy's severe abuse by his father, Mr. J., who was Lily's paramour. Eddy was admitted to the hospital in critical condition with head and abdominal injuries, and numerous scars and black and blue marks were noticed on his body. He was also filthy and lice-infested, as were his younger siblings.

During the initial interviews by our social worker, Lily seemed chronically depressed and unkempt in her appearance. She expressed a lot of resentment toward the child protective agency for taking her children away, and wondered how she could get "revenge." She admitted that her main objective was to "get the children back." She initially denied having problems, despite reports by the foster parents that Eddy and Julia were dirty and upset when they returned from visiting her. Lily seemed to drag herself to the appointments, and her attendance was quite irregular. She appeared to be socially isolated, and had no social contacts since Mr. J. left her. She thought about moving to another city where one of her sisters was living.

Lily was born in Puerto Rico but has been living in this country since she was five months old. She was the fourth of six children. She described a childhood marred by memories of beatings and scapegoating at the hands of her alcoholic father, who had also abused her mother. Her parents subsequently divorced and her mother remarried. Lily felt rejected by her peers while growing up, because she was "different." This feeling continued in adulthood, as she isolated herself from others because of her conviction that nobody would ever like her or help her. Lily quit school in the eleventh grade because her father had been overly strict and did not permit her to go out. She went to work in a factory when she was seventeen, and met Mr. J. She soon became pregnant with Eddy and went to visit her sister in the Midwest to have the baby. The relationship with Mr. J. was characterized by frequent arguments culminating in physical violence. He often beat her during his periodic bouts of alcoholism.

After her return to New York, Lily met and married Mr. N. She soon became pregnant with Julia, but their relationship ended when Mr. N. left her when she was four months pregnant. Lily had accused her husband of not working and refusing to support the household. When she was nine months pregnant, she met Eddy's father again, and they moved in together.

The initial intervention with Lily was supportive with an emphasis on providing her with concrete services. Home visiting was alternated with office interviews because of her difficulties with transportation. Her functioning seemed impaired in critical areas. She appeared to be intellectually limited, and her thinking was concrete, and became disorganized under stress. The strength of her narcissism and her orientation to the immediate present made it difficult for her to focus on her past and future relationships with her children. She seemed incapable of recognizing or dealing with her child-rearing problems. She expected the children to gratify her needs, and their inevitable failure to accomplish this resulted in intense feelings of frustration and rejection for which she had little tolerance. For example, she found it difficult to accept Eddy's anger toward her, which he vented by hitting and becoming verbally abusive during his weekend visits home. She failed to limit this aggressive behavior until she became overwhelmed with anger; this resulted frequently in her spanking him while out of control. Instead of being able to focus on the source of his anger, she was preoccupied with the fear that he might injure her when he grows up.

After several months of supportive psychotherapy with her psychiatric social worker, Lily began to exhibit some positive changes in several areas. Her physical hygiene and appearance improved noticeably, and she became more consistent in keeping her appointments. She was more open and less defensive in discussing her relationship with her children, and began to recognize her contribution to the problems with them. At this point, she stopped insisting on the immediate return of the children, and began to show an interest in improving her parenting skills by bringing specific problems for discussion, and even reading a book on child care. She became quite open about her need for help and was able to explore better ways of expressing her anger and increasing her assertiveness.

As Lily began to develop a positive response to her therapist and the treatment process, she accepted the referral to the parents' group as an additional treatment modality. She had adamantly refused group psychotherapy during her initial contact with the child protective agency. After one year in the program a student nurse, Karen, was assigned to Lily in order to help her with concrete household and parenting skills, in preparation for Julia's expected discharge from foster care. Karen helped Lily to deal with the children during their weekly visits.

While in foster care Juan, the youngest child, developed a malignant tumor of his eye, which required its removal. Lily realized that she was not yet able to provide him with optimal care, since she would soon care for Julia on a full-time basis. She decided to first concentrate on working toward Julia's and Eddy's return.

An indirect, but nevertheless significant, consequence of the successful intervention with Lily was her capacity for improved relationships with men. For the first time, she found a boyfriend who was kind to her rather than abusive. She was able to terminate this liaison when he was unable to adjust to her plans to gradually regain custody of her children. She subsequently fell in love with a supportive, giving man who is extremely fond of the children.

Fifteen months after her referral to the program, Lily regained custody of Julia. Buttressed by her social worker and fellow group members, and the home intervention by the student nurse, Lily has been managing quite well. Her current problems center around her relationship with Eddy, who has become predictably jealous following his sister's return home. Lily is also pregnant, and is expecting a baby within a month. This, of course, is another source of irritation for Eddy, and constitutes a major adaptive task for Lily.

With the exception of the H.'s, the preceding cases involved multiproblem families receiving public assistance. The psychological interventions which took place were supplemented by vigorous outreach efforts including visiting nurse contacts, and the provision of concrete social services designed to secure adequate food, clothing, housing, medical assistance, financial aid, and child care for each family. Assuming the role of parent-advocate in dealing with the welfare system helped the social worker/therapist in establishing a need-gratifying relationship with the maltreating parents. The consistent interest and availability of the therapist were pivotal in overcoming the parent's initial posture of suspiciousness and distrust. The basic "service" orientation for intervention with poor child-abusing families provided them initial motivation for participation in this type of program.

Intervention with more middle-class abusers, with more intact families and a minimum of neglect and family disorganization, requires the use of different tactics. These families need psychotherapeutic and child-rearing assistance but regard them as unnecessary and demeaning. All too often their major motivation for involvement in a therapeutic program is based upon pressure from the courts and the fear of losing custody of their children. Nevertheless this form of external coercion might be the only means of introducing these parents to a therapeutic environment, and provides the treatment staff with an opportunity to gradually increase the level of involvement with them.

The following two cases illustrate some of the difficulties in engaging resistant middle-class abusing parents in a therapeutic relationship.

Case 5. The D. family was referred to our clinic by the child protective services caseworker after the Family Court charged Mr. and Mrs. D. with the physical abuse of their baby boy, Mark. Mark was initially admitted to the hospital with broken ribs at the age of two months. Two additional injuries to his arm and head occurred during the next year. Mark was placed in foster care following the head injury, which he sustained at the age of four months.

Mr. and Mrs. D. both denied abusing Mark, and claimed to have no knowledge of how the injuries might have occurred. They reluctantly agreed to attend our treatment program. Their sole motivation was to satisfy the requirements of the court so they could regain custody of their child. Mr. D. initially admitted the abuse, but he maintained that he did so only on his lawyer's advise in order to help their case. Each parent participated in individual and joint psychotherapy sessions with a social worker.

Alice D., the mother, was a twenty-nine-year-old slightly built, petite woman of Italian-Catholic extraction. She was employed as a part-time bank teller. She formerly taught French in elementary school, but quit after two years because she found the children "too hard to handle." She felt she was "too easy" with them. Alice was born and raised in New York City and attended Catholic schools and colleges. She admitted being very dependent on her parents, having lived with them until she attended graduate school at an out-of-town university for her master's degree in French. She maintained that she had a good relationship with her parents. It became evident that Alice had no close personal ties outside of her family. She involved herself in solitary activities. Alice met Louis D. while he was in the army. They were married before he went overseas on an extended tour of duty. Their relationship was stormy, and Alice was angered by Louis's open discussion of his affairs with other women. Mark was born after three years of marriage. The pregnancy was not planned, but welcomed. Alice described Mark as an active infant and denied any difficulties caring for him. She sensed that he was affectionate and perceptive, because he could comfort her and cheer her up when she was sad. When describing her weekly visits with Mark at the foster care agency, Alice expressed an inability to tolerate the child's active and vigorous play. She was also unable to set any limits with him. She became visibly defensive when questioned about her interaction with Mark. Her difficulties in handling him were previously dealt with by delegating much of the child-care responsibility to her parents. When Mark was an infant, Alice allowed them to take him to Italy for several months because "he needed a vacation." The protective services caseworker believed that the child may have been taken out of the country to avoid detection of inflicted injuries.

Psychological testing revealed that Alice's object relations were shallow and impaired. She was described as narcissistic and infantile, and unable to acknowledge dependency and affectional needs. On card #3 of the TAT, Alice related a story of "a woman who tries to shoot her husband when she discovers he is having an affair, but kills her son instead." This indicates her readiness to displace rage toward her husband onto Mark. The psychiatric diagnosis was narcissistic personality with borderline features.

Louis D., the father, was a tall, reddish-blond, good-looking twenty-seven-year-old security guard. He was of Irish and Protestant background, a Vietnam veteran. He denied abusing Mark, but agreed that he might benefit from counseling because of his marital problems. Louis described dissatisfaction in his relationship with Alice, and his being attracted to other women. He indulged in frequent extramarital affairs quite openly, and suggested that Alice go out with other men. He was preoccupied with sexual fantasies about women in which he was the passive object of their seduction. He felt that women might want to be raped by him. He regarded other men as cruel, aggressive, and exploitative with women.

Louis had considerable difficulty in talking about his combat experience in Vietnam. He described two experiences involving deaths of fellow soldiers during combat. He became "hysterical" and tried to kill himself after one of these incidents. He admitted two earlier suicide attempts, by pill ingestion and carbon monoxide, following rejection by girlfriends.

Louis was raised in a small coastal New England town. His father worked in a shipyard and his mother was a Sunday school teacher in the Methodist church. One of Louis's early childhood memories was of hunting with his father and being forced to kill deer. He became a good marksman and an avid gun collector. When Louis was thirteen, his father encouraged him to study martial arts and wrestling. As a youth, he had numerous male friends, but confessed to having problems with girls. He was jealous and overly possessive with girlfriends, which often provoked them to reject him.

Psychological testing revealed major defenses of denial and projection of predominantly aggressive impulses. Louis exhibited a need to demonstrate his masculinity to women as a means of compensating for deep-seated feelings of emasculation. Louis's psychiatric diagnosis was "paranoid personality."

Although they firmly denied the charge of child abuse, Alice and Louis agreed to participate in treatment in order to deal with their marital problems and to provide a more harmonious atmosphere for Mark if he were to be returned to them. We decided to provide each parent with his or her own social worker, and also to see them together periodically for conjoint counseling. They were permitted to ventilate their anger toward the court and the foster care agency regarding Mark's placement. We hoped that as they perceived their therapists as advocates they would be able to relinquish their feelings of guardedness and mistrust. The intensity and pervasiveness of their denial made it imperative to avoid confrontations about their participation in the abuse. We wanted to find out how Alice and Louis functioned as marital partners and parents during this initial exploratory stage of our intervention.

Alice remained constricted and guarded during the early contacts with her social worker. She denied having problems and, as expected, used the sessions to express her feelings of rage and humiliation engendered by the various agencies she perceived as adversaries. It was much more difficult to get her to reveal her disappointment and anger at Louis and her feelings about Mark, to penetrate her facade of denial and intellectualization, and her constricted affect. On several occasions the social worker accompanied Alice on her visits to Mark at the foster agency, but she had little success in modifying her "mechanical" handling of the child. During the joint sessions with Louis, Alice was finally able to confront him with her anger regarding his numerous infidelities, which he inappropriately talked about with her.

Louis's treatment was characterized by his inability to talk about Mark or his actual problems with Alice. His blatantly seductive chatter with his female social worker about his sexual fantasies served as a defense against deeper feelings of anguish and turmoil regarding the deterioration of his marriage and his separation from Mark. Louis was finally able to tell Alice how much he resented her aloofness and detachment in their joint sessions. His feelings of deprivation precipitated his interest in other women.

During the fifteen months the D.'s remained in our treatment program they gradually became more open with one another and began to communicate more directly. As Louis's sexual acting out subsided, they could finally explore their mutual dissatisfactions, rooted in the personality traits of their partner. Unfortunately, the couple were never able to discuss their abuse of Mark, and the fact of his placement reduced the urgency of dealing with their difficulties with child rearing. The D.'s terminated with our program after the court and the foster care agency recommended that Mark be placed with his maternal grandparents. The failure of the judge to explicitly order the continuation of treatment as a condition for Mark's return to his grandparents removed the major motivating force which kept his parents in our program. We felt that the D.'s required much more treatment and specific parenting education before they could assume any responsibility for Mark's care. This case underscores the important role of the court or child protective agency in initiating and sustaining the treatment process with minimally motivated maltreating parents.

Case 6. Mr. and Mrs. F. and their eight-year-old daughter Clarisse were referred to us by a foster care agency. The child had been placed in one of their foster homes after she had been abused by her mother, Diane F. The abuse had been reported two years earlier by Clarisse's teacher, who noticed her reddened, swollen hands in the classroom. Clarisse told her teacher that her mother had beaten her with a telephone receiver. When Clarisse was taken to the hospital, a physical examination revealed numerous old scars, scrape marks, and healing lacerations all over her body. The hospital records revealed that she had been taken to the emergency room a year and a half previously with two black eyes, but physical abuse was not reported at that time. Clarisse told the doctor that her mother had beaten her frequently and forced her to kneel on a potato grater every day as a form of punishment. Diane admitted abusing Clarisse and rationalized her actions by insisting that this was the only way she could handle her daughter's provocative and aggressive behavior.

The F. family was referred to us at this time in order to determine the feasibility of returning Clarisse to them, and to help prepare the family for their reunion if this disposition seemed appropriate.

The F.'s were a middle-class black family of Haitian extraction. Jean F., the father, was a thirty-eight-year-old dispatcher for a drug company. Diane F., the mother, was a thirty-six-year-old housewife. The F.'s owned their two-family house in a middle-class section of the city, living in one half of it while renting the other part. Mr. and Mrs. F. had been married eleven years, and were strict Catholics. They were born and raised in Haiti.

Diane reported a happy and uneventful childhood. She was the seventh of nine siblings, six of whom lived in the United States or Canada, but none of them near her. Her mother, a beautician, still lived in Haiti, while her father, a successful attorney, had died of a heart attack four years earlier. Diane did well in school and enjoyed it. She had finished high school and begun to study nursing when she met Jean, who was an engineering student. She left school at the age of twenty-five when they were married, and became pregnant several months later. During the pregnancy, Jean was arrested and held without explanation by the Haitian regime. For four months Diane was not informed of her husband's whereabouts or the charges against him. She became extremely despondent and felt that this contributed to a difficult pregnancy during which she failed to gain weight and was nauseous for the entire nine months. Clarisse was a full-term, healthy baby, but Diane hemorrhaged extensively following the birth and was bedridden for several weeks. The paternal grandmother took care of Clarisse during this time.

Diane finally discovered where her husband was imprisoned, and was able to obtain his release through her father's influence. Jean left immediately for New York on a visitor's visa, feeling it was no longer safe for him to remain in Haiti. Diane soon joined him in New York, leaving the ten-month-old Clarisse in the care of her paternal grandmother and aunt. Diane explained that she was not able to take Clarisse with her because of her inability to obtain immigration status. It took her four years to arrange for the child's admission to the United States. Diane and Jean were reluctant to return to Haiti during this time because of the fear that they would not be able to leave again. Jean worked in a factory and continued studying for his engineering degree. Diane became pregnant again and gave birth to another daughter, Marie.

When Clarisse was five, she was finally brought to New York by her paternal grandmother and aunt. There was a struggle between these women and Diane about who would assume responsibility for Clarisse's care. Diane became enraged when she learned that the paternal relatives told Clarisse in Haiti that she was dead. Jean and Diane finally prevailed and Clarisse moved in with them. Diane claimed that Clarisse was difficult to manage from the beginning. She was "fresh" and disobedient at home, and was frequently in trouble for lying and fighting at school. Soon after Clarisse's return, another sibling, George, was born. The parents became preoccupied with this baby and their relationship with Clarisse deteriorated further. The beatings by Diane culminated in Clarisse's placement in a foster home less than two years after the reunion with her parents.

Clarisse made a good initial adjustment to her foster family, but her father attempted to coerce her into saying that she wanted to return home. The foster parents, on the other hand, indicated that Clarisse seemed frightened before the visits with her parents. After a while, Clarisse began to have temper tantrums with the foster parents and claimed that they hit her. She was transferred to another foster home in which her behavior improved. She displayed an increasing interest in returning home with her parents. Jean and Diane were also impatient to regain custody of Clarisse. It was at this point that the family was referred to us for treatment.

Diane became the main participant in the treatment program because Jean refused to attend our clinic. He clearly regarded us as another punitive agency which might further deprive him of the custody of his daughter. In her weekly sessions with her social worker, Diane gradually realized that Clarisse's problem behavior was not a sign of her inherent "badness," but was in response to a difficult early childhood, which included separation from her parents and substandard care by her husband's relatives. The social worker also helped Diane understand that Clarisse's placement in foster care had a traumatic impact on her. She was finally able to recognize her daughter's anger toward her for being removed from home, which was perceived as a second abandonment by the child. Diane also became aware of her basic ambivalence toward Clarisse because of the extremely stressful circumstances surrounding the pregnancy and postpartum period. She discovered that a great deal of her rage at her husband for his lack of support in her struggle with his family for Clarisse's custody had been displaced onto the child. In the latter stage of treatment, she began to express this anger directly toward him. She also insisted on his greater involvement in child care.

We decided to involve Clarisse in psychotherapy when she started regular weekend visits with her parents. The therapeutic handling of her feelings of anger, abandonment, and sibling rivalry facilitated her gradual reintegration into her family. After four months of intervention with Diane and Clarisse, the child was returned home on a full-time basis. As treatment continued another five months, Diane became increasingly able to empathize with Clarisse and recognize her needs. Clarisse's behavior and academic performance in school improved noticeably. This brief but significant progress was used by Jean as a pretext for terminating our intervention. He still regarded the treatment as demeaning, and sought to demonstrate that the family was ready to function on its own.

Although we felt that additional treatment would have been desirable to deal with the marital conflicts and consolidate the progress achieved thus far, we were satisfied that the basic improvement in Clarisse's interaction with her family and the relationship with her mother would be sustained.

11

Helping the Children

Psychiatric Treatment of Abused Children

Despite the documentation of severe developmental and psychological sequelae in abused children, the subject of individual psychotherapy for these children has been virtually absent from the child-abuse literature. Most descriptions of therapeutic intervention in child-abusing families fail to describe specific treatment techniques for the abused children. Kempe (1976b) concluded that individual treatment should not be attempted on a routine basis. Her emphasis remained on the alteration of the child's environment, through intervention with the parents and the establishment of therapeutic day-care programs for preschoolers. She recommended group therapy as the treatment of choice for abused latency children. We feel these efforts must be supplemented by individual treatment techniques when the child reaches school age, in order to improve the chances of reversing the long-standing ego deficits and psychopathology. This chapter will deal primarily with the specific psychotherapeutic strategies found to be effective in alleviating the psychological sequelae of child abuse and safeguarding the child's future development.

Previous studies of physically abused children have described various behavioral and cognitive difficulties resulting from their maltreatment (Elmer 1965, Morse, Sahler and Friedman 1970, Johnson and Morse 1968, Martin 1972). This author explored the complex group of variables comprising the child-abuse syndrome and assessed its impact on the psychological functioning of the abused children (Green et al. 1974b, Sandgrund et al. 1974), based on research and treatment experience. A pilot treatment program for abused children and their families, established at the Downstate Medical Center, was designed to explore the psychopathology and psychodynamics characteristic of abused children. The bulk of the treatment was performed by professionals with special training in child psychiatry, such as child psychiatry fellows and trainees in child psychology.

The research and treatment populations of abused children at Downstate originated from predominantly impoverished, slum-dwelling, inner-city minority group families. Their abuse had been inflicted upon a background of maternal deprivation and family disorganization. In addition to the noxious environment, the abused children were often burdened by deviant physical and psychological endowments which often precipitated their abuse and scapegoating. The acute and long-term effects of the traumatic child-rearing environment and constitutional vulnerability had a devastating impact on the ego functions, behavior and character structure of these abused children. (See chapter 3.) We found an overall impairment of ego functioning associated with intellectual and cognitive deficits, acute "traumatic" reactions, pathological object relationships, impaired impulse control, poor self-concept, masochistic and self-destructive behavior, impaired object constancy, and severe academic and behavioral difficulties in the school setting (Green 1976).

Although the abused children demonstrated a wide range of psychological impairment, their early traumatic experiences left a characteristic imprint on their personality and behavior. Some of the more typical symptoms, traits, and defenses were: a basic suspicion and mistrust of adults; low frustration tolerance with impulsivity; a need for immediate gratification; a need to exploit, manipulate, and control objects; and expression through motor activity rather than by verbalization and use of symbols. The children were preoccupied with violent fantasies depicting scenes of physical attack, spankings, and retaliation. These were elicited spontaneously in play with dolls and puppets, and were thinly disguised elaborations of the original abuse. The children demonstrated developmental lags, often in the area of speech and language, though unevenness of development was frequently observed. Defects were accompanied by precocious achievement in other areas, such as unusual motor ability, a premature capacity to perform such household duties as cooking, cleaning, and infant care, and an overall "streetwiseness." The abused children, especially the boys, avidly competed in tests of strength and skill in an attempt to feel powerful and secure. However, beneath the facade of pseudoindependence and omnipotence, one could see helpless, depressed, and enraged children, hungry for, but fearful of, contact, convinced of their "badness" and "worthlessness" because of the maltreatment they had received.

General Treatment Objectives for Abused Children

The initial goal of intervention with abused children is to prevent further maltreatment and scapegoating. This may be accomplished by strengthening parental functioning where possible, or by temporary removal from the home if the abusive environment proves refractory to change. The delivery of crisis-oriented comprehensive psychiatric, social, and medical services to abusing families, in order to maintain the integrity of the family unit and secure the safety of the children, must precede or accompany any direct psychotherapeutic involvement with the abused child. This type of family intervention has been previously described (Green 1976, Kempe and Helfer 1972, Pollock and Steele 1972, Steele 1975, Helfer 1975).

Once these children are in a safe environment, every effort should be made to reverse the serious emotional and cognitive impairment associated with their traumatic life experiences. A wide range of psychotherapeutic and educational techniques has proven successful in reducing their deficiencies and symptoms. Psychoanalytically oriented play therapy and psychotherapy have been utilized effectively in the Downstate Medical Center's treatment program for abused children. Certain modifications of therapeutic technique are required to deal with the high incidence of developmental deviation and psychopathology present in the abused children. Their ego deficits and cognitive impairment require an emphasis on ego integration, reality testing, containment of drives and impulses, and the strengthening of higher level defenses, similar to those techniques used with borderline and psychotic children.

Without therapeutic intervention, the abused child can be expected to perpetuate the traumatic condition by projecting his struggle with internalized bad parents onto new objects in his environment. Therefore once the abused child's personality is formed, modification of the traumatic conditions at home may not be sufficient to reverse his maladaptive behavior. This is illustrated by the large numbers of abused children whose aggressive and provocative behavior has contributed to their expulsion from foster homes which provided them with adequate parental figures and material supports.

Specific Treatment Goals

Therapeutic intervention must deal with each of the major psychopathological sequelae of child abuse: acute traumatic reactions, impaired ego functioning, distorted object relations, poor impulse control, low self-esteem with self-destructive behavior, extreme separation anxiety, and school difficulties associated with learning and behavior disorders.

Alleviating the Acute Traumatic Reactions

The therapist often encounters episodes of acute anxiety with phobic elements during the initial stages of treatment of the abused child, when the violent and assaultive behavior of the parents is still occurring. These anxiety states, in which the children experience feelings of panic and helplessness, are often manifested in anticipation of, during, or after a beating. Ego functioning is frequently paralyzed with a marked regression in behavior. The phobic anxiety is often transferred onto the therapist, who then becomes a frightening object.

Case 1. Josephine, age seven, had sustained several fractures during her first two years of life as a result of severe beatings by her alcoholic father. After the parents' marriage was annulled, the father remarried and had another daughter. Several months prior to Josephine's entering psychotherapy, her half-sister died after a beating by the father. During the opening hours of treatment, Josephine reenacted her violent experiences through doll play which depicted vivid scenes of fathers and robbers hitting, shooting, and running over babies and little girls. The fear of another murderous attack by her father was extended to the therapist. During the fourth session, she expressed a fear that the therapist might kill her and accused him of being drunk.

It is therapeutic to allow the child to master the trauma by repetition and symbolic reenactment with dolls, puppets, drawings, etc. Reassurance can only be effective if intervention with the parents has successfully controlled their assaultive behavior. Psychotic or alcoholic parents might remain quite unpredictable in their potential for violent behavior. Their children might exhibit traumatic reactions in anticipation of violence long after the cessation of beatings.

Case 2. Cindy, age nine, called the operator on a play phone during her session and informed her that she would be killed in her bed. She announced "first they killed your brother and now they'll kill you." Cindy recalled that she had a baby brother who died in his crib under mysterious circumstances. It was quite apparent that she feared being killed by her mother and father, each of whom had been impulsive and abusive in the past.

Strengthening of Ego Functions

Ego functions are strengthened in several ways. The therapist actively mobilizes the healthy areas of the child's personality and cognitive apparatus. He encourages verbalization and containment of impulse and action, and assists the child to gradually increase his tolerance for frustration. He helps the child with reality testing, promotes sublimation, and encourages participation in the typical, structured "latency" games. One major goal in this area is the establishment of more adaptive controls and defenses, so the child can finally experience a latency period relatively free from excessive external and internal stimulation.

A more gradual buttressing of ego structures occurs as a result of consolidation of the special relationship between the child and his therapist. The therapist acts more supportively and allows more gratification of dependency strivings with abused children than is the case with the average child patient. As the child's libidinal bond with the therapist develops, the therapist becomes idealized and serves as a benign, loving parental object for identification. The child slowly incorporates the ego and superego characteristics of the therapist. Gradual internalization of the therapist's attitudes and controls leads to the emergence of more effective defenses, such as repression, sublimation, and reaction formation. The child will finally begin to demonstrate internal conflict with neurotic symptom formation, with a corresponding diminution of acting out and externalization.

Improvement of Object Relations

The object world of the abused child is highly colored by the perceptions and images of hostile and malevolent parents, and by the primitive defenses by which he attempts to contain these threatening stimuli. The pervasive use of denial, projection, and splitting enables the child to maintain the fantasy of having a "good parent" while the "badness" is projected onto some other person or onto the child himself. The predominance of these defenses impairs the abused child's ability to integrate the loving and hostile aspects of his parents and others, leading to an overcategorization of objects into "good" and "bad."

This fluctuating polarization of the object world is extended to new encounters and becomes the leitmotif of the therapeutic relationship. The abused child's initial mistrust and suspicion usually gives way to an overidealization of the therapist in response to his acceptance and warmth. The child attempts to perpetuate this image of the therapist as "good parent" by utilizing familiar techniques of manipulation and seduction. He tries to please the therapist by demonstrating feats of skill, strength, and intelligence, or by offering to take care of the therapist's office and personal needs. This constitutes a reenactment of "role reversal," representing the child's obligation to gratify the parents by conforming to their premature and inappropriate demands for independent performance.

The enormity of the child's demands, in contrast to the therapist's limited availability as a real object, ultimately leads to frustration and a sense of betrayal. The child becomes enraged with the therapist, who begins to take on the attributes of a "bad parent." This shift is enhanced by the projection of some of the child's anger onto the therapist, with consequent fears of retaliation. The child's fears of punishment and annihilation often lead to a display of aggressive and provocative behavior in order to overcome feelings of helplessness. This identification with the aggressor (therapist, violent parent) intensifies his negative self-concept and exacerbates the "bad" self-image of the child.

The therapist must be active and supportive. The rapid shifts in the child's perception of the therapist from overidealized primary object to hated and feared "bad parent" should be correlated with alterations in the child's experience of gratification. It is helpful to clarify the child's initial wishes for rescue and nurturance and his anger when these wishes are frustrated. The therapist should interpret the child's use of identification with the aggressor as a compensation for conscious feelings of weakness and inadequacy and, in addition, interpret his subsequent sense of "badness" and fear of punishment.

Case illustration. Betsy, a ten-year-old girl, had been subjected to chronic scapegoating and abuse by her impulsive schizophrenic mother and her passive but explosive father. After several months of psychotherapy characterized by her overidealization of the therapist, Dr. G., she began to express feelings of deprivation and anger because of Dr. G.'s inability to satisfy her insatiable demands for love and attention. Betsy frequently refused to leave the playroom when the time was up, exclaiming, "If you love me, you'll let me stay." Her anger peaked after she witnessed another child in Dr. G.'s playroom prior to her appointment. She shouted, "You don't like me, the doll you gave me for Christmas was dirty and too small, the lollipop you gave me was poison." She threw herself on the floor and asked Dr. G. to pick her up, stating that she herself was "poison." In the following sessions, Betsy continued to express her rage by cursing and flooding Dr. G.'s plants. This was followed by self-deprecatory ideation and feelings of "badness." Dr. G. interpreted Betsy's jealousy of the child who preceded her and a sense of betrayal, which was correlated with Betsy's severe sibling rivalry with two younger sisters who were preferred by the parents. The fear of being poisoned by Dr. G. was explained as Betsy's fear of punishment because of the intensity of her own anger.

Impulse Control

Strengthening of impulse control is imperative to preserve the structure of the therapeutic relationship and to help the abused child develop the degree of socialization necessary for his adjustment to family, school, and peer-group activities. The abused child's aggressive and destructive behavior within and outside of the home is the major cause of referral for psychiatric evaluation. After the therapist has identified and acknowledged the child's need to feel important and powerful, he should limit direct manifestations of aggression, such as hitting or destroying toys and playroom materials. The child should be encouraged to verbalize anger or express it symbolically through play. Limit setting must be clearly defined with respect to entering and leaving the playroom, removing toys and materials, and the length of the sessions. The binding of aggression may be fostered through the introduction of sublimatory activities and typical "latency" games.

Case illustration. Ken, age seven, was beaten by his father for aggressive and violent behavior in school. Ken's school maladjustment led to his psychiatric referral. During the initial phase of his therapy, Ken often was preoccupied with violent themes. He frequently came into the playroom shooting his cap pistol, karate-chopping the toys and furniture, and turning out the lights in a counterphobic manner. After the therapist curtailed some of this behavior, he began to reenact violent scenes of hitting and punishment with puppets and dolls. He eventually was able to verbalize his fear and anger toward his father and his wish for revenge for the beatings he received. Ken's need to be powerful and in control of the playroom stemmed from his fear that the therapist might also beat and punish him. His initial wild and chaotic behavior gave way to attempts at mastery through games, toys, and drawings. He eventually became fascinated with a calculator and began to enjoy doing arithmetic with it.

The gradual identification with the therapist, and the internalization of his gentle and accepting attitudes, counteracts the child's tendency to use identification with the aggressor as a primary mode of communication. The abused child's capacity to "neutralize" aggression increases with the consolidation of his libidinal and affective bonds with the therapist. Therapeutic progress is characterized by a gradual internalization of controls and formation of superego structure.

If impulsivity is associated with hyperactivity and minimal cerebral dysfunction, psychotherapeutic techniques should be complemented by the use of amphetamines or ritalin.

Improvement of Self-Esteem

The poor self-concept of abused children results from chronic rejection, physical assault, and humiliation, and is reinforced by each new episode of abuse, rejection, or failure. The child's self-esteem gradually improves during his exposure to the climate of warmth and acceptance generated by the therapist, the child slowly modifying his self-concept to coincide with the therapist's positive view of him. Improvement in the child's overall ego functioning and behavior also has a beneficial impact on his self-esteem by virtue of his greater mastery in daily activities and his improved capacity to form gratifying object ties. These changes in self-esteem can be considered an integral part of the therapeutic relationship, but they can only be maintained if the parental scapegoating and abuse can be brought under control. At times, the therapist must be more active in challenging the child's readiness to assume the role of the scapegoat. The child needs to be told that his frequent beatings usually resulted from parental problems rather than as a consequence of his behavior, or his "badness."

Case illustration. Cindy's mother repeatedly humiliated her for her poor academic performance in school. Mrs. M. admitted, "I call her dumb and stupid because she's just like I was as a girl; she's passive and has no spunk." In reality Cindy's IQ was above average, but she manifested a reading disorder. Her therapist continually reassured her that she was not "stupid," and that her reading problems were improving because she had been placed in a special class. The therapist praised her when she read to him. When the parents demanded that she read to them, she would panic and could hardly speak. The

therapist also challenged her alleged "clumsiness" as he compli-
mented her for her skill in throwing and catching a ball in the
playroom.

The abused child whose self-concept remains impaired is
vulnerable to masochistic and self-destructive behavior. This
behavior represents the child's ultimate translation of self-
hatred into action, in compliance with parental wishes for his
destruction and/or disappearance.

Strengthening Object Constancy and the
Capacity to Tolerate Separation

With the marked decrease or cessation of child battering
which usually accompanies the abusing family's involvement in
a crisis-oriented comprehensive treatment program, the child's
fear of physical attack diminishes and he begins to show
increased concern about rejection and abandonment. This shift
is enhanced by changes in the parent-child relationship resulting from external intervention. Abusing parents commonly
withdraw from the scapegoated child as an initial alternative to
the punitive interaction. The abused child, who learned to
equate abuse with care and attention, becomes puzzled when
his provocative behavior no longer elicits maltreatment. This
also occurs within the therapeutic relationship. The failure of
the therapist to respond punitively to the child's "acting out" is
often regarded as a sign of his lack of interest. This increases
the child's fear of retaliation by rejection or abandonment. The
abused child often displays "hide-and-seek" behavior in an
attempt to gauge the therapist's interest and to master separation anxiety. Cancelled sessions, lateness, and interruptions in
treatment on the therapist's part are interpreted as punishment
and rejection. Evidence of the therapist's involvement with
other children is tolerated poorly. The child often finds it difficult to leave the playroom at the end of the session. He resists
terminating the play, and will often ask permission to take
home play materials. These children require active reassurance
on the part of the therapist concerning their ongoing interest

during absences of contact. If necessary these children should be allowed to take home token "symbols" of the therapist (drawings, candy, pencils, etc.) to promote internalization of his mental representation during separations. Interruptions of treatment should be kept to a minimum. Vacations and changes of therapists must be clearly presented and worked through.

Case illustration. Earl, age seven, was in his second foster home placement when he was referred for psychiatric treatment because of aggressive and disruptive behavior in school. He had been removed from his home after being hospitalized with severe burns and multiple injuries as a result of abuse by his mother and maternal grandmother. His aggressive and demanding behavior proved too difficult for his first set of foster parents, who returned him to the agency after one year. Unfortunately, Earl's sensitivity to separation was exacerbated by his therapist's leaving the hospital after six months of treatment. Earl's preoccupation with separation, abandonment, and associated feelings of helplessness was expressed very poignantly during the initial stages of treatment with his new therapist. He initially searched for Dr. S. (the first therapist), looked for his office and automobile, and wondered if he would ever see him again. He accused Dr. B., the current therapist, of having sent Dr. S. away. He soon became preoccupied with the magnetic letter B. and tried to take it out of the playroom, along with other play materials such as crayons, scissors, etc. When Dr. B. announced that he was taking a vacation, Earl started to draw "stop" signs, in order to stop Dr. B. from leaving. He also engaged in repetitive play in which he would place an ant on a piece of paper in a sink filled with water to see if it would drown, and then try to save it. Dr. B. commented on how difficult it was for him when people went away, and how he worried that he would leave him like Dr. S. and not return. Dr. B. reassured him that he was returning to see Earl and allowed him to take some paper and crayons home as a talisman and memento of Dr. B. during his absence. Following Dr. B.'s return, Earl expressed anger by threatening not to see him. He was also concerned with the other children who saw Dr. B. in the playroom on the days he wasn't there. He tried to take the toys home so the other children wouldn't have them, and taped the telephone receiver to "prevent Dr. B. from talking to anyone else." Another desperate attempt to control the object and prevent separation occurred when he tried to cut off some of Dr. B.'s hair with scissors and take it home with him.

Dr. B. was ultimately able to connect Earl's feelings of helplessness and abandonment by his therapists with the rejection and abandonment by his parents and foster parents. As Dr. B. realized Earl's difficulty with internalization, which interfered with his capacity to maintain a mental image of absent objects, he encouraged Earl to take home concrete mementos of himself and the playroom.

Improvement of School Performance

Most abused children of school age require psychological testing and educational assessment to document current and potential intellectual functioning and learning capacity. The presence of specific learning disabilities or behavior problems might require remedial intervention or placement in a special class. The therapist should maintain contact with the child's teacher and guidance counselor and act as an intermediary between the child's parents and the school. The child's adjustment at school should become a major focus of the treatment. The child's tendency to utilize classmates and teachers as targets of aggression originally directed toward the family may be interpreted. The parents need counseling about the origins of the child's academic deficiencies, which are rooted in his limited attention span, frequent hyperactivity, and cognitive impairment, since the parents feel that these learning problems are under the willful control of the child and are evidence of his stubbornness or defiance. Poor school performance is a major precipitant of child abuse in the school-age population. The vicious cycle of academic failure, physical abuse, and increased disruptiveness in school must be interrupted. Better functioning in school can be an important factor in the improvement of the child's self-esteem.

Intervention with Infants and Preschool Children

Since the incidence of reported maltreatment is greatest during infancy and early childhood and the documentation of developmental and emotional sequelae in this very young abused population has been increasing, intervention should occur as quickly as possible after case identification. The earlier the involvement with the parent, the more far reaching the potential impact of improved child rearing on the child's development. Early intervention with the child will improve the possibility of reversing pathological sequelae. Supportive involvement with the family can interrupt the vicious cycle of maltreatment, behavioral and developmental defiancy, further maltreatment, etc.

Crisis Nursery

Placement of the abused infant in a crisis nursery during the day, or on a twenty-four-hour basis, may be an effective therapeutic modality for both infant and parents. This type of nursery provides a safe environment for the infant, who might otherwise be exposed to harsh and punitive parents under stress. Placement of an infant in the nursery affords the parents temporary relief from a difficult child-rearing burden. The nursery staff acts as a social system for the parents, as mothers or fathers who abuse their infants are usually isolated from friends and family. The nursery may also serve as a center for education in child rearing and infant care, on an individual basis or in a parents' group. The nursery setting offers a controlled means of observing mother-infant interaction, which can be used as the basis for therapeutic intervention. The infant's presence in the nursery also facilitates the collection of relevant medical and developmental data.

Day-Care Centers for Abused
Preschool Children

A day-care program for abused preschoolers between two
and five can serve as the primary vehicle of intervention for
these children and their parents. This type of program has
advantages for the children and their parents which are similar
to those of the crisis nursery. It provides the parents some relief
from the stresses of child care and allows the child some respite
from an abusive environment which impedes his normal
development. In addition, the program may be designed to
meet the specific needs of the children, based on their special behavioral and developmental problems. Galdston (1971)
and Mirandy (1976) have described the various ways that day
care has proved beneficial to abused preschoolers. Special
therapeutic techniques may be devised to remedy the typical
pathological behaviors of these children. Children who are
withdrawn, hypervigilant, and constricted because they fear
and mistrust adults may be helped to achieve greater spontaneity as they develop a supportive and permissive relationship with an adult staff member. For many of these children,
the day-care program provides their first opportunity to
socialize with peers and adults outside of their family. Their
parents have typically discouraged their children from developing ties with others to insure their control over them. The
gradual establishment of basic trust and confidence with staff
members may extend to other relationships. Children with
deficits in speech and language might profit from special intervention by a speech therapist. Most of these young abused
children need to develop the capacity to use language, rather
than motor activity, to express needs and feelings. They often
seek recognition through aggressive and violent behavior,
which often has a driven quality and may represent the child's
need to repeat and master the parental violence they have endured. Through the combined therapeutic and educational
components of the day-care program, the children are
gradually helped to divert their aggressive energies into play
and the exploration of their environment. This type of program

is also designed to provide age-appropriate cognitive stimulation, in order to overcome developmental lags induced by
neglect and deprivation in the home. As these small children
improve in their social relationships and cognitive skills, they
begin to gain self-confidence and demonstrate a simultaneous
enhancement of their self-esteem.

Crisis nurseries and day-care programs may be established
in community centers, schools, churches, or in a hospital setting. They should be staffed by teachers and child-care workers
experienced in handling infants and toddlers. There should be
an adequate staff-child ratio, with back-up pediatric care and
developmental evaluation.

Perhaps the greatest value of these specialized day-care facilities for maltreated infants and preschoolers rests in their ability
to protect the child and relieve the overwhelming child-rearing
stresses during crises, while maintaining the intactness of the
family. This provides additional time for the establishment of
therapeutic contact with the parents, reducing the need to
place the children in foster homes and institutions.

Parental Factors Complicating the Treatment of Abused Children

Abusing parents display specific resistances to the psychiatric
treatment of their children. These are more formidable and
extensive than those exhibited by nonabusing parents whose
children are referred for psychiatric assistance.

Poor motivation. Abusing parents do not actively seek help
for their children. If the child's psychological difficulty is discovered during family contacts related to the investigation of
child abuse, the usual parental denial of the maltreatment will
be extended to the functioning of each family member. The
parents will maintain that there is "nothing wrong with any of
us." Acknowledgment of a child's problem will arouse guilt and
feelings of inadequacy. These parents struggle to maintain a
facade of normality.

Specific denial of psychological deviation of the child. The parents' need to view the child as a scapegoat results in the belief that all of his deviant behavior is under willful and voluntary control. Most abusing parents are consequently unable to understand the concept of psychological illness in children, perceiving them as "bad" rather than as "sick." This provides a rationalization for the continuation of the scapegoating process.

Fear of relinquishing their special relationship with the child. The parents are threatened by the child's attachment to the therapist. A warm, affectionate relationship between the child and his therapist is viewed as a betrayal of the child's special allegiance to the parent. Reaching out to other adults by the child is perceived by the parent as the gratification of the needs of these people instead of their own. In other words, the typical role reversal is threatened, and the parent fears the loss of his special control over the child.

Competing with the child for dependency gratification. The parents are often jealous of the interest and attention paid to their child by the therapist and other staff members. Gratification of the child stirs up their own memories of childhood deprivation.

Fear of the child's improvement. The parents fear that the child's improvement will alter their special relationship, resulting in his refusal to participate in the processes of scapegoating and role reversal. Unless the parents display similar improvement in their self-esteem and capacity to secure satisfaction from more appropriate sources, another child may be selected for scapegoating in order to maintain the homeostatic equilibrium.

These resistances are frequently unconscious, so they are communicated to the therapist in a typical, disguised fashion. For example, a parent will talk about terminating treatment just at the point that the child is deriving gratification from the therapist. The parent will exaggerate the inconvenient reality factors, such as time, travel, expense of treatment, etc. He will insist that the child is getting worse when he is actually beginning to show improvement.

Needless to say, successful treatment of abused children requires an awareness of these resistances, and a means of combatting them. This can only be accomplished if the parents are actively involved in the therapeutic process. As their own dependency needs are being satisfied, they will no longer need to turn to the child for the role reversal. As they experience an enhancement of their self-esteem and an acceptance of the "imperfections," their need to deny these faults and project them onto their children will diminish. Educating the parents about child rearing and child development will alter their premature expectations regarding the child's physical and emotional capacities.

Treatment Results

The results of our psychotherapeutic intervention with twenty abused children in the Downstate program have been encouraging. Fifteen of sixteen children remaining in treatment for at least nine months exhibited a significant improvement. Criteria for therapeutic success included a modification of the presenting symptoms, improvement in cognitive functioning, better control over impulses, and the achievement of more satisfactory object relations. These were based on a reduction of aggressive and destructive behavior at home and in school, improved academic performance, increased capacity for mutuality and trust, and improved self-esteem. Assessment of therapeutic change was made by the therapist, his supervisor, and the entire treatment staff during case presentation. Their impressions were derived from the child's behavior during treatment and with his family, reports from parents and teachers, and home observations. For clinical reasons, it was not possible to perform independent assessments using objective measurements. Parental participation in various aspects of the treatment program facilitated a favorable treatment outcome for the children. However successful treatment results were obtained with some children whose parents were minimally involved in the therapeutic network – providing that the abuse was controlled.

Our clinical impression suggests that the following variables affect the nature and outcome of the treatment process: age of the child at onset of abuse, duration of abuse, age at onset of the intervention, and sex of child and abuser. In general, the earlier the onset of maltreatment, the greater the severity of the developmental deviations and psychopathology. This observation is based on clinical comparisons of individual cases where abuse was reported during infancy and cases of children who were first abused after entering school. Similarly, psychotherapeutic intervention soon after the onset of abuse, preferably during the preschool years, is more likely to result in positive therapeutic change. Preadolescent and adolescent abused children who might have experienced institutional or foster home placements are liable to be more refractory to psychotherapeutic techniques. If the therapist is the same sex as the abusing parent, initial transference resistances will be intensified. If the abuser and the child are of opposite sex, the beatings are more likely to assume a sexual connotation. The length of treatment required for each child will vary with the child's age, extent of psychological impairment, and the degree of family pathology. The average period of treatment necessary to effect major changes in the child would seem to be about two years, although the cessation of abuse as a result of crisis intervention with the family might result in a rapid improvement of some of the symptomatology, such as acute panic states and phobic reactions.

Summary

The usual emphasis on modifying the harmful environment or placing the abused child in a secure foster setting might be necessary for the child's protection, but it is insufficient to alleviate his suffering and inner turmoil. The damage to his object relations, ego functions, cognitive performance, and self-esteem requires direct psychotherapeutic and psychoeducational intervention. The child will perpetuate the sadomasochistic pattern of abusive interaction in his relationships with parents or new caretakers, unless therapeutic intervention can effect changes in the child's pathological inner world. This original pattern recurs as the child projects the internalized destructive characteristics of his abusing parents onto other caretakers, teachers, and authority figures. The resulting fear and distrust of the new objects exacerbate his anger and resentment, and lead to provocative behavior which might elicit further punishment, which in turn intensifies the child's original sense of "badness."

The abused child's tendency to re-create his original traumatic experiences is a typical manifestation of the "repetition compulsion," by which he attempts to master the trauma he had passively endured during the infliction of abuse. This situation makes it almost impossible for the abused child to derive satisfaction from good objects, as witnessed by the frequent failure of abused children to adjust to foster care, their behavioral difficulties with teachers, and their sadistic behavior toward peers and siblings. Longer-term consequences of repeating the trauma include a risk for assaultive, homicidal, and suicidal behavior.

One of the main values of psychotherapeutic intervention with abused children is its ability to modify these persisting pathological internalized objects and identifications, so that the children can eventually accommodate to an average expectable environment and attain the capacity to love themselves and others. Counseling and special child-rearing advice for parents, foster parents, and those entrusted with the residential care of abused children should complement the child's individual treatment.

Only long-term follow-up studies can indicate whether this relatively brief psychotherapy with abused children is powerful enough to maintain their improvement and safeguard their normal psychological development during adolescence and adulthood. We know that failure to psychologically rehabilitate the abused child has grave consequences. Untreated abused children are a constant drain on the resources and finances of our communities, because of their vulnerability to mental illness, vocational and educational failure, proneness toward violence and criminality, and their tendency to repeat the abusive pattern with their own children in the following generation.

12

Treatment Programs and Service Delivery

Types of Treatment Programs

Child-abuse and neglect treatment programs may originate from protective service units of public social service agencies, hospitals, private service agencies, community based teams, and volunteer organizations. The objectives and focus of each program may vary according to the type of sponsor organization. The success of any program depends upon the amount of cooperation received from the community and the degree of coordination of its services and resources, such as the courts, schools, social services, and welfare agencies.

Protective Services Programs

Protective service units of public social service agencies have become providers of treatment services for abusive and neglectful families in many communities. These units are legally mandated to investigate reports of abuse and neglect and to provide care management and supervision if maltreatment is confirmed. However due to the large number of reported cases, protective services caseworkers traditionally have been burdened with unmanageable caseloads, so that the functions of intake and investigation have taken priority over treatment services. The overextended caseworkers also have been prone to poor morale and high job turnover. Some units have managed to overcome these obstacles by hiring sufficient personnel to insure smaller caseloads, and by expanding their staffs to include trained social workers, nurses, and psychiatrists. Other units have been able to generate treatment potential by collaborating with hospitals, day-care centers, and mental health facilities in the community offering specialized treatment services.

The protective services model has certain advantages. Since the agency is legally mandated to investigate and treat cases of abuse and neglect, it wields authority and a permanent source of funding is insured. The disadvantages stem from the frequent inefficiency and restrictiveness inherent in a civil service bureaucracy, and the reluctance of clients to divulge confidential material to an investigative and punitive body, which has the power to terminate their parental rights.

Some protective services treatment programs attempt to divorce their intake and investigation procedures from the treatment process, but this requires the client to deal with two caseworkers without really eliminating the punitive image of the agency.

Hospital-Based Programs

Many hospitals located in inner cities, where there is a high incidence of abuse and neglect, have initiated treatment services for maltreated children and their families. These multidisciplinary programs often use existing staff and facilities from the departments of pediatrics, social service, and nursing. Psychiatric consultation is usually available. A child-abuse team, usually consisting of a pediatrician, radiologist, social worker, and a child-abuse coordinator, reviews suspected cases of abuse and neglect on a regular basis. These cases are usually reported to the local protective services units by social workers from the department of pediatrics. One disadvantage of a hospital-based program is the frequent emphasis on diagnosis and medical management, rather than the provision of long-term supportive and psychological services to the families. Most hospitals require additional funding and community support in order to provide their own treatment services, such as parent groups, child-care programs, parent education, home visiting, counseling, and psychotherapy. An effective hospital-based program must maintain a close liaison with the local protective services agency and the family court.

The advantages of the hospital model include access to medical diagnosis and treatment for the maltreated children and their families, credibility as a service provider, and separation from investigative and law enforcement functions. Larger academic hospitals may increase their long-term service delivery by mobilizing evaluation and treatment resources from the departments of psychology, psychiatry, and child psychiatry. (Chapter 13 provides a detailed description of this type of program.)

Private Nonprofit Agency-Based Programs

Private service programs, which often obtain their funding through public social service agencies, offer individualized treatment services to abusing and neglectful families. These programs are usually smaller in scope than those sponsored by public agencies, and are more selective in their acceptance of referrals. They often maintain a home-like atmosphere and offer flexibility in meeting clients' needs. They usually provide group and individual therapy, telephone hot lines, and day-care components, and are geared to maintaining client anonymity.

Community-Based Team Programs

These programs are usually located in small rural communities where no single agency has the resources to provide effective services and rehabilitation to abusive and neglectful families. The public social service agencies in these communities usually limit their involvement to investigations and crisis intervention. The community teams are usually composed of representatives from the department of public welfare, the local hospital and health department, mental health center, elementary and preschool programs, and the county attorney's office. They meet regularly to review the reported cases of abuse and neglect. They provide consultation services to the department of public welfare regarding case management and advise the county attorney on recommendations to the court. They frequently coordinate the activities of local agencies interested in maltreatment and are involved in community education and training. Treatment services may be arranged through collaboration with local mental health centers and children's programs.

Volunteer Programs

These programs operate largely through volunteers, who may include former abusing and neglectful parents. These volunteer organizations have small budgets and are quite cost effective. They usually operate independently from other community agencies and professionals. Parents Anonymous is a typical volunteer organization operating therapy groups for abusing or neglectful parents staffed by rehabilitated abusers. The clients can benefit from the nonjudgmental approach, and can readily identify with the nonprofessional staff. Counseling by parent-aides and a twenty-four-hour hot line for emergencies are also typical services provided by volunteer groups. Disadvantages of these programs are a high turnover rate among the volunteers, and their lack of training, which often prevents them from dealing effectively with severe and difficult cases. Some volunteer programs utilize professional consultants to overcome this problem.

Coordination Programs

Some private and public agencies have adopted a coordination model, in which they assume the case management responsibility for clients, but the treatment services are provided by other agencies in the community. Some of these services are obtained on a purchases-of-service basis.

Types of Child-Abuse and Neglect Treatment Services

The type of therapeutic intervention offered to abused and neglected children and their families varies considerably from one program to another, depending upon the theoretical orientation of the staff, the type of agency or facility which sponsors the program, the programs' resources, the type of families to be served, and the needs of the community. Other considerations include caseload capacity, the established criteria for abuse, the decision to include or exclude various types of maltreatment (sexual abuse, failure to thrive, emotional abuse, etc.), commitment to short- or long-term treatment, the possible use of preventive intervention, the professional backgrounds and levels of training of staff members, and the capacity to deliver outreach services. The following sections describe the general categories of services utilized by child-abuse treatment programs.

Supportive and Advocacy Services

The availability of supportive and advocacy services is often required to consolidate the relationship with the parents during the early stages of intervention. These services are often indispensable for poor, disorganized inner-city families bogged down in the welfare system. As therapists assume an advocacy role in the numerous encounters with municipal and community agencies, such as the welfare department, the courts, protective services agency, housing administration, schools, and hospitals, the clients' initial mistrust and guardedness diminish. The staff of the treatment program must maintain an active collaboration with these agencies, which play such a crucial role in the lives of their clients, in order to guarantee that the appropriate services are rendered. Advocacy services may include the following:

Health care. The worker assists the family in obtaining medical and dental care and family-planning counseling. The worker might provide child-rearing education and health-care information directly to the family. Some staff members might be required to bring the family members to their hospital clinic appointments, and make sure that the children receive their periodic physical examinations and immunizations.

Housing assistance. The family is helped to maintain their house or apartment in a tidy and organized fashion. The worker assists the family in obtaining better housing, if necessary, and acts as an advocate in all dealings with the landlord or public housing administration.

Income and employment assistance. The worker might be required to help a client obtain welfare, vocational rehabilitation, or job training.

Legal assistance. The family might be helped in their dealings with the juvenile or family court, or with law enforcement personnel. Some treatment programs might hire a legal consultant for their clients.

The following supportive services may be provided by a treatment program:

Child care. The treatment staff may provide or arrange for child care or babysitting to permit the parents to have some time for themselves, or to enable them to keep important medical or therapeutic appointments. The program itself might operate a drop-in service or day-care program for infants and young children.

Transportation. Some families might require transportation to and from their treatment appointments, or to other important activities such as medical visits, court appearances, job interviews, etc.

Homemaking. A client might be provided with a homemaker to help with cooking, cleaning, child care, and home management during times of stress when the family is overburdened.

Visiting nurse. A visiting nurse might be made available for periodic home visits to families with medical problems or difficulties with infant and child care. Some mothers require visiting nurse assistance during the postpartum period after they return home from the hospital. Nurses are able to demonstrate techniques of infant care and provide health education in the home.

Emergency financial assistance. Families might experience a crisis situation which depletes their financial resources, such as a loss of employment, large medical expenses, fire, theft, etc. An emergency fund might be established in order to supply clients with small amounts of money during such crises.

Treatment Services for Adults

These services encompass a wide variety of modalities ranging from supportive and educational techniques to insight-oriented psychotherapy.

Individual psychotherapy. The parent meets with a therapist, usually a psychiatrist, psychologist, or social worker, once or twice weekly to discuss and try to gain some understanding of his or her problems. The issue of maltreatment is only one focus of the therapy, which attempts to deal with major underlying personality problems and conflicts as well. One of the goals of psychotherapy with abusing parents is to help them understand the link between their own childhood and their current dysfunctional parenting. Hopefully, the parent will eventually be able to perceive his children more realistically and achieve the capacity to empathize with them. Relationships with spouse, family, and peers are also explored. As the parent begins to develop trust and rapport with the therapist, he or she will find it easier to establish social contact with others.

Individual counseling. Counseling focuses more on a few of the parent's major difficulties. The emphasis is on current problems and relationships, with a more directive and educational thrust. The therapist might be quite active in making appropriate suggestions and recommendations to improve the client's functioning.

Lay-therapist counseling. Counseling of parents by lay persons or *parent-aides* is an innovative treatment modality which has become increasingly popular. The lay person is usually a volunteer, and a mature individual who has parented successfully. Most lay therapists are mothers or grandmothers, but men may also perform this service. The lay therapist is usually trained on the job. He or she attempts to establish a supportive and friendly relationship with the client, with much of the interaction taking place in the home. The lay therapist gives advice, and helps with child care and household management. Depending on the type of program, he or she might be the sole treatment contact for the client, or operate in conjunction with a treatment team which also provides intervention by trained professionals. The activities of the lay therapist are always under close supervision by professional staff members.

Group therapy. Therapeutic groups for abusing or neglectful parents usually meet on a weekly basis for one-and-a-half to two hours, and contain from six to ten members. They are led by staff members who are experienced in group psychodynamics and treatment. If possible, two leaders, a male and a female, are assigned to each group, in order to replicate a family constellation with two parents. Group therapy can be useful to maltreating parents in a number of ways. It may act as a bridge to therapeutic involvement in extremely defensive and mistrustful parents who are threatened by a one-to-one relationship. The realization that their problems are shared by others tends to diminish guilt and low self-esteem. The permissive atmosphere of frank and open discussion facilitates the expression of long-suppressed personal feelings, and reduces vulnerability to criticism. Finally, the establishment of personal ties with other group members fosters social contact with others. Group therapy is often valuable for abusing fathers, who are notoriously reluctant to seek help on an individual basis because of their difficulty in acknowledging passive-dependent wishes.

Self-help groups, such as Parents Anonymous, have been beneficial to individuals who are more comfortable in a peer-group milieu divorced from contact with professionals in an organized treatment center. This type of group might also serve as an aftercare facility in the community for those parents who have successfully terminated their outpatient treatment.

Marital or couples counseling. Since most child-abusing parents manifest prominent difficulties with their spouses or mates, they can often profit from joint-counseling sessions. Couples' counseling might be the major treatment service for the parents at a given time, or it may supplement individual or group therapy. Since unresolved friction and hostility between parents are readily displaced onto their children, a therapeutic exploration of their relationship would tend to reduce scapegoating and abuse. Couples' counseling might be the treatment of choice in families where child abuse is accompanied by spouse abuse.

Hot line. Many treatment programs have telephone lines operating on a twenty-four-hour basis so that a client may call for help at any time of the day or night. Some hot lines are limited to program participants, while others may be open to the public. Hot lines which service program participants should be manned by permanent members of the treatment staff in order to insure continuity of case management, as well as the immediate knowledge of the patient's prior history. This leads to more effective intervention in a particular crisis.

The hot line may be considered a rehabilitative mechanism within the context of the treatment program. Based upon the perceived need of the client at the time of the call and the resources available, a determination is made of the type of emergency services to be dispensed.

In addition to providing any of the services available within the treatment center, the hot line has been observed to have an anxiety-reducing effect upon the program participants, thereby facilitating both rapport and therapeutic intervention.

Crisis intervention. All treatment programs should have the capacity to meet with a client during any crisis. Optimally, crisis intervention should provide twenty-four-hour coverage, with the client's regular therapist or counselor on call, if possible. In addition to arranging nonscheduled meetings at the treatment center, effective crisis intervention should include home visiting whenever necessary.

Education in parenting. Although most types of intervention available to child abusers are geared to eventually improve their parenting skills, more specific training in parenting and child management is warranted. This can be achieved in numerous ways. A series of lectures or seminars might be organized around a specific curriculum dealing with child care and child development. A more informal approach would consist of small groups of parents sharing their child-rearing problems in the presence of a staff member trained in parent education. The parents might be asked to bring their children so that learning could be based upon direct observations of parent-child encounters. A day-care center or crisis nursery would provide an appropriate site for an educational program for the parents of the children in attendance.

Treatment Services for Children

Until recently, most of the treatment services in the field of child abuse and neglect have been extended to the adult perpetrators. Intervention with abused and neglected children has been limited to medical diagnosis and treatment, and their temporary or permanent placement in foster homes and institutions. Increasing reports of developmental, psychological, and cognitive impairment in maltreated children have induced more treatment programs to establish therapeutic and rehabilitative services, including individual psychotherapy and play therapy for older preschoolers and school-age children, group therapy for latency children, and day-care centers and crisis nurseries for infants and toddlers. (These treatment modalities were discussed in detail in chapter 9.) The child's treatment is coordinated with the intervention with the parents and siblings. The treatment should be preceded by a careful physical, psychological, and developmental evaluation which may be repeated at various intervals in order to evaluate the efficacy of treatment. Specialized forms of treatment might be necessary for children with problems in speech and language and with perceptual disorders due to CNS impairment.

Family-Oriented Treatment Services

Family-oriented intervention is geared toward rehabilitating the family as a unit. The most popular family-oriented services are residential treatment and family therapy. In residential treatment, the whole family is placed in a residential setting, which spares the children from placement in foster homes or institutions. Pathological parent-child interaction and dysfunctional family communication may be identified and modified in this therapeutic milieu. In family therapy, the whole family is seen together in an outpatient setting. The family is viewed as a functioning unit with no single member as the identified patient. Each member's contribution to the family problems is ascertained during the evaluation of their verbal and nonverbal communication.

Residential treatment. Residential treatment for abusing and neglecting families is an innovative form of intervention which has recently been initiated at several centers in the United States and Europe. This modality offers intensive short-term treatment for the whole family in a residential setting. Working parents, usually the fathers, are permitted to continue their employment during the period of treatment, but remain at the residence evenings and weekends. The fathers are encouraged to increase their participation in child-care activities. The New York Foundling Hospital program accepts fathers or boyfriends only on an outpatient basis.

These programs provide a therapeutic milieu in a supportive home-like setting which permits the families to pursue their usual routines under close observation by a skilled staff of trained professionals and paraprofessionals. The therapeutic impact of these programs is derived from the warm supportive climate of the milieu, which facilitates the establishment of a trusting relationship with staff members which can be extended to other agencies and individuals following discharge. A large part of the residential program consists of parent-child interaction sessions in which the parents are trained to utilize more effective and empathic techniques in caring for and playing with their children. Modification of parenting through observation of skilled adult models is another crucial therapeutic element. These programs also offer more traditional services, such as individual and group psychotherapy and marital counseling. The abused children and their siblings receive medical, developmental, and psychiatric assessment. Preschoolers usually participate in a structured child-care program during the day. The parents gradually assume more responsibility for the child's care, which may include spending weekends at home as the termination date approaches. Following discharge, the families return for periodic visits, and are usually followed as out-patients. Post-discharge home visiting by paraprofessionals is another service offered by most residential programs.

The results of the residential treatment programs are promising, but inconclusive. Lynch and Ounsted (1976) reported that forty of fifty families treated over a two-year period at the Park Hospital in Oxford, England, were able to return home with their children, while the remaining ten families required placement of their children during residential treatment after a short trial at home. Residential programs at the New York Foundling Hospital, the Circle House at Denver, and the Triangle program in Amsterdam have also had successful results.

Some major advantages of residential treatment are its reduction of the child-rearing burden and its capacity to preserve the family unit during crises. In addition, the residential setting provides a unique opportunity to systematically observe and correct pathological parent-child interaction. Disadvantages include its high cost, the limited number of families that can be served at a given time, and the difficulty in recruiting maltreating families sufficiently motivated to move into an inpatient setting. In this writer's experience, residential treatment would be appropriate for only a small percentage of maltreating families. More vigorous evaluation of the therapeutic efficacy and the cost-effectiveness of these programs is necessary before their widespread use can be recommended.

Family therapy. Family therapy has been used infrequently in the treatment of child abuse. This is surprising since family dysfunction has been frequently described as an important characteristic of abusing families (Green et al. 1974b, Helfer and Kempe 1976, Serrano et al. 1979). It would appear, then, that some of these families might benefit in some way from a family-systems approach. The understanding of the pathological family interaction and aberrant communication accompanying child abuse might compliment the more traditional focus on individual psychopathology and the stressors in the environment.

There are several reasons for the underutilization of this modality. Child abuse has been primarily regarded as a disturbance in the abusing parents rather than in the family system. In addition, family therapy traditionally has been used with intact families containing latency children or adolescents. The typical abusing family contains infants and preschool children who lack the verbal capacity and attention span required for this type of intervention. Also, many one-parent families are involved in child abuse. Even if the usual criteria can be satisfied, the marked deprivation of the abused children and their parents makes it difficult for them to share a single therapist. Therefore with some abusing families, family therapy might be more appropriately initiated after a preliminary multidisciplinary intervention with the parents and children separately, in order to satisfy some of their basic needs for dependency gratification and social supports.

Malone (1979) observed that family therapy could intensify and perpetuate pathological family patterns in cases of child abuse because of the prevalence of destructive and sadistic behavior. Family intervention might be more effective after the cessation of abuse and some attenuation of the acting out of overt hostility. For example, when the abuse of a scapegoated child is controlled, the resulting shift in the dynamic equilibrium between family members could result in the displacement of the violence and hostility previously directed toward the scapegoat onto another child or the spouse. At this point family treatment might be valuable in identifying the projective identifications involved in the establishment of a new scapegoat. Family therapy might also be used periodically to supplement individual modes of treatment during times of family crises, such as death, illness, separation from important members of the family, the birth of a child, the loss of employment, etc. Family treatment has been used successfully by the author in cases where children are returned to their parents after extended placement in foster care. These reunions can be inordinately stressful for the parents, the returning children, and the siblings who remained at home. Failure to provide family treatment during this period of dramatic change in the family equilibrium could jeopardize the reintegration of the returning children. Grodner (1977) and Levitt (1977) have recently reported on the value of combining family intervention with other treatment modalities, such as parent education, outreach, group therapy for parents, and educational and therapeutic involvement with the abused children.

Observation of family interaction in family interviews can be a valuable diagnostic tool during the initial evaluation. Knowledge of their patterns of interaction would facilitate the development of a treatment program for a given family and its individual members.

Parents Anonymous

Parents Anonymous is a self-help group for abusive parents founded in 1970 by Jolly K., a former abusing mother who had been dissatisfied with the lack of services available to abusing parents. Parents Anonymous groups also include families involved in neglect, emotional abuse, and sexual abuse. Group members rely on one another for support and guidance and attend weekly group meetings. This organization traditionally has divorced itself from professionals and community agencies, and places a high premium on confidentiality. However some Parents Anonymous chapters are used as referral sources by protective service units. Other chapters are loosely associated with professionals who act as consultants and dispense special services which the members cannot provide for themselves. The Parents Anonymous chapters also provide emergency telephone "lifelines," through which members may contact one another during times of stress.

13

A Hospital-Based
Comprehensive
Treatment Center

The following design for a hospital-based comprehensive treatment center for abused children and their families is based on the combined clinical experiences of numerous child-abuse treatment programs which have been developed recently in various parts of the country, and the author's own experience in initiating a pilot treatment program for abused children and their families at the Kings County Hospital/Downstate Medical Center complex. This pilot program, which required the coordination of a great many clinical services of the medical center, is gradually expanding to encompass the structure and functions of the larger center to be described in this chapter. An effective treatment program must deliver comprehensive immediate and long-term crisis-oriented mental health and social services, carefully adapted to the needs of maltreated children and their families.

The ideal hospital-based program is designed to involve abusing and neglecting families in a network of supportive and rehabilitative services from the moment of the detection of maltreatment, throughout the child's hospitalization, and following his discharge. Contact is maintained until the quality of parenting becomes reasonably adequate to meet the physical and emotional needs of the children. The program can be directed most effectively by a child psychiatrist, or a general psychiatrist with some experience with children and parental dysfunction. The director coordinates services from the departments of pediatrics and psychiatry and their social service and nursing components. The program operates in close liaison with the local child protective services agency and the family court. The pediatric staff is responsible for the detection and reporting of maltreatment, the initial contact with the parents, and the medical care and hospital management of the child. Prior to discharge, a multidisciplinary child-abuse consultation team reviews and evaluates the child's medical and psychiatric status during his hospitalization, and makes a psychiatric assessment of the parents and their child-rearing capacity. This team formulates the final discharge plan, which is based on the level of parental competency, the degree of risk in the home, and the parent's accessibility to intervention. The psychiatric staff provides psychiatric consultation and the evaluation of the child and family during the period of hospitalization as members of the child-abuse consultation team, and is responsible for the long-term delivery of mental health services and parenting education following discharge.

Role of Pediatrics

The pediatric in- and outpatient units identify and report all suspected cases of maltreatment to the local child protective services agency. Children seen in the outpatient clinic or emergency room who are suspected of maltreatment are admitted to the inpatient service. These children receive a thorough pediatric evaluation and medical treatment for their injuries. The nurses are trained to observe the children's behavior on the ward, and their involvement with peers and staff. They also record the visiting patterns of the parents, and the quality of the parent-child interaction. The pediatric staff must effect the crucial initial therapeutic contact with the parents. Following discharge, each child is assigned to his own pediatrician for periodic follow-up visits in the outpatient clinic, in order to identify any recurrence of maltreatment.

Role of Psychiatry

The psychiatrist, as a member of the child-abuse consultation team, assists in the formulation of an appropriate, immediate, and long-term intervention for the maltreating families. Psychiatrists and psychiatric social workers are also responsible for the implementation of this treatment plan. They conduct such therapeutic activities as counseling, psychotherapy, group therapy, parent education, home visiting, etc. The psychiatrists are also involved in the training and supervision of pediatricians and mental health professionals (social workers, psychologists, nurses, volunteers, etc.) in therapeutic intervention. The program director coordinates the activities of all of the components of the treatment program (pediatric care, child-abuse consultation team, outpatient mental health services) with other specialized services in the medical center especially relevant to the specific needs of the child-abuse population, such as addictive disease facilities, family medicine programs, and developmental evaluation and learning disability clinics for the abused children. Psychiatric consultation with child protective services, courts, schools, and community organizations improves service delivery, facilitates the flow of referrals from outside the hospital, and creates favorable publicity for the program.

Child-Abuse Consultation Team (CACT)

The child-abuse consultation team, which follows the Denver Model (Kempe and Helfer 1972), includes physicians, nurses, and social workers from the departments of pediatrics and psychiatry. This team reviews and evaluates all suspected cases of maltreatment seen in the pediatric OPD, emergency room, and inpatient service, and formulates a plan for intervention after discharge. This team supplies the major coordinating link between the medical and mental health components of the treatment center.

The child-abuse consultation team should consist of an attending pediatrician, a radiologist, a pediatric social worker, a pediatric nurse, a full-time team coordinator, a psychiatrist, a psychiatric social worker, and a representative from the local child protective service agency.

The *pediatrician* acts as a consultant to the emergency room and to staff physicians and nurses. He collects historical data, interprets physical findings and laboratory results, and maintains communication with the family, protective agency personnel, and community workers. He also coordinates follow-up medical care, and chairs the dispositional conference.

The *radiologist* with special expertise in pediatric radiology aids in the diagnosis of child abuse. He interprets X-ray findings and acts as a consultant to the pediatric staff. He also determines the most appropriate radiological procedures for each case.

The *pediatric social worker* develops a relationship with the family, and, if possible, assesses the family psychodynamics through careful observation and the subtle gathering of information. The worker maintains contact with the medical staff, child protective agency personnel, and various social agencies that might be involved with the family. She makes an assessment of the family's immediate and long-term requirements for medical care, child care, household management, financial assistance, counseling, psychiatric treatment, etc.

The *pediatric nurse* develops a relationship with the hospitalized children and their families. She observes the contact between child and family with the hospital staff and fellow patients. She discusses the social and psychological aspects of the family situation with the nursing staff and acts as liaison between them.

The *team coordinator*:

1. Establishes an early and ongoing relationship with children suspected of maltreatment and their parents in an effort to provide families with information regarding the status and expected progress of legal and medical procedures undertaken in their case. He also communicates the parent's wishes and needs to members of the child-abuse consultation team.

2. Meets as often as is necessary with members of the CACT so that the entire team is aware of existing case-related problems and the measures formulated to solve them.

3. Promotes as speedy and thorough an evaluation and disposition of instances of child abuse and neglect as possible.

4. Consults with all appropriate outside agencies and individuals indicated by the nature of each particular case.

5. Reports regularly to the CACT regarding the problems encountered in evaluating and arranging disposition of cases of child abuse and neglect.

6. Maintains a file of cases and suspected cases of child abuse and neglect, and issues periodic reports indicating the number of families evaluated and the results of the evaluations.

In providing these liaison and specific services, it is hoped that the coordinator might also increase the parent's motivation to enter the therapeutic program.

In addition to the CACT representatives from the Department of Pediatrics, a *psychiatrist* and a *psychiatric social worker* are members of the team and simultaneously serve as members of the Evaluation Unit of the Treatment Program, along with the Program Director. They act as the major link between the CACT and the Treatment Program. Subsequent to confirmation of abuse or neglect, the psychiatric social worker from the Evaluation Unit implements each referral by contacting the family and arranging for an evaluation. If a child has been hospitalized due to the severity of his injuries or need for protection, the evaluation is conducted prior to his return to the home.

A *representative from the child protective service agency* serving the area in which the hospital is located should be invited to join the child-abuse consultation team. This representative assists in the formulation of a discharge plan, based upon his estimate of the risk for further maltreatment, for maltreating families reported by the hospital to the agency. He can also implement the recommendations of the child-abuse consultation team. He is able to coordinate the protective case supervision with the activities of the treatment staff. Final disposition and case planning for families involved in the treatment program are discussed jointly by the treatment staff and the protective caseworker.

Evaluation Unit of the Treatment Program

This unit is composed of the program director, psychiatrist, and psychiatric social worker. In addition to referrals from pediatric and psychiatric in- and outpatient services, this unit receives additional referrals from child protective services, family court, neighboring hospitals, voluntary child-care agencies, and the local public schools.

Families screened by the Child-Abuse Team undergo a thorough psychiatric evaluation with consultation from other departments, e.g., neurology, when necessary. The evaluation consists of a diagnostic interview of either or both parents and the abused child, as well as a social service investigation into the family's psychosocial history. The family's current living situation is assessed through home visits by a member of the program's social work staff.

Following the evaluation, the unit recommends one of three plans for the abused child and his family (see Figure 1):

1. Child and family are amenable and appropriate for the treatment program and assigned to either the outpatient school-age component or the day-care component, depending on the age of the abused child.

2. Child and family do not warrant or would not profit from ongoing treatment at this time; however, crisis intervention in the form of parent counseling, visiting nurse, and concrete social work intervention (e.g., contacting the school guidance counselor) would be useful.

Figure 1

EXTRAMURAL REFERRING AGENCY	NONPEDIATRIC HOSPITAL REFERRALS	PEDIATRICS
Child protective services	Adult in- and outpatient services	Outpatient clinic ER
Family court		
Other hospitals	Child psychiatry in- and outpatient services	Inpatient services
Schools, day-care programs		

EVALUATION UNIT OF THE TREATMENT PROGRAM   CHILD-ABUSE CONSULTATION TEAM

1. ACCEPTED INTO TREATMENT PROGRAM   OUTPATIENT DAY CARE

2. CRISIS INTERVENTION AND PROVISION OF SOCIAL SERVICES

3. REFERRAL TO MEDICAL CENTER OR OUTSIDE FACILITY

3. Family is not amenable to comprehensive treatment or would be more appropriately followed by another specialized agency, e.g., Developmental Evaluation Clinic. Referrals are followed up to insure that they are implemented or, in cases where the parents refuse to cooperate, to enlist the assistance of the child protective service agency in order to provide supervision where treatment is not possible.

Psychologically deviant school-age abused children are assigned to the child psychiatry staff for psychotherapy and psychoeducational rehabilitation, while their parents receive either individual or group therapy. Parents of preschoolers similarly receive either one or both of these modalities.

Intervention with the Parents

Supportive psychotherapy. The therapist (psychiatrist, psychologist, or social worker) sees the parent one or twice a week. The psychotherapy is modified to accommodate the typical defensive patterns of abusing parents, which often include exaggerated narcissism, distrust of authority figures, and excessive use of denial and projection. Ultimately, the parent's misperceptions of the abused child, and the scapegoating process are explored. Contributions from pathological childhood experiences to the current abusive interaction are also identified.

Counseling. Psychiatric social workers provide weekly counseling to unsophisticated or poorly motivated parents who are less suitable for psychotherapy. Counseling may also be offered as an initial intervention in preparation for subsequent psychotherapy. Counseling might be focused on such important areas as spouse and family relationships, child rearing, and vocational issues.

Parent education. The overall aims of parent education are designed to sensitize the parents to the individual needs of their children, and to instruct the parents in appropriate child- and health-care practices. The parents are also taught methods of child control which do not depend upon physical punishment. Direct observations of parent-child interactions at the outpatient clinic, day-treatment center and crisis nursery help to point out maladaptive patterns of interaction and to reinforce adaptive and desirable methods of parenting.

Group therapy. Group therapy may be utilized by some parents receiving individual counseling or psychotherapy as an additional therapeutic modality, or may be offered as an initial intervention to some parents who are uncomfortable in a one-to-one relationship. Group therapy for both parents, or for fathers exclusively, might be appropriate for certain individuals.

Home intervention. Home intervention provides a setting for participation and instruction in appropriate child-rearing behaviors. This may be carried out by the parent's therapist or a visiting nurse. The home visitor will also be in a position to evaluate the progress of family treatment and to assess the degree of risk to the children at any given time.

Family therapy. This modality may be utilized, where appropriate, to identify, explore, and reverse scapegoating and aberrant communication systems. Intact families including older, verbal children derive the most benefit from this type of treatment.

Intervention with Children

Intervention with the children is specifically designed to deal with the common psychopathological sequelae of maltreatment, and is integrated with the outpatient and outreach-based treatment of the maltreating parents. Most of the maltreated children are referred directly from the pediatric inpatient service and the local child protective services unit. A variety of services are available to the maltreated children.

Diagnostic Evaluation

Medical diagnosis and pediatric evaluation are provided by the Department of Pediatrics for all children seen in outpatient settings. Developmental evaluations of infants and preschool children are performed upon their entry into the program and are repeated annually. Psychological testing of school-age children is also carried out initially, and is repeated at appropriate intervals. Test results from before and after the child's treatment are used as a measure of the program's efficacy.

Individualized Treatment of Preschool Children

Crisis-drop-in nursery. This facility, which may be located either in or near the hospital, provides a twenty-four-hour emergency shelter for children at risk for maltreatment who are involved in a family crisis. The nursery is capable of handling six to eight infants and preschool children on a twenty-four-hour basis. The average length of stay is three days. The nursery is subdivided into sections for infants and toddlers. Twenty-four-hour nursing intervention is available, as well as one-to-one contact with trained paraprofessionals. During the day the crisis-nursery children may participate in the day-treatment program.

Day-treatment program. A special day-treatment program for abused and neglected children serves as a resource for maltreating families who are overburdened with child-care demands. This program might accommodate ten to fifteen infants and preschool children for either whole or half days on an open-ended basis, while the acute family difficulties are being resolved.

The program provides a highly structured therapeutic milieu in which the children are taught socialization, cooperative play, and self-care in eating, dressing, and toileting. Language skills are also emphasized. The day-treatment program may include several of the crisis-nursery children during the daytime hours. The program is staffed by a full-time child-care specialist and two paraprofessional child-care assistants. Pediatric child psychiatry and developmental psychology consultants are available at both the crisis-nursery and day-treatment program. The staff is able to observe mother-child interaction in a controlled setting.

Treatment Modalities for School-Age Children

Modified psychotherapy. Individual psychotherapy on a once-or-twice-weekly basis is provided by the child psychiatrist and/or psychiatric social workers trained in child therapy. Play therapy with the younger children permits them to reenact and master in a controlled setting the traumatic events associated with their maltreatment. Special techniques such as behavior modification and role playing may be useful when there is a clear history of the child demonstrating rage reactions in frustrating situations. These techniques facilitate the development of alternative nonangry modes of reacting.

Group therapy. Group therapy is available to older, preadolescent and adolescent maltreated children. The presence of one male and one female cotherapist is effective in replicating a family configuration.

Psychopharmacological treatment. Specific psychopharmacological agents may be indicated for maltreated children manifesting evidence of depressive symptomatology or hyperactivity associated with the minimal brain damage syndrome.

School Consultation

The treatment staff consults with the teachers and guidance counselors of the school-age abused children, and with childcare personnel in cases of infants and young children attending day-care centers. The treatment staff gathers detailed information about the child's school performance and behavior, and provides consultation regarding classroom management and special class placement. The staff also assumes an educational role with the parents of local school districts by providing them with information about child abuse and neglect through meetings and discussion groups.

Psychoeducational Intervention

A high percentage of abused and neglected children require psychoeducational assistance because of their impaired cognition and language, which often contributes to their frequent functional retardation. Language competency should be assessed during the initial psychological evaluation. A learning disability specialist should work in liaison with the child's individual therapist and with his school. In many cases special class placement in the school system is required for abused and neglected children.

Primary Prevention

Physicians and nurses in the Departments of Pediatrics and Obstetrics and Gynecology are in a favorable position to identify mothers at risk for maltreatment. High-risk categories include: young and unsupported teenage mothers; parents of premature or abnormal infants who are unsupported and/or stressed; mothers with postpartum depression; isolated parents without adequate social support systems; and mothers who are substance abusers. Psychiatrically impaired or mentally retarded mothers are also at risk for parental dysfunction. These factors, in combination with an early history of maltreatment in the mothers themselves, would increase the risk for aberrant child-rearing behavior. High-risk parents will be eligible for the same types of services offered to the maltreating parents, with an emphasis on home intervention and parenting education.

Supportive Services

Homemaker services. Homemaking assistance and home visits are provided by female homemakers, who are assigned on the basis of family needs and receptivity. The mothers overburdened with the care of infants and preschool children might derive the greatest benefit from this service. The homemaking is integrated into the entire treatment program of the involved family, the homemakers receiving supervision and training from the psychiatric and social work staff. The presence of a homemaker might be pivotal in keeping a family intact during a crisis.

Parent-aide program. The successful use of parent-aides or lay therapists with abusing families was first described by Kempe and Helfer (1972). Parent-aides are assigned to certain families in which the mother's social isolation, maternal deprivation, immaturity, and failure to develop maternal feelings are outstanding. Parent-aides are usually mature women who have mothered successfully. They try to develop a non-critical supportive relationship with the abusive mothers and act as maternal role models. Parent-aides are trained by the psychiatric and social work staff and their intervention is integrated into the overall treatment program of the involved family. If possible, parent-aides and abusing parents should be matched according to socioeconomic level.

Nursing intervention. Nursing intervention is an integral part of the treatment program for the abusing and neglecting families. Nurses carry out the following functions during home visits.

1. Physical assessment of the children.

2. Consultation regarding physical illness of both children and adult family members, eventually making referrals to medical specialists.

3. Basic child-care education of the parents, including knowledge of the various stages of normal child development, assessment of developmental abnormality, information about feeding practices, nutrition, and home enrichment.

4. Supervision of medical care in case of the illness of a family member, e.g., supervising medication or help with special medical management, such as changing bandages, application of medical appliances, etc.

The nurses also act as instructors in a parent education program carried out in the outpatient or day-care setting. This program makes use of audio-visual equipment and materials.

The family intervention of the nurses is under the overall supervision of the treatment team consisting of the psychiatrist and social worker. If the treatment program is located in a hospital or medical center affiliated with a nursing school, student nurses may participate in the program as an elective during their training. A singular advantage of utilizing students rests in their youth, enthusiasm, and capacity to provide assistance with child care without evoking the image of the "critical mother" which usually occurs when an older woman intervenes in the home.

Hot line. A *hot line* is available for the use of all participants in the treatment program on a twenty-four-hour basis. The hot line is described in detail in chapter 12.

Vocational rehabilitation. The social work staff assesses the vocational needs and capabilities of the parents of abused children. Parents are encouraged to improve current, or learn new, vocational skills when appropriate. The staff assists the parents in seeking employment and continuing their education, if necessary. Liaison is established with the local Department of Vocational Rehabilitation in order to provide job training for those parents exhibiting psychiatric or physical impairment.

Legal assistance. The legal consultant secures rights not generally accorded without legal thrust, most specifically, direct services such as housing and increased welfare benefits when applicable. In this manner, the legal assistant is viewed by the parent as an integral member of the treatment team. The legal consultant does not participate in court-related activities of the parents.

Other Services

Intervention during placement of children. Far too often, placement of maltreated children in foster homes or institutions has become the expedient solution for overburdened and understaffed child protective facilities in large reporting areas. In many cases, this costly and uncertain remedy has been used largely because of the unavailability of home-based treatment modalities designed to stabilize families in crisis. The basic difficulties in adjustment facing the three major participants in the placement process have usually been ignored by the involved agencies.

The *maltreating parents* often receive no counseling or rehabilitation to help them prepare for the ultimate return of their children. Left to their own devices, these parents become depressed following the experience of humiliation and loss. Many of the mothers become pregnant within a year after removal of their children. The new infants will obviously be at risk for future scapegoating, role reversal, and abuse.

The *maltreated children* are traumatized by the forced separation from their families, and they face formidable problems in adjusting to unfamiliar foster parents and siblings. Their severe psychopathology increases the likelihood of an unsatisfactory placement experience. These children are notoriously prone to frequent changes in foster placement.

The *foster parents,* who are equally susceptible to the rescue fantasies manifested by the treatment staff, are often unaware of the difficulties posed by abused children. Foster care agencies often minimize the numerous problems of these children.

The facilities of the treatment program are, therefore, made available to abusing families from which the children have been temporarily removed to foster care. The main goal of treatment is the reversal of the pathological child-rearing climate so the children can ultimately return home.

The abused children are provided with day care or outpatient psychiatric treatment during their placement, with the emphasis on solving their problems of separation, foster care adjustment, and eventual reintroduction to their original homes.

The foster parents receive counseling regarding the specific management problems of the abused children and the relationship with the natural parents.

Training and education. A significant function of the hospital-based treatment program is the training and education of professionals, paraprofessionals, and students in the area of child maltreatment and family violence. Professionals and workers in the fields of medicine, pediatrics, psychiatry, child psychiatry, psychology, social work, nursing, education, child protection, law enforcement, and the courts would benefit from such training.

Community liaison. The hospital-based treatment program must collaborate closely with the major sources of referral in the community, the public protective service agency, private social service agencies, public schools, and the family court. Families jointly involved in the treatment program and in protective services supervision will benefit from frequent contacts and consultation between staffs of the two organizations. The significant numbers of maltreating parents whose children are in placement require frequent contact between the treatment program and the foster care agencies.

Program Evaluation

Since intervention with maltreated children and their families is in its infancy, it is important to assess the therapeutic impact of the various treatment techniques. The frequency and duration of the different types of patient contacts should be recorded, including lapses from treatment and premature or unilateral termination of contact. The following evaluation measures may be utilized to document changes in the children and their parents.

Evaluation of the Children

Assessment of developmental progress. A developmental assessment appropriate to the child's age should be performed upon entry into the treatment program. In the case of younger children this may take the form of a Bayley or Gesell. Among older children the WPPSI or WISC and a reading test, such as the Peabody Individual Achievement Test, which emphasizes both mechanical reading and language comprehension skills, are appropriate instruments. These evaluations should be repeated annually.

Physical status of the child. The child's percentile for height and weight should be recorded during intake and repeated at six-month intervals. Change in physical growth should be recorded on appropriate percentile charts. A standardized evaluation of the child's neurological status should also be recorded upon entry into the program.

Changes in behavior. Assessment of the behavior of the child may be carried out in the following ways:

1. For *pre-school children* a standardized interview method such as that described by Richman and Graham (1971) may be used to evaluate the child's functioning in a number of different areas. This instrument has been shown to be sensitive and

reliable to a wide range of behavior abnormalities in preschool children. In addition, a quantitative measurement of behavior disturbance could be obtained on a questionnaire such as the Behar (1977).

2. In *school-age children* a standardized interview may be administered to the parent or principal informant which covers a wide range of behavioral and social functioning. An evaluation from the teacher could be obtained by using the forty-three-item Teacher Questionnaire developed by Conners (1973). The parents might also be asked to complete a quantifiable instrument such as the Conners or the Peterson-Quay. In addition, the children could be interviewed in a standardized fashion using an instrument developed by Kestenbaum and Bird (1978). The main function of these instruments is to provide a reliable and standardized level of initial functioning against which subsequent change can be evaluated, rather than for assistance in diagnosis or treatment planning.

Evaluation of the Parents

Recurrence of maltreatment. All episodes of repeated abuse and neglect should be systematically recorded. These episodes might be reported by the parents or children or by the mandated reporting source, or might be noted by staff members. All children participating in the program should receive a pediatric examination every four months as a routine or whenever maltreatment is suspected.

Quality of parenting. The Caldwell Home Stimulation Inventory (1966) may be applied to the maltreating families upon admission to the treatment program, and should be repeated annually throughout their participation. This inventory is standardized for different ages of children and provides a reliable index of parenting independent of attitudinal reports.

Staff estimates of parental change. Periodic staff evaluation conferences may provide a standardized estimate of change in parental behavior and quality of child rearing.

Incidence of placement. The incidence of placing children in foster homes and institutions from families involved in the treatment program may be compared with the incidence of placement in maltreating families not served by a comparable treatment program.

Parents acceptance. Parents may be interviewed periodically and asked to rate different components of the program in terms of their usefulness and acceptability.

Parents participation. The number of visits of each parent and child may be recorded along with lapses from treatment. Premature or unilateral termination of contact should be recorded and explored.

Staffing Pattern: Outpatient Treatment Center

The *program director* is responsible for the total treatment program, including the screening and evaluation, the various outpatient treatment modalities, supportive services, and the day-care program. He is also responsible for coordinating the activities of the child-abuse consultation team and the components of the outpatient treatment program, requiring integration of services from the departments of pediatrics, psychiatry, social service, and nursing. The director also supervises the treatment center's liaison with referral and collaborating agencies in the community: the child protective services agency, family court, Society for the Prevention of Cruelty to Children, schools, and other public and private social agencies providing services to the treatment population. The director organizes and supervises training and educational programs for staff members of the treatment center, professional staff and trainees of the medical center, and child- and family-care professionals in the community.

The program director may be a pediatrician or psychiatrist with extensive experience with the various types of child maltreatment and parental dysfunction. A psychiatrist or child psychiatrist would have a special advantage owing to his or her expertise in the delivery of crisis-oriented and long-term health services to parents and children.

The *psychiatrist* participates as a consultant to the child-abuse consultation team and the screening and evaluation unit of the outpatient treatment program. He also performs psychiatric evaluations of the parents and adult family members, and is involved in decision-making processes concerning the acceptance of families into the program, the types of treatment modalities appropriate for them, and their discharge. The psychiatrist also may provide psychiatric treatment for more disturbed parents, and supervises psychotherapy and counseling carried out by psychiatric residents and fellows and social workers. He also supervises the medication received by adult patients.

The *child psychiatrist* supervises the day-care program and is responsible for the admission of children to the program. He provides training for the day-care professional staff and supervision for staff members and trainees involved in outpatient psychotherapy with school-age abused children. He also performs psychiatric evaluations of abused children and their siblings, when necessary, and supervises all medication given to the children.

The *social work supervisor* coordinates the various treatment services of the program, maintains liaison with and initiates referrals to other divisions within the hospital – pediatrics, pediatric social service, family medicine, addictive disease hospital, etc. – and effects liaison with the child protective services unit, the family court, community agencies, and the schools. He or she is also responsible for the training and supervision of social workers, social work students, nursing students, homemakers, and paraprofessionals, and provides individual psychotherapy and counseling of parents. This individual may also participate in group and family therapy.

The *psychiatric social workers* provide supportive casework, psychotherapy and group therapy with parents, including home visits when indicated, and are involved with play therapy and psychotherapy of the children under supervision. The social workers also participate in liaison activities with the participating departments of the hospital and community agencies serving their clients.

The *public health nurse* directs the nursing intervention program, supervises home visiting by parent-aides, homemakers, and student nurses, makes home visits to assess the health and child-care needs of families, provides parenting and health-care instruction, and coordinates nursing intervention with pediatric, psychiatric, and social work components. If the hospital maintains a college of nursing, the public health nurse should have a position on the faculty, and be involved with the development of a curriculum for child-abuse studies and the recruitment and training of student-nurse volunteers.

A *teacher* specializing in preschool education directs the day-care program and supervises the paraprofessional child-care workers. The teacher communicates regularly with members of the treatment staff who are involved with parents of the day-care children.

In addition to the primary services provided by the key staff members listed above, a comprehensive treatment center must also have access to specialized diagnostic and evaluative services such as developmental evaluation, psychological testing, speech and language evaluation, and pediatric neurology. These are usually supplied by the departments of pediatrics and psychiatry. All children serviced by the outpatient and day-care programs should routinely be given periodic physical examinations by the pediatric staff.

14

Placement of
Maltreated Children

The dramatic increase in the nationwide incidence of reported child maltreatment during the past decade has contributed to the widening gap between the number of maltreating families requiring crisis-oriented psychiatric and social services and our society's limited capacity to deliver these services. In New York City, although twenty-seven thousand children were reported abused or neglected in 1978, only a few treatment programs currently exist which can provide maltreating families with comprehensive home-based therapeutic and social service intervention. Overburdened and inadequately staffed child protective service units throughout the country have been unable to deal therapeutically and constructively with the large majority of maltreating families during and after completion of the mandatory investigations. Adequate supervision of even a small percentage of the families in which maltreatment was confirmed has not yet been attainable. By default, placement of abused and neglected children in foster homes and institutions has become the expedient way of attempting to solve the problem. Almost five thousand of the twenty-seven thousand New York City children currently in foster care were placed for reasons of abuse or neglect (Fanshel 1976). As a result of this policy, many families charged with maltreatment have been prematurely dissolved by court-ordered placement of their children, instead of receiving timely therapeutic intervention which might have strengthened and preserved the family unit. When placement is effected, the therapeutic focus shifts from the natural parents onto the child and his new milieu, while the underlying problems and pathological environment of the maltreating parents are ignored. Unfortunately, large numbers of abused and neglected children are eventually returned to their natural parents with no change in the original pathological child-rearing climate.

The purpose of this chapter is to demonstrate the need for a change from the current reliance on placement to an emphasis on crisis intervention and the provision of comprehensive psychiatric and social services for maltreated children and their families. Many of the "neglected" parents of maltreated children are ultimately reinvolved in the "system" when they are reunited with their children or when they become new parents. Our material is derived from maltreating parents, primarily abusing mothers, who have participated in the Comprehensive Treatment Program for Abused Children and Their Families at the Downstate Medical Center. For most of the parents in our program, the placement of their children created new problems and sequelae for both them and their children, for which no adequate help was available.

The parents may be divided into the following categories according to their involvement in the placement process:

1. They are under investigation by a local child protective service unit due to the seriousness of the maltreatment or the degree of family pathology, and are awaiting family court action regarding the possible placement of their children.

2. Their children have been placed in temporary or permanent custody of a relative, foster home, or institution. Involvement in a treatment program has been suggested as an initial step in exploring the possibility of the eventual return of their children.

3. They are actively petitioning the family court to regain custody of the children in temporary placement.

In all of the above situations, the abusing parents regard personnel from the agencies and courts as agents for the children, rather than advocates for themselves.

The Threat of Placement

Parents whose children are taken from them because of maltreatment or parents threatened with placement proceedings initially respond to this situation with anger and frustration. They are involved in an adversary relationship with a bureaucracy which determines their guilt and responsibility, and is empowered to sever their relationship with their children. The initial court proceedings are usually frightening and humiliating to the parents, and result in a prolonged or permanent distrust of court and agency personnel. In labeling these parents "inadequate" and "unfit," the child protective unit adds to the lifelong humiliation these individuals have experienced at the hands of their own critical parents. The anger and frustration are succeeded by shame, guilt, and a loss of self-esteem.

Removal of children from the home also constitutes a major object loss for the abusing parent. It must be remembered that unlike some extremely neglecting parents who might be relieved by having a burdensome child removed from their care, abusing parents have strong positive ties to the very same child they assault and humiliate. Studies of abusing parents (Morris and Gould 1963, Steele and Pollock 1968, Green et al. 1974b) have documented their extraordinary dependency on the children they scapegoat. Through this phenomenon of role reversal the abused child provides his parent with gratification and support not forthcoming from more appropriate sources, such as spouse, parents, and friends. The loss of this ambivalently regarded "special" child constitutes a major psychological trauma for the parents, which hardly seems to be recognized by protective service staffs, foster care agencies, and the courts.

Sequelae of Placement

The following sequelae have been frequently observed after the removal of one or more children from abusing parents, due to changes in the psychodynamic equilibrium of the family:

Depressive reaction. The separation from child(ren) regarded as need-fulfilling objects may constitute a significant object loss for the parent, often leading to grief and mourning. The loss of self-esteem resulting from the realization that one has failed as a parent evokes earlier memories of failure and inadequacy, and adds to the depressive affect. A final determinant of depression is the internalization of anger, which can no longer be directed toward the scapegoated child.

Search for a new scapegoat. After the removal of the abused child from the home, the parent's unacceptable wishes and attributes can no longer be projected onto a scapegoat. These feelings are threatening to the parent's fragile self-esteem, so a new scapegoat is sought to act as a target for the parental anger and frustration. Any child remaining in the home is vulnerable to future scapegoating.

Increased conflict with spouse. If all of the children are removed from abusing parents, the abuser will often displace his rage and frustration onto the spouse, who may assume the role of the new scapegoat. The nonabusing spouse blames the abusing partner for the loss of the children. The increased aggression and friction between the partners often lead to disintegration of the relationship and ultimate separation.

Pregnancy. Within a year after placement of her children as a consequence of child abuse, the characteristic mother becomes pregnant. This phenomenon is also typical of the mothers enrolled in our program with the hopes of having their children returned from placement. This urgent need to have a baby often remains unconscious, and can be understood as a means of coping with the depression and sense of loss resulting from the placement of the children. The new baby replaces the original child(ren) and restores the previous equilibrium in the family. If the family environment and the parental psychopathology remain unchanged, there is a strong likelihood that the new baby will be abused and scapegoated. Sometimes the parents use the replacement child to prove their rehabilitation and renewed capacity for parenting. The more this child is conceived to fulfill dependency needs and magical expectations of the parents, the greater is the possibility of parental frustration, disillusionment, and eventual maltreatment.

Due to the shift in focus after placement from the abusing parent to the child and his foster parents, these sequelae often remain unnoticed by the agencies, so necessary social service and psychiatric intervention is not initiated.

Reclaiming Children from Placement

Most abusing parents are insufficiently prepared for reunion with their children who have been in placement. In many cases, the parents and children must negotiate the difficult readjustment process without professional assistance. The reunion of the children with their natural parents can be extremely difficult, especially when the child has been in placement during the height of the development of attachment behavior (between six and eighteen months). When this occurs, the child's attachment to the foster parent is much greater than to his biological parent and a return to the latter constitutes a major separation experience. Such a child will exhibit separation anxiety and depression and will often express his resentment toward the natural parent by withdrawal of affection and provocative behavior. The marked contrast between the difficult adjustment of the recently uprooted child to his natural parents and the latter's fantasy of blissful reunion may provoke feelings of anger, despair, and betrayal in the parent. The child's strong ties to his foster family and initial unresponsiveness at home also reevoke the parent's deeply ingrained sense of inadequacy. The foster parents often contribute to the stressfulness of this readjustment period by actively competing with the natural parent for the child's affection and loyalty. This is often a consequence of the foster parent's strong attachment to these children, which is relinquished only with great difficulty.

It is clear that the termination of placement and restoration of the abused child's ties with the natural family constitute a unique stress for the natural parent, foster parent, and displaced child, which appears to be insufficiently appreciated by the agencies responsible for these decisions. Unfortunately, the welfare and rights of the natural parents receive the least advocacy in this situation.

Case Illustrations

The following case histories will demonstrate some of the typical problems confronting abusing parents who have been stigmatized but not assisted by the "system," which regarded them as adversaries. In beating their children, these parents attempted to master the trauma that had been inflicted on them during their own childhood. If the scapegoated children were taken away, others were substituted. Some modification of this repetitive cycle was achieved by persistent, crisis-oriented therapeutic intervention.

Case 1. Patricia L., a thirty-four-year-old unmarried woman, was referred to our treatment program by a local child protective agency. The caseworker felt that Patricia required psychotherapy to help her cope with severe personal difficulties and to assist in her attempt to regain custody of her two-year-old daughter, now in temporary foster care. Patricia had abused the child at the age of six months. Patricia had discontinued the relationship with the child's father during her pregnancy, even though he demonstrated interest in her and the child. At this time, she had recently come to New York from the South, and allowed a girlfriend with three children to move in with her. The entire household tried to subsist on Patricia's welfare allowance, and the girlfriend often left her children in her care. She became depressed, began to drink to excess, and exhibited self-deprecatory ideation. Patricia was unable to confront her friend about her inability to tolerate the increased financial pressures and child-care responsibilities which resulted from their living agreement. She took out her frustrations on the baby instead. She admitted hitting the child while she was "high" on alcohol. She recalled the incident: "We had no food, it was Christmas time. I got high, I slugged her in the face and she bounced on the bed. I kept hitting her."

Patricia's background revealed that she had been her mother's fourth child. Three older siblings were fathered by her mother's first husband. Patricia was born after her mother remarried. Her father was an alcoholic who frequently abused and humiliated her, and treated her as the scapegoat of the family. Patricia has a four-year-old son who is currently living with her parents in the South.

After entering our program, Patricia seemed strongly motivated to regain custody of her child, whom she visited regularly. She recognized the need to separate from her friend, took her own apartment, and sought employment. At this point, however, she became plagued with loneliness, low self-esteem, and guilt about having beaten her baby. During the initial months of psychotherapy, she made two suicidal gestures while intoxicated, first putting her fist through a window and then cutting her wrists.

These self-destructive episodes were precipitated by drinking and guilt-ridden "flashbacks" of beating her infant, and resulted in brief psychiatric hospitalizations, after which her psychotherapy resumed. They were understood as manifestations of rage directed toward her "bad" self-image, under the influence of her punitive superego. In the five-month period of psychotherapy after the last suicidal gesture, Patricia was able to explore her masochistic lifestyle and its roots in the humiliating experiences of early childhood. She was able to stop drinking and now recognizes that there are alternatives to the explosive aggression or self-destructive rage which have caused her such difficulty in the past. Patricia is currently seeing a boyfriend she met during her last hospitalization. At the present time, her therapist and the foster care agency have arranged to permit her daughter to visit her at home. Current therapeutic goals will focus on her parental functioning and interaction with her daughter during forthcoming home visits, and on her attempts to maintain more rewarding personal relationships. Patricia's recent involvement in group psychotherapy is geared toward overcoming her social isolation. If home visits prove manageable for her, return of the daughter to her custody could be considered. It is clear, however, that her characterological problems and lifestyle leave Patricia poorly equipped to care for her child under stressful conditions. Therefore we expect to provide her with a visiting student nurse who will be able to give her direct child-rearing assistance at home.

Case 2. Doris L., a twenty-one-year-old unmarried woman, was referred to our program following the alleged abuse of James, her five-year-old son. This incident occurred only four months after James had been returned to her from foster care. James was placed in a foster home after his birth. Doris was fifteen at that time, and was in a foster home herself. Her foster mother threw Doris out of the house after she became pregnant, and persuaded her to give up the baby after the delivery.

Doris had been deserted by her mother when she was two, and placed in a foster home at the age of four after briefly living with her alcoholic father. She felt "unloved" by her foster mother, whom she described as a rigid, strict, and punitive woman. Doris had been subjected to physical abuse and was often confined in the apartment and forced to do all the housework. The foster mother was enraged when Doris became pregnant and forced her to enter a residence for unwed mothers. Doris finally left when she was eighteen because her foster mother remained restrictive and wouldn't permit her to bring friends to the home. Doris still reports repetitive nightmares about being trapped at home with her foster mother.

During the initial sessions with her therapist, Doris appeared to be angry and considerably depressed about her son's replacement in the foster home. She poured out her resentment toward the protective service worker and the foster care agency, by whom she felt betrayed. Her initial motivation for coming to us was clear. She wanted us as allies in her power struggle with the agencies which, according to her, had once again deprived her of her child. She was initially incapable of dealing with the numerous difficulties complicating her relationship with James. Doris became quite angry with her therapist when she informed the protective service agency that sufficient progress had not been made to warrant James's return home, and threatened to discontinue her contact.

It became obvious that Doris reacted to her therapist as another punitive, critical, and depriving figure, similar to all of the important adults in her life (her mother, foster mother, caseworkers from protective services and foster care agency). Faced with the "loss" of her son, Doris became pregnant at this time. In her fantasy, the baby would provide her with the love and attention that she couldn't get elsewhere. She decided to have an abortion, however, when the actual consequences of a new baby were explored. Doris was finally able to work through her basic mistrust of the therapist, as well as all authorities, and eventually could regard her as an ally. At this point she could focus on her relationship with James. She observed, "Since I didn't raise him, I never felt like a mother." Doris and her therapist reviewed each of the visits with James in detail. The major difficulties in their interaction centered around Doris's perception of the child's constricted affect and fearful responses to her as signs of rejection and disinterest. She contrasted this "holding back" with his ability to behave more spontaneously and enthusiastically with others. Doris felt hurt and betrayed whenever James expressed affection for his foster parents. Doris endowed her son with the skills and capacities of a much older child, a clear example of role reversal. For example, she remarked, "James is very mature; he talks like a nine year old. He's real nice to everyone else but me." Doris and James were perpetually involved in a power struggle the entire day, which began when Doris insisted that the boy make his bed. There were fights over most of the daily activities, such as eating, cleaning up, playing, and bedtime. The more intrusive she became, the more the child responded with withdrawal and such passive-aggressive behavior as hiding, wetting his pants, and refusing to eat or go to sleep. Doris related to James as if he were a rejecting peer or an ungiving parent, instead of recognizing his enormous difficulty in separating from his foster home, and the only real parents he knew. She failed to recognize that in her son's eyes, she was a stranger and an object of dread, rather than the long lost mother for whom he yearned. As the therapist provided Doris with information and advice about child rearing and child development, her unrealistic expectations of James began to diminish.

Just recently, Doris regained full custody of James, a visiting student nurse was assigned to the family, and James began his own therapy. The period of adjustment has continued to be difficult, but with her therapist's help, Doris is beginning to understand her misperception of her child and the special problems he faces because of maltreatment and the early disruption of parental ties, something she was all too familiar with during her own childhood. With special help, Doris and James have a second chance to "make it" together. But, as Doris recently observed, "No one ever told me before how hard it was going to be."

Discussion and Conclusion

The placement of dependent children in institutions and foster homes and the subsequent changes of caretakers pose major problems of adjustment for the children, parents, and fostering individuals. Therefore the use of placement as a major therapeutic intervention in maltreating families is recommended only as a last resort. The vigorous deployment of crisis-oriented social and psychiatric services to these families should be the main therapeutic modality, with the emphasis on home involvement. Maintaining the stability and integrity of abusing and neglecting families, where possible, should be the primary focus of treatment. This type of service delivery can also save considerable sums of money by sharply reducing the number of children requiring placement, and by reducing the length of hospitalization for maltreated children ("boarder babies").

Hospital-based treatment programs, like the Comprehensive Treatment Program at Downstate Medical Center, are inexpensive to maintain because they rely largely on existing personnel from the departments of psychiatry, social service, pediatrics, and nursing. These centers could be self-supporting if third-party payments could be recovered and diverted back into the program.

When placement of maltreated children proves necessary, more vigorous social service and therapeutic involvement with the natural parents and the children is warranted. Better training and education of foster parents are also required. In our experience, the prospective foster parents have little or no knowledge about the special problems and difficulties the maltreated children will pose for them. In some cases, the foster care agencies deliberately conceal major cognitive and emotional difficulties of the children so as not to jeopardize their chance of placement.

Since placement of abused children not only fails to solve the original parental problems but contributes to additional sequelae, providing the parents with ongoing social and therapeutic services is essential for strengthening their child-rearing capacity. It is likely that they will have to cope with new offspring or with the eventual return of their maltreated children from temporary placement.

Finally, therapeutic intervention with the abused children is often indicated, whether they remain at home or in foster care. Younger children may benefit from such services as special nursery or day-care programs, while many school-age children can utilize psychotherapy to good advantage. Psychological assistance might be indispensable in helping these children adjust to the stress of separation, placement, and readjustment to unfamiliar family environments.

15

Prevention

Our ideal objective in studying and treating child abuse on a nationwide scale is, as with any major public health problem, the development of a strategy for prevention. Thus far, early case findings and protective intervention in abusing families have been the primary areas of interest for workers in this field. As more basic knowledge about the child-abuse syndrome is accumulated through clinical experience and research, a shift in focus from treatment and rehabilitation (secondary prevention) to primary intervention can be expected to occur.

General Educational Programs

Our society's inadequate preparation for infant and child care has been revealed by the enormous popularity of "how to" books about children and child rearing. With the demise of the

extended family in this country, Spock and other child-rearing
specialists have replaced grandparents among the general
public as the traditional source of wisdom about raising children. Educational programs concerned with child development and parenting, therefore, might satisfy a basic need of
our society. Socioeconomically and educationally deprived
segments of the population might particularly benefit from such
programs. The subject matter could be introduced through
adult education programs, community organizations, religious
groups, day-care centers, and obstetric and pediatric clinics.
These programs would include information about community
resources for child care and provide education about child
abuse and neglect.

More specific programs would be valuable to special groups.
Classes for expectant mothers and fathers could be made available in hospitals as an integral part of prenatal care. The parents would be taught about pregnancy and prenatal and
newborn care. Educational programs for the parents should be
continued after the birth of the child with a change in focus to
infant and early child care. These classes could be held at the
same hospital, or at a pediatric or well-baby clinic.

Identification of Parents at Risk
for Child Abuse

The recent advances in our clinical and theoretical understanding of the child-abuse syndrome, stimulated by an
increased national preoccupation with this problem, have
facilitated the identification of families at risk for maltreatment.
Experienced professionals are now capable of identifying
abuse-prone parents who are likely to maltreat their children
under certain stressful conditions. Parents with low self-
esteem, who are isolated and lack gratifying relationships with
spouse and family, will often make excessive and inappropriate demands on their children in order to fulfill their own
unsatisfied needs. These faulty child-rearing practices are more
likely to culminate in maltreatment under conditions of stress if
the parents are impulsive and had been exposed to violent or

exploitative parenting when they were children. It is also possible to predict the children most likely to be abused or scapegoated in a given high-risk family. It is usually the most difficult, demanding, or deviant child who is unable to satisfy the premature expectations of the parents. Predictive judgments can be made through a variety of techniques. Interviewing the parents, observation of the parent-child interaction, and assessment of the home environment may provide sufficient information to justify an attempt at preventive intervention. There have been recent attempts to develop predictive questionnaires to identify abuse-prone parents (Schneider, Hoffmeister, and Helfer 1976, Gaines et al. 1978). However, this type of instrument has several drawbacks. Thus far many nonabusing parents have similar responses to the questionnaire as those parents who have abused their children. The high number of "false-positive" responses might indicate that a questionnaire can only detect parents with deviant or unusual child-rearing attitudes and practices, but cannot reliably predict child abuse. Research with predictive instruments carried out at the Downstate Medical Center (Gaines et al. 1978) utilized the Helfer questionnaire and a similar instrument adapted for use with a low socioeconomic minority group inner-city population. Neither questionnaire was able to differentiate abusing and nonmaltreating control mothers. It is evident that current predictive instruments have not yet achieved the validity and reliability necessary for use as a serious screening device. In addition, Gaines et al. (1978) described several difficulties with the questionnaire format in low socioeconomic populations, where low intelligence, poor reading ability, and a lack of test sophistication could interfere with the validity of the results.

Perhaps the most reliable means of assessing parents at risk for maltreatment is through a sensitive clinical interview of the parent accompanied by careful history taking, which should include the parent's home situation, the nature of relationships with important figures, availability of support systems, attitudes toward and expectations from the children, perception of current self-image, and the manner in which the parent viewed his own childhood and child rearing. The interview and history taking should be followed by an observation of the family's interaction, which might include interaction between the parents, parents and children, and high-risk parent and target child. The potentially maltreating parent may be identified at various stages of the child's development, but early detection is preferable. The earliest opportunity for high-risk screening is during pregnancy, where the mother can be assessed during routine prenatal visits. Observations can continue during labor, delivery, and postpartum hospitalization. After the mother returns home with her baby, the next opportunity for observation will be during the infant's visits to the pediatrician for illness or well-baby care. Abuse proneness might also be detected during mother-child interaction in a nursery school or day-care setting. The staff of preschool programs should receive training in the recognition of children who are at risk for maltreatment. Later in childhood, the elementary school teachers and pediatrician are the professionals in the best position to detect potential maltreatment. Since parents and young children are in frequent contact with preschool and elementary school programs and health-care facilities, it is important that teachers, school personnel, and pediatricians receive training in the area of child maltreatment.

Early Assessment of Maternal Competency and Abuse Proneness

The prolonged period of contact between prospective mothers and the medical and nursing staff during pregnancy, labor, delivery, and postpartum period, provides a unique opportunity for the assessment of maternal competency.

Prenatal Period

A thorough medical, social, and psychiatric history may be gradually obtained through the mother's attendance at the prenatal clinic. Information about the mother should include an appraisal of her current relationships with spouse, parents, previous children, and peers, and a history of her childhood. One should be aware of the current home environment, socioeconomic and cultural factors, and major sources of stress. The mother should be encouraged to express her feeling and anxieties about the pregnancy and childbirth. The quality of the relationship with the spouse can often be determined during this period through discussion and by observation of their interaction when the husband is present. The extent of the mother's anticipation and planning for the baby's birth should be ascertained, as well as her expectations of the infant. It is important to know if abortion was considered or attempted. The mother's level of cooperation during the clinic visits should be noted, including keeping of appointments, following of medical advice regarding diet, self-care, etc. The availability and reliability of the mother's support system may be explored at this time. The assignment of the mother to one supportive staff member can facilitate the gathering of this information and promote a positive relationship with the clinic.

The following high-risk signals may be observed in the prenatal clinic:

Denial of the pregnancy. In extreme cases, the mother is unable to accept the reality of the pregnancy. She might be unwilling to gain weight or wear maternity clothes when appropriate, and fail to plan for the baby's living arrangements in the home. Denial is more commonly expressed by the mother's inability to react to the pregnancy on an emotional level, dealing with the pregnancy in an intellectual and detached manner instead.

Preoccupation with abortion or relinquishment of the baby. This usually signifies a lack of preparedness for the pregnancy and doubts about the ability to care for the infant. The reasons for the mother's ambivalence or rejection of the pregnancy should be explored.

Depression during the pregnancy. This symptom might be related to conflicts about the pregnancy, unconscious hostility toward the fetus, feelings of helplessness due to a lack of support from spouse or family, etc. It also might represent a more general reaction to the stress of pregnancy in a mother with a predilection for depression.

Lack of support systems. The unavailability of the spouse, parents, family, or friends as reliable sources of support at a time when the mother's passive-receptive wishes are mobilized may increase her negative feelings toward the pregnancy and exaggerate the burdensome aspects of motherhood. A sense of isolation will increase the likelihood of a compensatory reliance on the baby for dependency gratification, and thus facilitate the development of role reversal. The mother's hunger for contact may be expressed by an overdependence on a doctor or nurse or by an increase in physical complaints requiring extra clinic visits.

Inappropriately high expectations of the baby. Mothers who expect that their infants will prematurely achieve developmental milestones or display precocious performance in other areas of functioning are unable to deal with the baby's long period of helplessness. Underlying their impatience with the developmental process is the fantasy that the infant become independent and take care of them.

Overconcern with the sex of the unborn baby. The mother's overriding and persistent wish for a baby of a certain sex usually indicates the presence of unresolved conflicts from childhood. The undesired sex might be associated with a negatively perceived significant individual of the same sex. The rejection of a female infant by the mother is often associated with a poor self-concept and a negative sexual identification. Regardless of the underlying significance of the sex preference, the mother is depending upon the baby to inappropriately satisfy her own needs.

Labor and Delivery

Most parents interact with their newborn for the first time in the delivery room. This initial contact is important for the bonding process. Observations of the mother's responses during labor and her interaction with the newborn after delivery may be of predictive value for her maternal capacity. A positive initial response to the baby might be conveyed by the mother's excitement and pleasure, including affectionate remarks, kissing and hugging the baby, and the establishment of eye contact. The following maternal responses may indicate a high-risk situation:

1. Hostile remarks about the baby's looks or sex. For example, a mother might say that the baby is ugly, make a disparaging comment about how the baby resembles the father, etc.

2. A lack of interest in the baby, which might be expressed by a refusal to look at or to hold it, or a sudden change in plans about breastfeeding.

3. Anger toward the father which might be expressed by blaming him for the pregnancy.

Postpartum Period

The mother's initial attempts at caring for her infant may be assessed during the postpartum period. Observations of mother-infant interaction are facilitated by the widespread availability of rooming-in facilities. Impressions of maternal behavior may be provided by such caretaking activities as feeding, diapering, and bathing the infant. Some mothers are quite adept at anticipating the needs of their infant during this period, while others require more active assistance by the nursery personnel in caring for their newborns. Some mothers are effective in comforting and soothing their crying babies; others become anxious and perplexed in this situation.

Some high-risk signals in the postpartum period are:

Delay in naming the baby, or inappropriate naming of the baby. This may indicate a lack of preparation for the baby, some ambivalence about accepting it, or insufficient attachment.

Poor tolerance or inappropriate response to the baby's crying. Some mothers react angrily and impatiently to the cries of their baby, whom they regard as unnecessarily demanding. At times, mothers interpret the crying as a critical attack on their caretaking ability, resulting in feelings of inadequacy and helplessness. Certain mothers make little or no effort to comfort their crying infant, while others go to extremes to make the crying stop. Mothers in the latter category should be observed carefully, because many instances of physical abuse are triggered by persistent crying. Some mothers regard the crying infant as a rival who would preempt their own need for nurturance.

Difficulty in handling and sustaining contact with the baby. Abuse-prone mothers might handle their infants roughly, while relating to them in a harsh and irritable manner. These mothers are often unable to establish and maintain eye contact with their babies, and do not engage them in an en face position. They regard their babies as primarily burdensome and are unable to experience pleasurable aspects of infant care. Some mothers refrain from handling their infants as a defense against impulses to injure them.

Intolerance of the baby's messiness. Mothers who experience difficulty in attaching to their infants react to feeding and diapering with disgust. Abuse-prone mothers will frequently regard the messiness as a willful act under the baby's control. These mothers have little patience with the helplessness of their babies, and often prematurely institute toilet training and demands for cleanliness. To some mothers, the messy baby is symbolic of their own negative self-image from childhood.

Inordinate expectations of the baby in relation to its developmental capacity. Mothers who already exhibited unrealistic expectations of their baby during the pregnancy may respond with anger and frustration when the infant fails to perform as anticipated during the stages of early development. This spoils the mother's fantasy that the infant will take care of her and might also be interpreted as a confirmation of her parental inadequacy.

Numerous unverifiable complaints about the infant. Excessive fears about the baby's health and development on the mother's part may indicate a reaction formation against unconscious hostility toward the infant, as well as a lack of confidence about her caretaking ability.

Fears of accidentally or intentionally injuring the baby. This symptom occurring during the postpartum period might indicate the presence of a postpartum depressive or psychotic reaction and warrant a psychiatric evaluation. This threatened breakthrough of destructive impulses toward the baby must be taken seriously, as there is a risk for infanticide and/or suicide. These mothers often have a history of prior depressive illness or psychotic behavior, but sometimes these symptoms represent the first evidence of psychiatric decompensation. This symptom should be differentiated from the frequently observed anxiety in new mothers about their newborn's vulnerability to injury because of their apparent fragility.

Later Identification of High-Risk Parents

After the mother and newborn are discharged from the hospital, the pediatrician becomes the community's major link with the parent-child unit. Pediatricians in hospitals, clinics, and private offices have the best opportunity to identify high-risk symptoms of abuse-prone parents when the infants are presented for illness or routine examinations and immunizations. Preschool programs such as nursery schools and day-care centers become an important source of information about child-rearing practices as the infant becomes a toddler and progresses into early childhood. By the time the child begins elementary school, the opportunity for direct observation of parent-child interaction at the school diminishes and the pediatricians are once again in the best position to identify aberrant parent practices.

High-Risk Signals During Infant and Child Care

Many mothers who had been placed in the high-risk category during the perinatal period could be expected to perpetuate ineffective or inappropriate infant or child care in the absence of specific intervention or a reduction of stress. These mothers display a marked intolerance for their babies' irritability and discomfort. They are easily frustrated when their infants are messy, cranky, or need to be fed or changed. Persistent crying might precipitate their striking out at the baby. They also find it difficult to tolerate regressive patterns in an older child, such as bedwetting, soiling, clinging, and tantrumlike behavior. Other originally high-risk mothers with unresolved dependency needs might demonstrate a rather spontaneous improvement in parenting as the child gradually becomes less demanding and more self-sufficient and independent. These older children often assume the burden of gratifying their parents. Another group of mothers might respond more favorably to a helpless, dependent infant but develop harsh and punitive child-rearing patterns at the height of the child's oppositional behavior during the latter part of the second year. These mothers might display major conflicts in the area of control and cleanliness, with obsessive-compulsive symptomatology. The child's rebelliousness and need for autonomy might precipitate major struggles over toilet training. Still another group of parents might display adequate child rearing during the child's first three years and begin to act punitively in response to age-appropriate expressions of sexuality during the oedipal period (age three to five). These parents have unresolved conflicts regarding their own sexuality which are projected onto the child. Little girls who display a normal amount of seductive behavior at this time are accused of being "whores," and masturbation is viewed as a confirmation of their sexual precocity.

Interaction with School-age Children

High-risk parents with unrealistic expectations concerning their child's performance often become abusive when their children enter school. These parents often project their own intellectual and vocational inadequacy onto the child and punish him for not compensating for their defects. They cannot tolerate poor academic performance or behavioral misconduct by the child because it reminds them too painfully of their own inadequacies. On the other hand, children who are rigidly disciplined or physically punished often displace their aggression onto the school setting, creating a vicious cycle of misbehavior in school, more parental punishment, and increased acting out in the classroom.

School personnel are in a good position to identify signs of neglect, such as the failure to provide a child with adequate food, clothing, or personal care. Such children might arrive at school hungry because they are not given breakfast, or they might be inadequately dressed for cold weather or appear dirty and disheveled. Another indication of possible neglect is the child's excessive unexplained absence from school. Some children will appear malnourished or far below average in height and weight. Others might show signs of inflicted injury, such as bruises, welts, or burns.

Preventive Intervention

Modification of the Childbirth Experience

Since the mother's experiences during pregnancy, delivery, and the postpartum period may be crucial for the development of affectional bonds with her infant, one should strive for a sensitive, family-centered delivery of maternity and newborn care, designed to maximize contact between the mother and her spouse and baby. Attendance at childbirth classes and mothers' groups, and participation of the father during prenatal visits, can enhance the mother's preparation for the birth process. The father's presence during labor and delivery is supportive and reassuring. The mother should be permitted physical contact with her baby and spouse immediately after delivery. Alertness of the mother and baby can be facilitated by minimizing the use of anesthesia and medication. In cases of normal birth, extended contact between mother and infant through rooming-in is preferable to arrangements in which the mother only receives the child for routine feedings. Mothers of premature babies or neonates requiring special care should be encouraged to visit as frequently as possible. Upon discharge from the hospital, one should be certain that an adequate support network exists in the home to assist the mother with infant care.

Intervention During Infancy

Families identified as at risk for abnormal parenting through careful assessment during pregnancy, labor, delivery, and the lying-in period require a continuation of the supportive contacts between the parents and the hospital staff after the mother and newborn are discharged. This can be achieved through the assignment of a visiting nurse to the high-risk family. The nurse can play a supportive, encouraging role with both parents, while demonstrating and dispensing information about infant care and child development. This should facilitate the bonding process. The nurse should be in a position to initiate referrals for social services or psychotherapy and/or counseling if necessary. Kempe and Helfer (1972) described the routine placement of health visitors (visiting nurses) in Aberdeen, Scotland, in all homes following the birth of a child. These nurses provide assistance with infant care and are also trained to identify high-risk families. Gray et al. (1976) reported research which demonstrated the beneficial impact of intervention with high-risk parents identified during the perinatal period. None of the infants of parents at risk who were visited regularly by a physician or nurse suffered serious injury, while 10 percent of the babies of the high-risk parents without intervention required hospitalization for serious injuries thought to be the result of abnormal child-rearing practices. The assignment of a visiting nurse might be especially valuable for an inexperienced new mother who is unable to depend upon her own family or friends for assistance with infant care. The nurse might be indispensable for a high-risk mother with a vulnerable infant, one who is premature, colicky, chronically ill, or difficult to comfort.

Participation in mothers' or parent groups can be another effective preventive modality. Such groups may be primarily educational in orientation, where feelings about parenthood and general problems are explored and discussed. Other groups might focus mainly on education concerning infant care and child development. Parents attending groups can benefit from the awareness that their problems are shared by others.

Group participation can also overcome feelings of isolation, and serve as a bridge to social contact.

The following categories of high-risk mothers, identified at the prenatal clinics and maternity floors at the Kings County Hospital/Downstate Medical Center, were able to benefit from the services of a visiting nurse or student-nurse volunteer, and from participation in groups. First of all, young teenagers who decide to keep their babies are encouraged to mother their infants rather than delegate the caretaking responsibility to their own mothers or relatives. (Girls under sixteen account for 6 percent of all Kings County Hospital deliveries.) Another group of high-risk mothers are those who have been cited for abuse or neglect of previous children. Some of these mothers conceive in order to replace the previously maltreated children who have been legally removed from the home. Mothers with prominent psychiatric disturbances are likely to have inappropriate or unrealistic expectations of their infants. Some of these women are chronically psychotic or depressed, or are mentally retarded. Others have experienced postpartum psychoses or depressions. The stress of infant care often causes paralyzing anxiety in these women, who find the presence of a visiting nurse most reassuring. Since the majority of these mothers require psychiatric care, the nurse often collaborates directly with the psychiatrist in the implementation of the treatment plan. Alcoholic and drug-addicted mothers constitute a special subgroup of emotionally impaired high-risk parents who have benefited from home intervention with visiting nurses. These women have been simultaneously enrolled in drug rehabilitation programs at Kings County Hospital.

The temporary placement of an infant or young child in a special nursery (crisis nursery) during times of parental stress is another type of intervention which can be beneficial to both the parents and the child. Such a nursery may provide day-care or operate on a twenty-four-hour basis. The nursery provides a safe environment for the infants and toddlers, while giving the parents a temporary respite from the pressures of infant and child care. Residence in the nursery provides an opportunity for the medical and developmental evaluation of the child and observation of mother-child interaction. The nursery may also serve as a center for parent groups and for training in infant and child care.

Later Intervention with High-Risk Parents

When the high-risk family and target child have been identified during contact with pediatricians, schools, or social agencies, an appropriate intervention strategy can be developed according to the relative contributions of the three major factors of the maltreatment syndrome. This conceptual model allows preventive interventions to be employed where they will have the greatest impact. For example, if parents' personality variables were found to be more significant than either child deviancy or stress, psychotherapy or casework might be considered the treatment of choice. If, on the other hand, environmental and family stresses were found to have made the greatest contribution, the placement of parent-aides, homemakers, or visiting nurses in the home could present a more effective intervention. In families particularly burdened with a difficult or deviant child, a medical and/or psychiatric and psychological evaluation of the child would be performed followed by a referral to the appropriate treatment modality. This would complement the intervention with the parents. Parents of deviant children can benefit from a careful explanation of their child's disability and limitations, which often contribute to their scapegoating.

A multidisciplinary hospital or community-based comprehensive treatment program for maltreating families is best equipped to provide preventive intervention for high-risk families. It can deliver the crisis-oriented mental health and social services required by these families, including a strong outreach component consisting of visiting nurses, homemakers, and parent-aides stationed in the home. The home-based staff member can not only dispense important child-rearing assistance to the parents, but may be an invaluable source of information about the physical and emotional climate in the home and the degree of risk for the children, which can then be relayed to the treatment staff at team conferences.

A day-care center for the preschool children of high-risk parents can be an important modality for the prevention of maltreatment. The center provides the young child with a secure environment and promotes socialization with peers and adults. It also relieves overstressed parents of the burdens of child care during the day. This type of program is ideal for a child who is deviant or difficult to manage, and for the mother who is psychologically unprepared for child rearing on a full-time basis. The availability of day care also frees the mother for part-time or full-time employment, schooling, or vocational training, which might contribute to the enhancement of her self-esteem.

The last section of this book deals with research, legal issues, and the conclusions and recommendations of the author. Chapter 16 reviews some of the current research in the area of child abuse and neglect, and its application for treatment. Chapter 17 describes some of the important legal aspects of child maltreatment, including reporting laws, investigation procedures, and the judicial process in the family or juvenile court. The final chapter presents the author's observation on the quality of the current national response to our epidemic of child abuse, and his recommendations to mental health and child-care professionals for more effective prevention and treatment.

Part IV

Other Aspects of
Maltreatment

16

Current Research in
Child Maltreatment

Overview

Kempe's description of the *battered child syndrome* in 1962 generated widespread interest in the area of child abuse and neglect. The late 1960s witnessed the growth of a sizeable literature on the characteristics of maltreating parents. The quantity and scope of clinical studies in this area increased dramatically during the 1970s, and have recently included observations of abused children and parent-child interaction in maltreating families. The initial studies in this field were impressionistic and naive, and largely consisted of observations of a few abusing parents. Many of the early investigators sought to discover a single personality trait or psychological abnormality which could explain the phenomenon of child abuse. Their failure to include control groups in their studies led to faulty conclusions and generalizations. Many of the characteristics ascribed to abusing parents, such as immaturity, impulsivity, social isolation, and a tendency to depend too much on their children, were too general, and were present in large numbers of nonabusing parents. Other clinicians, unduly biased by the prevailing punitive atmosphere and their own angry feelings toward the parents, described them as psychopaths who were refractory to treatment. Fortunately, the quality of the research in this area has improved during the past few years. The federal government began to actively support research through its National Center for Child Abuse and Neglect, which was established in 1974. The more recent research has been based on the theory of multiple causality. The relative contributions of parental personality factors, demographic data, environmental and socioeconomic variables, and the characteristics of the target children have been assessed through discriminant function analyses. More of the current studies use appropriate controls, and several well-planned prospective studies have been completed. Nevertheless, the study of child maltreatment is still in its infancy. In order to develop effective strategies for intervention we require a much greater understanding of these combinations of factors which, when catalyzed by certain precipitants, result in maltreatment.

Specific Difficulties Inherent in Child-Abuse and Neglect Research

Problems in Definition

It is quite difficult to establish a universally acceptable definition of child abuse in a culture which supports the use of physical discipline. Physical punishment, though regarded as a norm in one subculture, may be labelled as physical abuse in another. There is also a common tendency to ascribe only more severe injuries to abuse, when, in fact, the most common types of abuse cause relatively minor injuries, such as contusions or strap marks. Neglect is often hard to define in poor, large, disorganized inner-city families, in which the level of material and psychological resources for child care falls far below the national average. Neglect can also be defined as "intentional" or "unintentional." The latter category would include substandard child care resulting from poverty, large numbers of children, poor housing, or subnormal parental intelligence.

Problems of Identification

It is generally agreed that only a small percentage of the actual cases of child abuse and neglect are identified and reported. Therefore it is difficult to exclude the possibility that "normal controls" might include families in which unreported abuse or neglect has taken place. It is also difficult to distinguish between accidental and inflicted injuries in small children, which makes the use of "accidentally" injured children as comparison groups of questionable value.

Problems in the Patient Population

Maltreating parents make extremely poor research subjects. They are likely to be poor historians, especially regarding previous incidents of abuse or neglect. Their frequent use of denial and their concerns with confidentiality impair the reliability of their responses on questionnaires or during interviews. The parents are likely to be hostile and mistrustful of the researchers, who are usually identified with those professionals (reporting physicians, protective service personnel) regarded as adversaries. Maltreating families are also unstable and hard to reach. They move frequently and often do not have telephones. Their relative inaccessibility interferes with follow-up studies, and results in a high drop-out rate in prospective longitudinal research. Since reports of maltreatment originate most frequently from public agencies (municipal hospitals, child-health stations, public schools, etc.) the poor are overrepresented in child-abuse registries. This can lead to faulty generalizations which would unjustifiably equate poor reported maltreators with their more middle-class unreported counterparts.

Problems of Confidentiality

The honesty and spontaneity of maltreating parents are often compromised by their fear that the information they divulge might be used against them. They might also strive to produce socially desirable or "normal" responses in order to improve their position vis-à-vis child protective services and the courts. The issue of confidentiality is often used by protective service or private agencies to deny researchers access to case records, in order to safeguard their clients' right to privacy. Research on maltreatment requires cooperative liaison between the research staff and the child protective services personnel. The researchers must guarantee the confidentiality of the data gathered from the parents, while reassuring the protective services that their records would not be subjected to unauthorized exposure.

Failure to Differentiate Maltreatment

Many research studies regard "maltreatment" as a single independent variable, failing to distinguish between physical abuse, neglect, or failure to thrive. When this occurs, the findings are impossible to interpret. The types of maltreatment under investigation should be carefully defined and delineated. Unfortunately, the frequent coexistence of physical abuse and neglect makes this a difficult task. If neglect is the variable to be studied, care should be taken to rule out the coexistence of physical abuse. This may be dealt with by using a comparison group in which neglect without abuse has taken place.

Weaknesses of Retrospective Studies

The major studies in the area of child abuse and neglect have been retrospective in nature, which poses certain difficulties. First of all, it is impossible to separate the preexisting family characteristics, which may have contributed to maltreatment, from those resulting from abuse or neglect. Secondly, the significant amount of time which has elapsed between the incidents of maltreatment and the collection of data prevents accurate and reliable measurement of variables. For example, it is difficult to retrospectively assess the level of familial stress operating during maltreatment which occurred several years prior to the inquiry. Another obstacle is the frequent change in the circumstances and composition of maltreating families during the interval between the reporting and the time of study. Some of the families will demonstrate the effects of treatment, while others will manifest a new family constellation resulting from placement of the target children, new offspring, or separation from spouse or mate.

Major Areas of Research

Studies of Maltreating Parents

Whereas the earlier studies of abusing parents focused on rather general personality characteristics which interfered with their child-rearing capacities, more recent research has considered parents' personality variables as only one of numerous factors in the complex etiology of child abuse. Some of the recent research attempted to test the early clinical observations of the parents in a more objective manner, and also explored various demographic, social, and stress-related variables in maltreating parents and normal controls, using multivariate analyses. Many of the studies documented differences for abusing parents. Starr et al. (1978) found abusive parents significantly more alienated and nonconforming than norms for the population as a whole on two subscales of the Psychological Screening Inventory. Abusing mothers had significantly lower IQ scores than matched control mothers of children hospitalized for nontraumatic medical emergencies. The abusing mothers also reported significantly more stressful events during the past year, had lower annual incomes, and were more socially isolated than the controls. The abusers also scored higher on "denial of the complexity of child rearing" as measured by the Choler Maternal Attitudes Scale. Wolock and Horowitz (1977) interviewed single-parent welfare mothers, who were divided into categories of abuse only, neglect and abuse, neglect only, and nonmaltreating comparison mothers. The abusing mothers differed from the comparisons in that they experienced greater difficulties growing up (poverty, beatings, inadequate food and clothing, etc.), reported less positive attitudes toward their children, and were more socially isolated. This last observation was also described by Ceresnie and Starr. The neglecting families were differentiated from comparison families by having larger numbers of children. Burgess and Conger (1977) analyzed observations of verbal and physical family interactions in both one- and two-parent abusing, neglecting, and control families. They found overall levels of communications significantly less frequent and less positive between mothers and children in abusing and neglecting families. Abusing and neglecting mothers made significantly fewer verbal statements toward family members in general and children in particular, and fewer positive verbal and physical interactions overall. Children in abusing and neglecting families made less verbal contact with their mothers than control children.

In another mother-infant interaction study, Dietrich (1977) observed that abusing mothers were less stimulating and more passive in handling their infants. They provided significantly less tactile and auditory stimulation than control mothers.

Gaines et al. (1978) attempted to verify the multifactor theory of child abuse and neglect, which explains maltreatment as a function of parental personality characteristics, child characteristics, and environmental stress, with eighty abusing, neglecting, and closely matched comparison mothers. Each of the mothers was measured on twelve variables derived from child-rearing questionnaires, stress measures, and infant risk. A multiple discriminant analysis revealed that stress factors, including items such as unemployment, evictions, and arrests, measured by a project developed questionnaire and the Schedule of Recent Experience (Holmes and Rahe 1967) accounted for most of the between-group variance. The neglecting mothers also had the most difficulty meeting emotional needs. Although the abusing mothers actually scored high on stress, the neglecting mothers exceeded them. The abusing mothers were less able to cope with stress than the neglecting and control mothers, as measured by Helfer's Michigan Screening Profile of Parenting (1977). Demographic data revealed that significantly more neglecting mothers had been separated from their own mothers before the age of eleven. The abusing and neglecting mothers had significantly more children than the comparisons, and were less likely to have a telephone, suggesting social isolation. The authors concluded that, due to the retrospective nature of the study, stressful life events coincident with the abuse may have dissipated by the time of data collection, while among chronically disorganized, neglecting families, stress may be an omnipresent phenomenon more easily detected by questionnaires.

Chapa (1978) compared seventy-six families involved with maltreatment (either abuse or neglect) with ninety-two comparison families selected at random from a street directory. Data were collected by a three-hundred sixty-item project-developed interview. Twenty-two factors were derived from the data, measuring the parents' attitudes toward children and child rearing, impressions of the family, and demographic variables relating to stress. The results indicated that two to three times as many maltreators as controls reported that at times they couldn't cope with life. Fewer maltreating parents had lived with both natural parents and more had experienced greater physical punishment as children. With regard to child-rearing variables, two to three times as many maltreators as controls reported feeling inadequate as parents and finding child-care responsibilities too burdensome for them. The maltreating parents were more restrictive and used harsher child-rearing measures than the controls. Chapa also reported large between-group differences on items relating to the phenomenon of role reversal. The maltreators stated more than the controls that their children should love them more, should be more helpful to parents with their problems, and should spend more time with parents.

Green (1976) compared sixty mothers of abused children with thirty neglecting mothers and thirty normal controls obtained from a pediatric outpatient clinic. The majority of the mothers were black or Hispanic and resided in the inner-city slums. A structured interview was conducted with each mother to gather information regarding family background and early childhood experience; dating, courtship, and marital history; obstetrical and perinatal history; child-rearing attitudes; the mother's behavioral assessment of the child; and the presence of outstanding maternal deviancy. The results indicated that the mothers of the abused children most frequently reported these children to be problems at home and in school. These mothers also reported more marital difficulties than the neglecting and control mothers, and a higher incidence of being beaten by their husbands or boyfriends. A significantly higher percentage of these mothers described a poor relationship with their own parents. The mothers of the neglected children reported the highest percentage of unplanned pregnancies and the absence of a husband or male companion at home. The neglecting mothers also exhibited the highest incidence of alcoholism, psychosis, and chronic physical illness.

Prospective Studies

Egeland and Brunnquell (1979) followed two-hundred seventy-five high-risk mothers and infants throughout the child's first year of life. Characteristics of the mothers, infant temperament and the organization of neonatal behavior, environmental stress factors, and the interaction of the caretaker and infant were examined in an attempt to identify differences between mothers who mistreated their children and those who did not. A subsample of twenty-five mothers providing good quality care and twenty-six mothers who abused or mistreated their child was identified. This 10 percent maltreatment rate exceeded the 2 percent rate for abuse and neglect of the Minneapolis public health clinic population. Data regarding demographic and medical characteristics were obtained from the prenatal clinic and the hospital delivery files. The factors distinguishing the two groups of mothers were environmental support for the mother, general education, and specific preparation for the baby by the mother. Only 37 percent of the good mothers were single at the time of delivery, compared to 84 percent of the inadequate mothers. Supportiveness of the father's and mother's family was significantly higher for the adequate mothers. The good mothers received more schooling than the inadequate mothers, and 100 percent of the good mothers attended childbirth classes, compared to only 30 percent of the maltreating mothers. Public health nurses rated a significantly higher percentage of the adequate mothers as prepared for their babies and as having realistic expectations about infant care. Before delivery, 73 percent of the good mothers intended to breast feed, compared to only 28 percent of the maltreating mothers. The maternal age difference was striking: the mean age of the good mothers was 24.5 years while the mean age of the inadequate mothers was 19.3 years. This age difference seemed to be related to the mothers' differing abilities preparing for and meeting the demands of pregnancy and child rearing. Separate discriminant function analyses were performed using the mother, infant, and mother-infant interaction variables, in an attempt to differentiate between the good and inadequate mother groups. The variables that best differentiated the two groups were:

1. The mother's understanding of the psychological complexity of the infant, based on scales developed by Cohler, Weiss, and Grunebaum (1970), which measure the appropriateness of the mother's attitude toward the child's aggression, her attitude toward encouraging reciprocity, and her acceptance of the ambivalent feelings that accompany pregnancy and mothering.

2. A factor based on the nurse's ratings assessing the mother's interest in the child.

3. Factors based on mothers' behavior and babies' social behavior assessed in the three-month feeding observation.

Egeland and Brunnquell were able to predict group membership with 88.2 percent accuracy, based on the ten variables representing information from the evaluation of the baby, the evaluation of the mother, and the evaluation of mother-child interaction. Variables taken from the interactive situation were the most useful in distinguishing the good from the inadequate mothers. There were generally no differences in the amount of stress experienced by the two groups of mothers. The differences that did occur had to do with the inadequate mothers experiencing more stress of a chaotic and disruptive nature, including involvement in physical fights, heavy drinking of a family member or close friends, and breaking up with a husband or boyfriend.

In another controlled prospective study, Altemeier et al. (1979) assessed fourteen-hundred pregnant women registered in the prenatal clinic of a city hospital in Nashville, using a standardized interview designed to elicit parental factors associated with child maltreatment. The categories of interview questions included: the mother's perception about her nurturance as a child; her personality, including self-image, isolation, and stress tolerance; her support systems; her feelings about the pregnancy; her ideas about parenting and discipline; alcohol, drug and health stresses; her expectations and knowledge of child development; and a Life Stress Inventory of herself and the baby's father, adapted from Holmes and Rahe (1967). Twenty percent or two-hundred seventy-three of the mothers were estimated to be at highest risk for abuse and neglect based on their responses to the interview. A comparison group of two-hundred twenty-five low-risk mothers was composed of 20 percent of the remaining mothers selected at random. After delivery, the infants and siblings of the high- and low-risk mothers were followed for evidence of child abuse, neglect, and failure to thrive in a double bind fashion. The average age of the infants was 12.8 months when the data concerning maltreatment were obtained. The results indicated that all three parenting disorders were found significantly more often in high-risk compared to comparison families. Reported abuse was found in 4.4 percent of the high-risk families, and in 0.4 percent of the comparison families; neglect occurred in

5.1 percent of the high-risk families and in 1.1 percent of the comparison families; and failure to thrive was found in 14 percent of the high-risk infants compared to 4.2 percent of the low-risk infants. A total of 18.7 percent of all high-risk children had some evidence of a parenting disorder. The interview was more reliable in predicting abuse. The interview category "mothers nurture during childhood" had the highest correlation with selection for high risk. Mothers who reported being battered as children felt significantly more isolated, had a poorer self-image, less tolerance to stress, and were more likely to have been physically attacked recently than the nonbattered mothers.

Hunter et al. (1978) studied the families of two-hundred fifty-five premature infants who had been hospitalized in a newborn intensive-care unit prior to being discharged by their parents. Psychosocial characteristics of each family were assessed during the infant's hospitalization by a family psychosocial risk inventory. Ten of the infants were subsequently reported as victims of maltreatment (two abused, eight neglected) during the first year of life. Thirteen family psychosocial characteristics were significantly associated with later maltreatment. These included social isolation, a family history of child abuse and neglect, serious marital problems, inadequate child-care arrangements, apathetic and dependent personality styles, and inadequate child spacing. The maltreated infants differed from other babies admitted to the intensive care nursery during the same time period. They were significantly less mature at birth (mean gestational age 31.5 weeks) than the infants who were not maltreated (mean gestational age 35.3 weeks). Mean birth weights were less for the reported group (1,477 gm.) compared with their nonreported nursery mates (2,224 gm.). In addition, congenital defects were noted in six of the ten infants later reported for maltreatment. The maltreated infants were more likely than their nursery mates to have remained in the intensive-care nursery for longer than forty days. The maltreated babies also received less frequent visits than the nonreported babies.

Dean et al. (1978) assessed early maternal attitudes of seventy-seven hundred mothers in Aberdeen, Scotland, during an observation of the mother-infant interaction when the infants were three to four months of age. Of the seventy-seven hundred children, thirteen-hundred eighty-eight (29 percent) were taken to the hospital with an injury or failure to thrive during the first two years of life. These thirteen-hundred eighty-eight index children were matched for age and sex with thirteen-hundred eighty-eight control children from the original population pool when they reached the age of two. The health visitor's assessment indicated either no concern (68 percent), mild concern (21 percent), moderate concern (7 percent), or great concern (3 percent), according to the mothers' competency in handling her baby. Twice as many injured or failure-to-thrive children were in the "moderate" or "great" concern groups than the control children. A significantly higher percentage of mothers for whom the level of concern was "moderate" or "great" had their children's injuries classified as "nonaccidental." When the suspected nonaccidental injuries were classified according to the degree of seriousness, the more serious injuries were overrepresented in the children of the less adequate mothers (moderate or great concern). These investigators recommended that families designated as high risk by the health visitor's assessment be provided with outreach services.

Studies of Abused and Neglected Children

Dietrich (1977) compared matched samples of fourteen abused infants with fourteen control infants admitted to a hospital emergency room for a medical illness, using the Bayley Scales of Infant Development. The abused infants scored significantly lower on the mental development index (mean score 90.00) than the control infants (mean score 106.28). The abused infants also scored lower on the psychomotor development index, but the results were not quite so significant. The abused infants also manifested significantly lower blood hemoglobin levels than the controls. 79 percent of the abused infants displayed an iron deficiency anemia compared to none of the control infants. Dietrich postulated that the anemia might have resulted from prolonged bottle feeding and a delayed introduction to solid foods on the part of the abusing mothers. No differences were found between the two groups of infants regarding birth weight or prematurity. This failure to confirm the higher prematurity and low birth-weight rates found in previous studies was attributed to their high incidence in the lower-class population, from which the control group was recruited.

In a follow-up study of three-hundred twenty-eight families cited for abuse, Herrenkohl and Herrenkohl (1979) compared two-hundred eighty-four abused children with two-hundred ninety-five nonabused siblings, with reference to birth data and maternal perceptions of the birth and subsequent development of the child. 6.9 percent of the abused children were born prematurely as compared to 1.5 percent of their nonabused siblings. Fewer of the mothers of children born earlier than thirty-six weeks gestation saw their babies immediately after delivery than the mothers of full-term babies. The mothers of the premature babies also reported significantly greater time lags before touching or holding their infants, lending support to the theory that increased separation of premature infants from their mothers may increase their risk for subsequent abuse by adding obstacles to the bonds of attachment between mother and child. Children who were described by their mothers as having more problems in infancy (e.g., excessive crying, slow development, slow weight gain) were more likely than their siblings to have been targets of gross, or life-threatening, neglect. In addition, infants whose first Apgar scores were less than eight were significantly more frequent targets of gross neglect than those with Apgar scores of eight or above. Mothers of abused children perceived themselves as having less control or influence over these children than their non-abused siblings. Herrenkohl's study also demonstrated that the babies of teenage mothers were at higher risk for subsequent abuse and neglect. 32.4 percent of the abused children were born to mothers under twenty, compared to 14.9 percent of their nonabused siblings.

Martin and Beezley (1977) carried out a follow-up study of fifty abused children. The behavior of the children and the characteristics of their environment were assessed at a mean of four and a half years after physical abuse was first identified. Differences in behavior of the fifty children were noted according to the frequency and pervasiveness of such symptoms as temper tantrums, aggression, enuresis, sleep disturbance, hyperactivity, poor peer relationships, potentially delinquent behavior, and socially inappropriate behavior. The children were classified in one of four categories: no symptoms, few (1-2) symptoms, numerous (3-4) symptoms, and severe disturbance (3 or more symptoms of severe intensity). The severity and frequency of symptoms were significantly related to the number of home changes since the abuse was identified. The more symptoms the child had, the more likely he was to have had three or more home changes. The degree of behavioral disturbance was also related to the child's sense of impermanence in his current home, the instability of the home, the amount of punitiveness in the home, and parental emotional disturbance. Children who remained in their natural homes were more likely to be living in punitive and unstable environments than children in foster or adoptive homes. These investigators concluded that the children's behavioral symptoms may have resulted from the parental punitiveness and home instability, which in turn would further disrupt the home environment and incite additional punishment from the parents.

DeCastro et al. (1978) conducted a one-year follow-up study of one-hundred fifty-six abused children. In one-third of the sample, abuse continued after the identifying incident. Girls under three years of age had the greatest risk for reinjury. After one year, 12 percent of the children were much improved, 52 percent showed some improvement, and 35 percent manifested no improvement. A greater proportion of children in foster care showed improvement than children remaining at home. This was felt to be associated with the very limited number of supportive home visits by social agencies following the return home of abused children. The observers recommended that the families of abused children who return home should receive more than twenty supportive visits during a year.

Parent-Child Interaction in Abusing Families

The failure to adequately explain the phenomenon of child abuse solely on the basis of parental character traits, predisposing factors in the child, or environmental stress has led to a recent interest in observing parent-child interaction within maltreating families. These observations permit us to study the reciprocal impact of parent and child upon one another during varying levels of stress.

Burgess and Conger (1977) studied daily interaction in abusing, neglecting, and control families. The families were observed in their homes by trained, naive observers. The abusing and neglecting families displayed lower rates of overall interaction. Abusing and neglecting mothers exhibited positive interaction (affectionate and supportive behavior) significantly less frequently than the mothers in the control families. On the other hand, the abusing and neglecting mothers displayed much higher rates of negative behavior (threats and complaints, etc.) toward their children than the control mothers. Reid and Taplin (1977) found that abusive families exhibited significantly higher rates of aversive behavior than did families with no history of abuse. Egeland and Brunnquell (1978) demonstrated that ratings of a mother-infant feeding interaction at the age of three months were a good predictor of subsequent maternal caretaking in a group of high-risk mothers and infants. Some of the behavior observed included quality of verbalization, expressiveness, quality of physical contact, sensitivity, responsiveness to baby's initiation of interactions, facility in caretaking, and positive and negative regard. Deficiency in maternal caretaking skills was the best predictor of subsequent child abuse or maltreatment. Gaensbauer et al. (1978) observed that the reciprocity of mother-infant interaction was impaired in cases of child abuse. The infants often failed to respond to their mother's attempts to initiate interaction, often resulting in parallel play in which sustained reciprocal interactions are rare. When social contact was left to the infant's initiative, proximity seeking to the mother and bids for attention were less frequent than in the normal population.

Impairment of maternal caretaking skills not only increases the current stress experienced by the mother and infant, but constitutes a unique stress by itself. This child-rearing stress might trigger the mother's impulsivity or stimulate her own regressive dependent fantasies. The resulting asynchrony between mother and infant might be interpreted by the mother as a rejection by the child. A vicious cycle might ensue, consisting of cumulative environmental stress in the mother (from child-rearing and nonchild-rearing sources), increased infantile stress and discomfort, reactive maternal anxiety and hostility or abuse, leading to further asynchrony between mother and infant, etc.

Evaluation of the Treatment Process

Cohn (1979) evaluated eleven three-year child-abuse and neglect demonstration projects. Data were collected on seventeen-hundred twenty-four adults and seventy children served by the projects. The clients were in treatment for an average of six to seven months and received therapeutic contact about once a week. Approximately 30 percent of the clients received lay or parent-aide counseling and/or Parents Anonymous, along with individual counseling. 12 percent received group treatment (including group therapy or parent education classes) along with other services. Over half (54 percent) received an individual counseling model of service delivery which excluded lay or group services. The limitations of this study included a lack of a nontreatment or control group. The data were collected from the treatment staff, and may contain clinical biases. The data were collected only until the time of termination, so that the long-term effects of treatment could not be assessed. Of the seventeen-hundred twenty-four parents studied, 30 percent severely reabused or neglected their children while they were in treatment. The best single predictor or reincidence appeared to be the severity of the case at intake. The reincidence was lowest in those projects that used highly trained professionals to handle intake, initial diagnosis, and treatment planning. Only 42 percent of the parents studied demonstrated a reduced potential for future abuse or neglect, according to the opinion of their workers. Therefore, less than half of the cases showed improvement. Parents receiving lay or parent-aid counseling and/or Parents Anonymous demonstrated a slightly higher incidence of improvement (53 percent). The lay-service model was also found to be more cost effective than individual counseling.

The major problem areas of the seventy children who were treated at three demonstration programs were: inability to give and receive affection; general unhappiness; poor attention span; poor sense of self; poor reaction to frustration; and impaired interaction with adults and peers. Analysis of the clinician-reported gains made by the abused and neglected children in problem areas indicated that 79 percent of the children with problems giving and receiving affection were improved. Two-thirds of those children with problems interacting with adults and with general unhappiness were reported to be improved. Fifty-seven percent of the children with short attention spans and with poor self-images showed improvement, while 59 percent of the children with interactional problems with peers also made positive gains. Although fewer children received treatment at the demonstration centers, those who did exhibited higher rates of improvement than their parents. The author cited the need to discover more effective therapeutic techniques in working with both maltreating parents and maltreated children.

Herrenkohl and Herrenkohl (1979) conducted a follow-up study of three-hundred twenty-eight families cited for child abuse in Lehigh and Northampton Counties in Pennsylvania during the period of 1967-1976. All of the families received casework services and 18 percent were involved in either individual or group therapy. This population displayed a high recidivism rate. 52.8 percent of the parents repeated physical abuse and 50 percent of the parents repeated sexual abuse, while 44.5 percent of the parents repeated gross neglect. Beatings of adults occurred in 25.3 percent of the families. The total number of abuse incidents for the families was significantly correlated with the total number of stresses mentioned by the parents. The most important stressors were found to be social isolation, conflict with others, and physical and legal problems. Fifty-eight of the three-hundred twenty-eight families who received individual or group therapy demonstrated a reduced propensity for futher abuse. Sixty-three percent of this population exhibited no further abuse either after the last therapy contact or after one year or more following the first therapy contact. 25.6 percent had one or more child-abuse incidents after the last therapy contact. The families who did not repeat abuse had substantially more therapy contacts than those where there was recidivism. Repetition of abuse in families involved in treatment occurred most frequently in resistant individuals who displayed poor attendance at therapy sessions. The Herrenkohls' data suggested the value of individual and/or group therapy in reducing recidivism in abusing parents.

Green et al. (1979) recently completed an evaluation of their comprehensive treatment program for abused children and their families at the Downstate Medical Center in Brooklyn, New York. Seventy-nine abusing parents were evaluated. The criteria for selection specified that the parents attended six or more therapeutic sessions with a member of the treatment staff. 79 percent of the parents remained in treatment over five months, with a maximum duration of thirty-six months.

Each parent received a rating of either slight improvement, significant improvement, or no improvement, based on a joint decision by the therapist and the other members of the permanent treatment staff, following an extensive case review. The criteria for these ratings were:

1. *Slight improvement* – progress was limited to symptomatic improvement, which included a reduction or elimination of child abuse and scapegoating, and modification of such symptoms as poor impulse control, depression, disorganization, and social isolation.

2. *Significant improvement* – elimination of child abuse, scapegoating, and misperception of the child, with additional progress, exceeding symptomatic improvement, in the parent's capacity for insight, self-observation, and empathy with the child and others. Significant improvement also included more effective child-rearing practices with a diminished reliance on

physical punishment, improved management of the household, improved relationships with spouse, family, and peers, and a reduction in the use of denial and projection as major defenses.

3. *No improvement* – lack of change in the parent's symptoms, deviant child rearing and scapegoating, and pathological relationships with spouse and family.

The impact of demographic variables, parental personality and child-rearing variables, variables pertaining to the child, and treatment variables on the treatment outcome were also assessed. The results indicated that slightly over two-thirds of the sample demonstrated some improvement. 40.5 percent of the parents demonstrated slight improvement, while 27.8 percent exhibited significant improvement. The reabuse rate was 16 percent. The demographic data reflected the impoverishment and low socioeconomic status of this inner-city population. The majority of the population was composed of blacks (57 percent), while Hispanics accounted for 21.5 percent of the sample. Three-quarters of the families had incomes below $6,000 or were on welfare, and less than one-third of the families were intact, with both parents at home. Ninety-four percent of the cases were reported to the central registry for child abuse while 68 percent of the cases were involved in the courts. The parents with court involvement manifested a lower incidence of significant improvement than those without court contact. Examination of the child-rearing variables revealed that parents exhibiting marked misperceptions and premature expectations of their children displayed a significantly higher incidence of "no improvement" than parents with moderate or no misperceptions and premature expectations. Parents who had previously abused the target child and who had inflicted the most serious injuries were also less likely to show any improvement during the treatment. The correlations between overall improvement, and improvement in the quality of child rearing, relationships with significant objects, insight, and self-observation, and modification of denial and projection, were all highly significant.

Analysis of the treatment variables indicated that the length of treatment was significantly related to the treatment outcome. The patients who remained in treatment over twelve months demonstrated a higher rate of improvement than those who stayed for less than twelve months. Very few of the patients who terminated the treatment against the advice of the therapist displayed any improvement, while the treatment outcome was more successful for the patients who terminated with their therapist's consent or who were still in treatment at the time of the evaluation. Patients who improved demonstrated a higher percentage of kept appointments than the "no improvement" group. Patients who entered treatment voluntarily exhibited more successful treatment outcomes than those ordered to attend by the protective service agency or the court.

The overall data from this study suggested general profiles of abusing parents who responded favorably and unfavorably to treatment. Abusing parents with a previous record of maltreatment, who entered the program on an involuntary basis, who never acknowledged the maltreatment or the existence of any other problems, and who inflicted more severe injuries, tended to be less responsive to rehabilitation. They frequently ended treatment prematurely, often against advice. These types of parents were also characterized by persistent use of denial and projection associated with misperceptions and abnormal expectations of their children and impaired relationships with significant adult objects. They had frequent court involvement and tended to have children in placement. On the other hand, parents with a less chronic history of mild to moderate maltreatment, who sought help voluntarily and were able to acknowledge the abuse as well as other problems, had a much greater potential for improvement. Their denial, projection, and misperceptions were perhaps less ingrained and accessible to therapeutic influence. These contrasting profiles indicated the importance of early therapeutic intervention with child-abusing families. The study also suggested that the amenability to treatment of many abusing parents progressively decreases with more and more punitively perceived hostile contacts with protective service caseworkers, the police, probation officers, and foster care personnel in the absence of a supportive and therapeutic environment.

The fact that patients who were provided with supplementary home visiting and service-oriented telephone advocacy fared better in treatment than patients receiving outpatient treatment alone demonstrated the value of outreach and advocacy as pivotal components of child-abuse intervention. This was consistent with Cohn's (1979) report of a higher rate of treatment success in clients receiving ancillary lay services in the form of parent-aide counseling and/or Parents Anonymous. The home visiting in the Downstate program was performed by either the primary therapists (social workers, social work students, psychologists) or student nurses, who acted as parent-aides.

17

Legal Issues in Child Maltreatment

Reporting Laws

In 1963, The Children's Bureau (1961) and the American Humane Association (1963) publicized model legislative guidelines to assist states in drafting laws which would encourage physicians to report cases of suspected child abuse. The impact was impressive. From 1964 to 1968, all fifty states, the District of Columbia, the Virgin Islands, and Guam enacted child-abuse reporting laws. Physicians are specifically designated as mandated reporters in most states, along with other professionals such as osteopaths, dentists, chiropractors, pharmacists, nurses, hospital administrators, religious healers, teachers, and social workers. All reporting laws provide immunity from criminal and civil liability for mandated reporters. The laws of most states include penalties for nonreporting.

Friends, relatives, and neighbors are also encouraged to report suspected cases of child abuse and neglect. These nonmandated reporters are not required to identify themselves. The agency legally designated to receive reports bears the prime responsibility for protecting children in the state. In twenty-three states the laws specify a single agency to receive all reports. In more than half the states mandated reporters may choose between two or more specified agencies. In the twenty-three states that require reporting to a single source, seventeen designate a child protective agency, five specify a law enforcement agency, and one reports to the juvenile court. The agency receiving reports of child abuse and neglect should be able to fulfill the following criteria: It should be able to handle reports twenty-four hours a day, seven days a week, and should be able to investigate reports within a day. It should also maintain a central register of reports at the local or state level. Several states have initiated statewide reporting systems which use one toll-free telephone number for reports from anywhere in the state. Certain states, such as Connecticut, New York, and Florida, require reports to be made to the local child protective agency, which must then report to the central register.

Reporting to child protective agencies is preferable to notifying a law enforcement agency because they are able to provide supportive and crisis-oriented social services which may prevent further abuse and strengthen family functioning. Reporting to the police, sheriff, or prosecuting attorney would be perceived as a punitive act by the parents, and would seldom lead to rehabilitative efforts. Child protective agencies are usually authorized to notify the appropriate district attorney in cases of abuse or neglect leading to the death of the child or accompanied by a felony.

The major objective of reporting laws is to increase case finding, which in itself does not solve the problem of child abuse. However without legal coercion, most of the maltreating families would not voluntarily seek help. The identification of larger numbers of abused and neglected children is of dubious importance if it is not followed by immediate investigation and remedial action.

The psychiatrist or mental health professional involved in the treatment of a family in which physical abuse or neglect takes place is required by law to report such maltreatment, as is any other professional. Reporting is also mandatory for any recurrence of abuse by parents who are receiving help for previous maltreatment. The reporting laws take precedence over the privileged doctor-patient relationship, and therefore constitute a breach of confidentiality. But when abuse takes place, the legal rights of the child immediately precede those of the parents. The potential negative therapeutic impact of the reporting laws can be minimized if the therapist clarifies his obligation to report abuse at the onset of any intervention with maltreating parents. The great strain that reporting abuse imposes on an ongoing therapeutic relationship requires the clinician to make the difficult distinction between physical abuse and physical punishment which constitutes an "acceptable" level of discipline.

Investigation

The child protective agency, generally located in the county or state department of social services, is usually authorized by law to investigate reported cases of abuse in order to determine the validity of the allegations. The investigation includes an intake process by a protective services caseworker, who tries to obtain information concerning the suspected maltreatment. The worker may contact neighbors, relatives, schools, and other agencies to obtain information about the family. He also checks the central register for any previous reports of maltreatment involving the child, his siblings, or the parents. All information collected about a family should be available to other agencies and professionals involved in the case.

If the investigation confirms the presence of maltreatment, the child may be protected in one of several ways. Depending on the severity of the case, the child can be hospitalized, can remain home under supervision of the child protective agency while the family is provided with supportive services, or can be placed in a shelter or foster home on an emergency basis. If the report of abuse or neglect cannot be verified, the case is closed and the report is expunged from the central register.

Parental Rights

The parent or any person alleged to have maltreated a child should be informed of his legal rights by the local authority. These usually include the right to receive written notice of one's record in the central register and of court orders and petitions filed, the right to consult legal counsel, the right to a court hearing prior to removal of the child, the right to refuse agency services unless mandated by a court, and the right to appeal child protective case determinations. The parents should also be protected from unauthorized disclosure of identifying information by limiting access to the records to the authorities designated in the state law.

Rights of the Child

All children alleged to be abused or neglected should be entitled to representation in all legal proceedings. Many states require that the court appoint a special guardian, or guardian ad litem, to protect the child's interest. The guardian ad litem, usually an attorney, is responsible to the court that appointed him. As the child's advocate, he insures that the court receives all relevant data. He also acts as an investigator, gathering relevant information about the causes, nature, and extent of the abuse or neglect inflicted on the child. He must ensure that the child's immediate and long-range interests are protected by the law, as a counterpart to the attorneys for the parents and protective agencies, who act as advocates for the parents and community, respectively.

The Judicial Process in the Juvenile or Family Court

Child protection proceedings are initiated when a petition alleging child abuse or neglect is filed. A *pretrial conference* may be held prior to any hearing, in order to examine the issues and determine which reports and evidence will be admissable. The judge and the attorneys for all parties evaluate all evidence, without subjecting the participants to the trauma of an adversary trial. The vast majority of cases are settled at the pretrial conference by some form of consent decree, in which the parent agrees to cooperate with the child protective agency.

If a case cannot be settled in a pretrial conference, an *adjudicatory hearing* is held. This is the "trial" stage of the proceedings, in which the charges of abuse and neglect are examined and argued. At the conclusion of the trial, the judge decides whether the allegations have been proven.

A *dispositional hearing* follows the adjudication. At this hearing, the agency managing the case, usually the local child protective agency, presents a case plan to the court and the parents. The plan usually stipulates conditions and arrangements designed to guarantee the child's protection, and a time schedule within which the plan is to be carried out. The dispositional order might require counseling, psychiatric treatment, or the provision of social services for the parents. If the child is placed outside the home, a schedule for visitation should be included in the case plan. Once the plan is agreed upon, the court should insure parental compliance by periodically reviewing the participation of the parents in the rehabilitative process.

At the periodic *review hearings,* the court should determine the level of progress made by the parents in complying with the dispositional order. The case plan may be modified as needed. Parents who fail to follow through with their commitments may be threatened with termination of parental rights.

If the child's health or safety is in danger, he can be removed from the home on an emergency basis by the court following the filing of a petition for *temporary custody* by the child protective service agency. Temporary custody of the child is usually awarded to the local social service agency for placement of the child in a foster home, home of a relative, or emergency shelter.

Termination of parental rights is a legal proceeding freeing the child from parental custody so that the child can be adopted by others without the parents' written consent. The legal grounds for termination differ from state to state, but most statutes include abandonment. Other indications are institutionalization of parents, reabuse, voluntary placement for over two years without visits by the parents, and refractoriness or repeated resistance to treatment.

Returning the Child to His Natural Parents After Placement Outside of the Home

Positive changes in the child-rearing climate must take place before the child can be reunited with his parents. First of all, the parents should be able to demonstrate impulse control adequate enough to allow them to utilize nonphysical forms of discipline. Other signs of improvement are a growing capacity to derive pleasure from the children, a cessation of unrealistic expectations of the children (role reversal), and some capacity for self-observation. Decreased social isolation and improved self-esteem of the parents would also reduce the likelihood of scapegoating and abuse. The capacity to utilize therapeutic intervention in a constructive manner should significantly improve parental functioning. Increased parental tolerance for the child's independence and expression of negative feelings should also be a prerequisite for the return of abused children to their parents. Final plans for the reunion should only be made after a gradually increasing schedule of parent visits outside of the home under supervision.

Testifying in Court

Various mental health and child-care professionals are called upon to testify in court as regular or expert witnesses in cases

of child abuse and neglect. Pediatricians are requested to provide medical testimony confirming the presence of abuse or
neglect. Psychiatrists are frequently asked to assess the presence and degree of psychiatric disorders in maltreating parents
which might seriously impair their child-rearing capacities.
Psychiatrists might also be able to predict the risk for abuse in a
given family, based on such factors as marital conflict, parental
impulsivity, external stress, and the availability of support systems. Child psychiatrists may be called upon to document the
adverse impact of abuse and neglect on the child's development and psychological functioning, and to recommend the
most suitable environment for the child's physical and emotional welfare. Social workers, nurses, psychiatrists, and other
members of a multidisciplinary treatment staff may be required
to describe the parent's motivation and response to therapeutic
intervention, and report on the current child-rearing climate in
the home.

Good court testimony requires a thorough knowledge of the
case, based on careful examination, evaluations, and treatment when applicable. Complete medical, evaluation, and
treatment records required by the court should be reviewed by
the witness. Prior to his court appearance, the witness should
have a definite idea about what is best for the child and family,
and be prepared to recommend this opinion to the court in a
clear and concise manner, avoiding the use of medical or
psychiatric jargon. All reports and recommendations should be
shared with the parents prior to the court appearance, and
they should be encouraged to attend the hearings. In cases
where the testimony may be viewed by the parents as against
their interest, one should avoid an accusatory or adversarial
tone, which could impair the parents' relationships with the
current or a future treatment facility.

18

Conclusions and
Recommendations

Child abuse and neglect, representing extreme forms of parental dysfunction, have reached epidemic proportions in this country. The underlying factors contributing to maltreatment are complex, and seem to be rooted in specific personality traits of the parents derived from their own adverse childhood experiences, special characteristics of the children which make them vulnerable to scapegoating, and a stressful and inadequate family environment which fails to meet basic emotional needs of its members. The poverty, unemployment, and violence rampant in our inner cities contribute to family disorganization. Caretaking patterns of socially isolated parents break down during times of stress when support systems are lacking. The typical childhood histories of physical abuse, neglect, and exploitation in the majority of maltreating parents, and the violent behavior of maltreated children, leave no doubt about the transmission of maltreatment from one generation to the next. This vicious cycle can be interrupted by vigorous multidisciplinary intervention, geared to alleviate the interacting problems of the parents, children, and environment.

The federal government has taken the lead in combating child abuse by appropriating millions for public awareness programs to increase the reporting of maltreatment, and by improving the quality of protective services through local grants. Regional demonstration projects, employing numerous treatment modalities, have been established through the National Center on Child Abuse and Neglect.

The body of knowledge in the area of maltreatment has increased tremendously during the past decade as a result of case studies, clinical investigation and research, and through the experiences of centers for treatment and training. Professionals from the fields of pediatrics, radiology, psychiatry, social work, nursing, child care, psychology, sociology, and law have made important contributions. Yet as far as meaningful intervention and service delivery are concerned, this field is in its infancy.

The current national focus on child maltreatment and the development of programs to strengthen family functioning offer a unique opportunity for adult and child psychiatrists, psychologists, and social workers to apply their expertise in this area. In a recent Department of Health, Education, and Welfare monograph based on site visits to various child-abuse and neglect programs throughout the country, Holmes (1977) identified child abuse as a major mental health problem and made specific recommendations concerning the role of mental health facilities in dealing with child maltreatment. She advocated the inclusion in each community mental health center of a child-abuse team composed of at least two child-abuse specialists, who could provide expertise in group and family therapy, in addition to individual treatment of adults and children. She also recommended that each center maintain a strong outreach component providing frequent home contact. Additional suggestions included the development of therapeutic programs for abused children, including day-care facilities for maltreated preschoolers. The child-abuse team would also provide training for mental health professionals and protective service workers.

At our hospital-based comprehensive multidisciplinary treatment program for abused children and their families in the Department of Psychiatry at the Downstate Medical Center, psychiatrists and other mental health professionals have participated in the following areas: individual and group psychotherapy and counseling of maltreating parents; psychotherapy and play therapy with maltreated children; family therapy; home visiting and crisis intervention; preventive intervention with high-risk mothers (teenagers, drug addicts, psychiatrically impaired, mothers of deviant children, etc.); evaluation of maltreated children and their families prior to admission to the treatment program. For outside agencies we have provided counseling of foster parents of maltreated children, and consultation with and training of personnel from protective service agencies, family court, foster care agencies, day-care centers, and elementary schools. Training of homemakers for placement with maltreating families and training of other psychiatrists, pediatricians, family-practice physicians, medical students, and social workers are included in the educational functions of our psychiatric child-abuse specialists.

Working with maltreated children offers psychoanalytically oriented psychiatrists an opportunity to test psychoanalytic and developmental theories concerning the impact of trauma and maltreatment on object relationships, identifications, self-esteem regulation, and control of aggression. Psychiatrists and mental health specialists can also make important contributions in the area of research. Pertinent areas of investigation include: the mother-child interaction in various types of maltreatment (abuse, neglect, failure to thrive, sexual abuse, etc.); the impact of maltreatment on the child at different stages of his development; longitudinal studies of high-risk and maltreating mothers and their children; studies of abusing fathers; environmental factors associated with maltreatment; and the effectiveness of various types of therapeutic intervention.

Psychiatrists should be taking a more active role in directing and coordinating multidisciplinary treatment programs for abusing families based in hospitals and community mental health centers, with components from the fields of pediatrics, nursing, and social work. These programs can often be self-supporting through the collection of third party payments. Mental health professionals could also be more involved in prevention of child abuse by organizing educational programs and acting as consultants on child rearing and child development to parents, young adults, and teenagers. These training activities could be carried out in schools, churches, and child-care centers, with an emphasis on early intervention, before maltreatment occurs. In the long run, crisis-oriented prevention and therapeutic intervention with maltreated children and their parents, focusing on strengthening parental functioning and maintaining the intactness of families, might be a more efficient, humane, and economical way of dealing with child abuse than the traditional punitive approach leading to the placement of the children and the dissolution of families. Through greater participation in improving service delivery to maltreating families, psychiatrists also have a unique opportunity in influencing public opinion and legislation toward the improvement of family life in our society.

At this point, I would like to make the following recommendations concerning the major changes that need to be implemented in the areas of child abuse and neglect:

1. An overall shift in policy emphasis from investigation to prevention and early intervention. Due to the overburdening of protective service investigators and the unavailability of treatment resources, many equivocal or less severe cases of maltreatment are closed because the family appears to be superficially intact and stable after a home visit. Yet we might expect that the next stressful event will trigger the violent interaction between the abuse-prone parent and the vulnerable-to-scapegoating child, unless change occurs through counseling, therapy, or crisis intervention in the home.

2. A shift in dispositional policy from temporary or long-term placement of the children to strengthening the family

unit by providing comprehensive mental health and social services, including home intervention by nurses, social workers, and paraprofessionals. Large sums of money could be saved by the reduction in the numbers of maltreated children requiring placement in foster homes and institutions. Furthermore, therapeutic programs can be financially self-sufficient through medicaid reimbursements.

3. Stationing of comprehensive treatment programs for maltreating families in hospitals, medical centers, and community mental health centers. Programs in hospitals and medical centers might operate as a special unit within the department of psychiatry. These programs might be designated as "family centers" rather than adopting a psychiatric label.

4. Each comprehensive treatment program would maintain liaison with the local child protective services unit, community organizations, schools, and the Family Court. Involvement with protective service units and the courts would facilitate ongoing case supervision and the procurement of psychological evaluations and psychiatric referrals. Each center would provide training and education of physicians, mental health workers, child-care professionals, and service-oriented groups in the community.

5. The provision of outpatient psychiatric treatment for maltreated children, consisting of play therapy, psychotherapy, and drug treatment when necessary.

6. The establishment of day-care facilities for preschool abused and neglected children as an integral component of the comprehensive treatment program. If feasible, crisis nurseries might be created to relieve the pressure of infant care for over-burdened families during the day. These day-care facilities also offer the staff a unique opportunity to observe the child's developmental progress on a daily basis, and witness the parent-child interaction.

7. The comprehensive treatment programs should provide for the rehabilitation of maltreating parents whose children are in placement and who are planning for their return.

8. The program should similarly be involved in counseling foster parents in those cases in which placement is necessary.

Foster parents are often unaware of the difficult problems and special needs of abused and neglected children.

9. A hospital-based treatment program should provide preventive services, consisting of counseling and supportive measures for high-risk mothers seen in the prenatal clinic and following childbirth. This group might include teenage mothers, drug-abusing mothers, mothers previously cited for abuse or neglect, and mothers with obvious physical or psychiatric problems. Mothers of premature or handicapped neonates, with congenital or physical abnormalities, require similar supportive intervention. Careful observation of mother-infant interaction during routine visits to well-baby clinics can detect abnormalities in maternal behavior which may signal impending maltreatment. The deployment of visiting nurses to assist high-risk mothers with infant care is indispensable for the primary prevention of child abuse and neglect.

References

Adelson, L. (1961). Slaughter of the innocent: a study of forty-six homicides in which the victims were children. *New England Journal of Medicine* 264:1345-1349.

Alfaro, J. D. (1977). Report on the relationship between child abuse and neglect and later socially deviant behavior. New York State Assembly Select Committee on Child Abuse. New York, New York.

Allen, H., Ten Bensel, R., and Raile, R. (1969). The battered child syndrome. *Minnesota Medicine* 52:155-156.

Altemeier, W. S., Vietze, P. M., Cherrod, K. B., Sandler, H. M., and O'Connor, S. (1979). Prediction of child maltreatment during pregnancy. *Journal of the American Academy of Child Psychiatry* 18:205-218.

The American Humane Association, Children's Division (1963). Denver.

Bakwin, H. (1949). Emotional deprivation in infants. *Journal of Pediatrics* 35:512-521.

Barbero, G. J. (1975). Failure to thrive. In *Maternal Attachment and Mothering Disorders*, ed. M. H. Klaus, T. Leger, and M. A. Trause, pp. 9-19. Johnson and Johnson Baby Products Co.

Barbero, G. J., Morris, M. G., and Redford, M. T. (1963). Malidentification of mother-baby-father relationships expressed in infant failure to thrive. *Child Welfare* 42:13-18.

Baron, M. A., Bejar, R. L., and Sheaff, P. J. (1970). Neurological manifestations of the battered child syndrome. *Pediatrics* 45:1003-1007.

Behar, L. B. (1977). The preschool behavior questionnaire. *Journal of Abnormal Child Psychology* 5:265-275.

Bender, L. (1947). Psychopathic behavior disorders in children. In *Handbook of Correctional Psychology*, ed. R. M. Lindner and R. V. Seliger. New York.

Bender, L. and Blau, A. (1937). The reaction of children to sexual relations with adults. *American Journal of Orthopsychiatry* 7:500-518.

Benedek, T. (1949). The psychosomatic implications of the primary unit: mother-child. *American Journal of Orthopsychiatry* 19:642-654.

————(1970). *Motherhood and Nurturing in Parenthood, Its Psychology and Psychopathology*, ed. E. J. Anthony and T. Benedek. Boston: Little and Brown.

————(1973). On the organization of the reproductive drive. In *Psychoanalytic Investigations*, pp. 412-445. New York: Quadrangle.

Bennie, E. H., and Sclare, A. B. (1969). The battered child syndrome. *American Journal of Psychiatry* 125:975-979.

Besharov, D. (1975). *The New York Times*, Nov. 30.

Bibring, G. L., Dwyer, T. F., Huntington, D. S., and Valenstein, A. F. (1971). A study of the psychological processes in pregnancy and of the earliest mother-child relationship. I. Some propositions and comments. *Psychoanalytic Study of the Child* 16:9-27.

Birch, H. G. (1972). Malnutrition, learning, and intelligence. *American Journal of Public Health* 62:773-784.

Birrell, R. G., and Birrell, J. H. W. (1968). The maltreatment syndrome in children: a hospital survey. *Medical Journal of Australia* 2:1023-1029.

Bowlby, J. (1951). Maternal care and mental health. *Bulletin of the World Health Organization* 31:355-533.

————(1958). The nature of the child's tie to his mother. *International Journal of Psycho-Analysis* 39:350-373.

Brazelton, T. B. (1973). Effect of maternal expectations on early infant behavior. *Early Child Development and Care* 2:259-273.

Bronfenbrenner, U. (1974). The origins of alienation. *Scientific American* 231:53-61.

Bullard, D. M., Glasser, H. H., Heagarty, M. C., and Pivchik, E. C. (1967). Failure to thrive in the neglected child. *American Journal of Orthopsychiatry* 37:680-690.

Burgess, R. L., and Conger, R. D. (1977). Family interaction patterns related to child abuse and neglect: some preliminary findings. *Child Abuse and Neglect: The International Journal* 1: 269-277.

————(1980). Family interaction in abusive, neglectful, and normal families. *Child Development* 49.

Burlingham, D., and Freud, A. (1944). *Infants Without Families.* London: Allen and Unwin.

Caffey, J. (1946). Multiple fractures in the long bones of infants suffering from chronic subdural hematoma. *American Journal of Roentgenology* 56:163-173.

————(1972). On the theory and practice of shaking infants: its potential residual effects of permanent brain damage and mental retardation. *American Journal of Diseases of Children* 124: 161-169.

Caldwell, B. M., Herder, J., and Kaplan, B. (1966). The inventory of home stimulation. Presented at meeting of American Psychological Association, New York, September.

Chapa, D. (1978). The relationship between child abuse/neglect and substance abuse contrasting Mexican-American and Anglo families. Interim Report of San Antonio Child Abuse Project Civic Organization. San Antonio, Texas.

Children's Bureau, U.S. Department of Health, Education, and Welfare (1961). Legislative guides to termination of parental rights and responsibilities and the adoption of children. Washington, D.C.: U.S. Government Printing Office.

Cohen, M., Raphling, D., and Green, P. (1966). Psychological aspects of the maltreatment syndrome of childhood. *Journal of Pediatrics* 62:279-284.

Cohler, B., Weiss, J., and Grunebaum, H. (1970). Child-care attitudes and emotional disturbance among mothers of young children. *Psychological Monograph* 82:3-47.

Cohn, A. H. (1979). An evaluation of three demonstration child abuse and neglect treatment programs. *Journal of the American Academy of Child Psychiatry* 18:283-291.

Coleman, R., and Provence, S. A. (1957). Developmental retardation (hospitalism) in infants living in families. *Pediatrics* 19: 285-292.

Condon, W. S., and Sander, L. W. (1974). Neonate movement is synchronized with adult speech: interactional participation and language acquisition. *Science* 183:99-101.

Conners, C. K. (1973). Psychological assessment of children with minimal brain dysfunction. *Annals of the New York Academy of Sciences* 205:283-302.

Dean, J. G., MacQueen, I. A. G., Mitchell, R. G., and Kempe, C. H. (1978). Health visitor's role in prediction of early childhood injuries and failure to thrive. *Child Abuse and Neglect: The International Journal* 2:1-17.

DeCastro, F. J., Rolfe, U. T., and Heppe, M. (1978). Child abuse: an operational longitudinal study. *Child Abuse and Neglect: The International Journal* 2:51-55.

DeFrancis, V. (1972). The status of child protective services. In *Helping the Battered Child and his Family*, ed. C. H. Kempe and R. H. Helfer. Philadelphia: Lippincott.

Dietrich, K. N., and Starr, R. H. Maternal stimulation of abused infants. Unpublished manuscript.

Duncan, G. M. (1958). Etiological factors – first degree murder. *Journal of the American Medical Association* 168:1755-1758.

Egeland, B., and Brunnquell, D. (1979). An at-risk approach to the study of child abuse: some preliminary findings. *Journal of the American Academy of Child Psychiatry* 18:219-235.

Elmer, E. (1960). Failure to thrive, role of the mother. *Pediatrics* 25:717-725.

———(1963). Identification of abused children. *Children* 10: 180-184.

———(1965). The fifty families study: summary of phase 1, neglected and abused children and their families. Pittsburgh: Children's Hospital.

———(1967). *Children in Jeopardy: A Study of Abused Minors and Their Families*. Pittsburgh: University of Pittsburgh Press.

———(1971). Child abuse: a symptom of family crisis. In *Crisis of Family Disorganization*, ed. E. Pavenstedt. New York: Behavioral Publications.

Elmer, E., and Gregg, C. S. (1967). Developmental characteristics of abused children. *Pediatrics* 40:596-602.

Erikson, E. H. (1950). *Childhood and Society.* New York: Norton.

Evans, S. L., Reinhard, J. B., and Succop, R. A. (1972). Failure to thrive: a study of 45 children and their families. *Journal of the American Academy of Child Psychiatry* 11:440-457.

Fanshel, D. (1976). Status changes of children in foster care: final results of the Columbia University longitudinal study. *Child Welfare* 55:143-171.

Faranoff, A., Kennell, J., and Klaus, M. (1972). Follow-up of low birth weight infants – the productive value of maternal visiting patterns. *Pediatrics* 49:287-290.

Feinstein, H., Paul, N., and Pattison, E. (1964). Group therapy for mothers with infanticide impulses. *American Journal of Psychiatry* 120:882-886.

Fischoff, J. (1973). Failure to thrive and maternal deprivation. In *Care of the High Risk Neonate,* ed. M. H. Klaus and A. A. Fenaroff. Philadelphia: Saunders.

Fischoff, J., Whitten, C. F., and Pettit, M. G. (1971). A psychiatric study of mothers of infants with growth failure secondary to maternal deprivation. *Journal of Pediatrics* 79:209-215.

Fontana, V. (1964). *The Maltreated Child.* Springfield, Illinois: Charles C Thomas.

Friedrich, W., and Boriskin, J. (1976). The role of the child in abuse: a review of the literature. *American Journal of Orthopsychiatry* 46:580-590.

Gaensbauer, T. J., and Sands, K. (1979). Distorted communications in abused/neglected infants and their potential impact on caretakers. *Journal of the American Academy of Child Psychiatry* 18:236-250.

Gagnon, J. (1965). Female child victims of sex offenses. *Social Problems* 13:176-192.

Gaines, R., Sandgrund, A., Green, A. H., and Power, E. (1978). Etiological factors in child maltreatment: a multivariate study of abusing and neglecting and normal mothers. *Journal of Abnormal Psychology* 87:531-540.

Galdston, R. (1965). Observations on children who have been physically abused and their parents. *American Journal of Psychiatry* 122:440-443.

———(1968). Dysfunctions of parenting: the battered child, the neglected child, the exploited child. In *Modern Perspectives of*

International Child Psychiatry, ed. J. G. Howells, pp. 571-586. Edinburgh: Oliver and Boyd.

———(1971). Violence begins at home. *Journal of the American Academy of Child Psychiatry* 10:336-350.

Garbarino, J. (1976). A preliminary study of some ecological correlates of child abuse: the impact of socioeconomic stress on mother. *Child Development* 47:178-185.

Gayford, J. J. (1975). Wife battering: a preliminary survey of 100 cases. *British Medical Journal* 1:194-197.

Geller, R. J. (1976). Abused wives: why do they stay? *Journal of Marriage and the Family* 38:659-668.

George, C., and Main, M. (1979). Social interactions of young abused children: approach, avoidance, and aggression. *Child Development* 50:306-318.

Giarretto, H. (1976). Humanistic treatment of father-daughter incest. In *Child Abuse and Neglect, the Family and the Community*, ed. R. E. Helfer and C. H. Kempe, pp. 143-158. Cambridge: Ballinger.

Gil, D. (1968). Incidence of child abuse and demographic characteristics of persons involved. In *The Battered Child*, ed. R. E. Helfer and C. H. Kempe. Chicago: University of Chicago Press.

———(1970). *Violence Against Children*. Cambridge: Harvard University Press.

———(1974). A holistic perspective on child abuse and its prevention. Paper presented at the Conference on Research on Child Abuse, National Institute of Child Health and Human Development.

Giovannoni, J. M., and Billingsley, A. (1970). Child neglect among the poor: a study of parental adequacy in families of three ethnic groups. *Child Welfare* 49:196-204.

Glaser, H. H., Heagarty, M. C., Bullard, D. M., Jr., and Pivchik, E. C. (1968). Physical and psychological development of children with early failure to thrive. *Journal of Pediatrics* 73:690-698.

Golden, M., Birns, B., Bridger, W., and Moss, A. (1971). Social-class differentiation in cognitive development of black preschool children. *Child Development* 42:37-45.

Goldfarb, W. (1945). Psychological privation in infancy and subsequent adjustment. *American Journal of Orthopsychiatry* 102: 247-255.

Gordon, A. H., and Jameson, J. C. (1979). Infant-mother attachment in patients with nonorganic failure to thrive syndrome. *Journal of the American Academy of Child Psychiatry* 18:251-259.

Gray, J., Cutler, C., Dean, J., and Kempe, C. H. (1976). Perinatal assessment of mother-baby interaction. In *Child Abuse and Neglect, the Family and the Community*, ed. R. E. Helfer and C. H. Kempe, pp. 377-392. Cambridge: Ballinger.

Green, A. H. (1968). Self-destructive behavior in physically abused schizophrenic children. *Archives of General Psychiatry* 19: 171-179.

————(1976). A psychodynamic approach to the study and treatment of child abusing parents. *Journal of the American Academy of Child Psychiatry* 15:414-429.

————(1978a). Psychopathology of abused children. *Journal of the American Academy of Child Psychiatry* 17:92-103.

————(1978b). Psychiatric treatment of abused children. *Journal of the American Academy of Child Psychiatry* 17:356-371.

————(1979). Child abusing fathers. *Journal of the American Academy of Child Psychiatry* 18:270-282.

Green, A. H., Gaines, R. W., and Sandgrund, A. (1974a). Child abuse: pathological syndrome of family interaction. *American Journal of Psychiatry* 131:882-886.

Green, A. H., Power, E., Gaines, R. W., and Steinbook, B. (1979). Factors associated with successful and unsuccessful intervention with child abusing families. Paper presented at the Annual Meeting of the American Academy of Child Psychiatry, Atlanta, Georgia, October 26.

Green, A. H., Sandgrund, A., Gaines, R. W., and Haberfeld, H. (1974b). Psychological sequelae of child abuse and neglect. *Proceedings of the American Psychiatric Association Annual Meeting*, p. 191 (abstract).

Green, A. H., Voeller, K., Gaines, R., and Kubie, J. (1978). Neurological impairment in maltreated children. Paper presented at the Annual Meeting of the American Academy of Child Psychiatry. San Diego, California, October.

Greenberg, M., and Morris, N. (1974). Engrossment: the newborn's impact upon the father. *American Journal of Orthopsychiatry* 44: 520-531.

Greenberg, M., Rosenberg, I., and Lind, J. (1973). First mothers rooming-in with their newborns: its impact on the mother. *American Journal of Orthopsychiatry* 43:783-788.

Grodner, B. (1977). A family systems approach to treatment of child abuse: etiology and intervention. *Child Abuse and Neglect: Issues on Innovation and Implementation*. DHEW Publication No.

(OHDS) 78-30148. Proceedings of the Second National Conference on Child Abuse and Neglect, April 17-20. Vol. 2,
pp. 331-336.

Helfer, R. E. (1975). The diagnostic process and treatment pro-
grams. DHEW Publication No. (OHD) 75-69. Washington, D.C.:
U.S. Department of Health, Education, and Welfare, National
Center for Child Abuse and Neglect.

Helfer, R. E. and Kempe, E. H., eds. (1968). *The Battered Child.*
Chicago: University of Chicago Press.

————(1976). *Child Abuse and Neglect: The Family and the
Community.* Cambridge: Ballinger.

Helfer, R., Schneider, C., and Hoffmeister, J. (1977). *Manual for
the use of the Michigan Screening Profile of Parenting.* East
Lansing, Michigan: Department of Human Development, Michigan State University.

Herrenkohl, E. C., and Herrenkohl, R. D. (1979). A comparison
of abused children and their nonabused siblings. *Journal of the
American Academy of Child Psychiatry* 18:260-269.

Hilberman, E., and Munson, K. (1977-1978). Sixty battered
women. *Victimology* 2:460-470.

Holmes, M. (1977). Child abuse and neglect programs: practice
and theory. DHEW Publication No. (ADM) 77-344. Washington,
D.C.: U.S. Department of Health, Education, and Welfare.

Holmes, T., and Rahe, R. (1967). The social readjustment rating
scale. *Journal of Psychosomatic Medicine* 11:213-218.

Holter, J., and Friedman, S. (1968). Principles of management in
child abuse cases. *American Journal of Orthopsychiatry* 38:
127-136.

Hufton, I. W., and Oates, R. K. (1977). Non-organic failure to
thrive: a long-term follow-up. *Pediatrics* 59:73-77.

Hunter, R. S., Kilstrom, N., Kraybill, E. N., and Loda, F. (1978).
Antecedents of child abuse and neglect in premature infants:
a prospective in a newborn intensive care unit. *Pediatrics* 61:
629-635.

Jaffe, A., Dynneson, L., and Ten Bensel, R. (1975). Sexual abuse
of children: an epidemiologic study. *American Journal of Diseases of Children* 129:689-692.

Jacobson, E. (1964). *The Self and the Object World.* New York:
International Universities Press.

Johnson, B., and Morse, H. (1968). Injured children and their
parents. *Children* 15:147-152.

Justice, B., and Duncan, D. F. (1976). Life crisis as a precursor to child abuse. *Public Health Reports* 91:110-115.

Justice, B., and Justice, R. (1976). *The Abusing Family.* New York: Human Sciences Press.

Kempe, C. H., and Helfer, R. E., eds. (1972). *Helping the Battered Child and his Family.* Philadelphia: Lippincott.

Kempe, C. H., Silverman, F., Steele, B., Droegemueller, W., and Silver, H. (1962). The battered child syndrome. *Journal of the American Medical Association* 181:17-24.

Kempe, R. (1976a). Arresting or freezing the developmental process. In *Child Abuse and Neglect, the Family and Community,* ed. R. E. Helfer and C. H. Kempe, pp. 64-73. Cambridge: Ballinger.

————(1976b). Play therapy, issues and commentary. National Child Protection Newsletter Vol. IV., No. 1, pp. 3-4. Department of Pediatrics, University of Colorado Medical Center.

Kennell, J. H., Jerauld, R., Wolfe, H., Chesler, D., Kreger, N. C., McAlpine, W., Steffa, M., and Klaus, M. H. (1974). Maternal behavior one year after early and extended post-partum contact. *Developmental Medicine and Child Neurology* 16:172-179.

Kennell, J. H., Slyter, H., and Klaus, M. H. (1970). The mourning response of parents to the death of a newborn infant. *New England Journal of Medicine* 283:344-349.

Kerr, G. R., Chamove, A. S., and Harlow, H. F. (1969). Environmental deprivation: its effect on the growth of infant monkeys. *Journal of Pediatrics* 75:833-837.

Kestenbaum, C. J., and Bird, H. R. (1978). A reliability study of the mental health assessment form for school-age children. *Journal of the American Academy of Child Psychiatry* 17:338-347.

Khan, M. (1963). The concept of cumulative trauma. *Psychoanalytic Study of the Child* 18:286-306.

Klaus, M. H., and Kennell, J. H. (1970). Mothers separated from their newborn infants. *Pediatric Clinics of North America* 17: 1015-1037.

————(1976). *Maternal-Infant Bonding.* St. Louis: C. V. Mosby.

Klein, M., and Stern, L. (1971). Low birth weight and the battered child syndrome. *American Journal of Diseases of Children* 122: 15-18.

Kotelchuck, M., and Newberger, E. H. (1977). Failure to thrive: a controlled study of familial characteristics. Unpublished Manuscript.

Kris, E. (1956). The recovery of childhood memories in psychoanalysis. *Psychoanalytic Study of the Child* 11:58-88.

Lang, R. (1972). *Birth Book*. Ben Lomond, Calif.: Genesis Press.

Leifer, A. D., Leiderman, P. H., Barnett, C. R., and Williams, J. A. (1972). Effects of mother-infant separation on maternal attachment behavior. *Child Development* 43:1203-1218.

Leonard, M., Rhymes, J., and Solnit, A. (1966). Failure to thrive in infants: a family problem. *American Journal of Diseases of Children* 111:600-612.

Levitt, J. M. (1977). A family systems approach to treatment of child abuse. *Child Abuse and Neglect: Issues on Innovation and Implementation*. DHEW Publication No. (OHDS) 78-30148. Proeedings of the Second National Conference on Child Abuse and Neglect, April 17-20, Vol. 2, pp. 321-330.

Light, R. J. (1973). Abused and neglected children in America: a study of alternative policies. *Harvard Educational Review* 43: 556-598.

Lind, J., Vuorenkoski, V., Wasz-Hackert, O. and Morris, N., eds. (1973). *Psychosomatic Medicine in Obstetrics and Gynaecology*. Basel: S. Karger.

Lourie, I. L. (1977). The phenomenon of the abused adolescent: a clinical study. *Victimology* 2:268-276.

Lynch, M. A. (1975). Ill-health and child abuse. *Lancet* 2:317-319.

Lynch, M. A., and Roberts, J. (1977). Predicting child abuse: signs of bonding failure in the maternity hospital. *British Medical Journal* 1:624-626.

Lystad, M. (1975). Violence at home: a review of the literature. *American Journal of Orthopsychiatry* 45:328-345.

Mahler, M. S. (1968). *On Human Symbiosis and the Vicissitudes of Individuation. Vol. 1: Infantile Psychosis*. New York: International Universities Press.

Malone, C. A. (1967). Developmental deviations considered in the light of environmental forces. In *The Drifters: Children of Disorganized Lower-Class Families*, ed. E. Pavenstedt, pp. 125-161. Boston: Little, Brown.

———(1979). Child psychiatry and family therapy. *Journal of the American Academy of Child Psychiatry* 18:4-21.

Marans, A. E., and Lourie, R. (1967). Hypotheses regarding the effects of child-rearing patterns on the disadvantaged child. In *Disadvantaged Child*, ed. J. Hellmuth, pp. 19-41. New York: Brunner/Mazel.

Martin, H. P. (1972). The child and his development. In *Helping the Battered Child and His Family*, ed. C. H. Kempe and R. E. Helfer. Philadelphia: Lippincott.

Martin, H. P., ed. (1976). *The Abused Child, A Multidisciplinary Approach to Developmental Issues and Treatment.* Cambridge: Ballinger.

Martin, H. P., and Beezley, P. (1976). Personality of abused children. In *The Abused Child*, ed. H. P. Martin, pp. 105-111. Cambridge: Ballinger.

———(1977). Behavioral observations of abused children. *Developmental Medicine in Child Neurology* 19:373-387.

Martin, H. P., Beezley, P., Conway, E. F., and Kempe, C. H. (1974). The development of abused children. *Advances in Pediatrics* 21:25-73.

McBryde, A. (1951). Compulsory rooming-in in the ward and private newborn service at Duke Hospital. *Journal of the American Medical Association* 145:625-628.

Melnick, B., and Hurley, J. (1969). Distinctive personality attributes of child abusing mothers. *Journal of Consulting and Clinical Psychology* 33:746-749.

Merrill, E. (1962). Physical abuse of children: an agency study. In *Protecting the Battered Child*, ed. V. DeFrancis. Denver: American Humane Association.

Milowe, I. D., and Lourie, R. S. (1964). The child's role in the battered child syndrome. *Journal of Pediatrics* 65:1079-1081.

Mirandy, J. (1976). Preschool for abused children. In *The Abused Child: A Multidisciplinary Approach to Developmental Issues and Treatment*, ed. H. P. Martin, pp. 215-224. Cambridge: Ballinger.

Mohr, J. (1962). The pedophilias: their clinical, social, and legal implications. *Canadian Psychiatric Association* 7:255-260.

Morris, M., and Gould, R. (1963). Role reversal: a necessary concept in dealing with the battered child syndrome. *American Journal of Orthopsychiatry* 33:298-299.

Morse, W., Sahler, O. J., and Friedman, S. B. (1970). A three-year follow-up study of abused and neglected children. *American Journal of Diseases of Children* 120:439-446.

Nagi, S. (1975). Child abuse and neglect programs: a national overview. *Children Today.* DHEW publication 75-14.

New York City Central Registry for Child Abuse (1977).

Ounsted, C., Oppenheimer, R., and Lindsay, J. (1974). Aspects of bonding failure: the psychopathology and psychotherapeutic treatment of families of battered children. *Developmental Medicine and Child Neurology* 16:446-456.

Oviatt, B. (1972). After child abuse reporting legislation – what? In *Helping the Battered Child and His Family*, ed. C. H. Kempe and R. E. Helfer. Philadelphia: Lippincott.

Parke, R. (1974). Father-infant interaction. In *Maternal Attachment and Mothering Disorders: a Round Table*, ed. M. H. Klaus, T. Leger, and M. A. Trause. Sausalito: Johnson and Johnson Co.

Paulson, M., and Blake, P. (1969). The physically abused child: a focus on prevention. *Child Welfare* 48:86-95.

Pavenstedt, E., ed. (1967). *The Drifters – Children of Disorganized Lower-class Families*. Boston: Little, Brown.

Peters, J. J. (1976). Children who were victims of sexual assault and the psychology of offenders. *American Journal of Psychotherapy* 30:398-412.

Polansky, N. A., DeSaix, C., Wing, M., and Patton, J. D. (1968). Child neglect in a rural community. *Social Casework*, Oct., pp. 467-474.

Pollitt, E., and Eichler, A. (1976). Behavioral disturbance among failure-to-thrive children. *American Journal of Diseases of Children* 130:24-29.

Pollitt, E., Eichler, A. W., and Chan, C. (1975). Psychosocial development and behavior of mothers of failure-to-thrive children. *American Journal of Orthopsychiatry* 45:525-537.

Pollock, C., and Steele, B. (1972). A therapeutic approach to parents. In *Helping the Battered Child and His Family*, ed. C. H. Kempe and R. E. Helfer. Philadelphia: Lippincott.

Prugh, D. G., and Harlow, R. G. (1962). "Masked deprivation" in infants and young children. In *Deprivation of Maternal Care: A Reassessment of its Effects*. Geneva: World Health Organization.

Rascovsky, M., and Rascovsky, A. (1950). On consummated incest. *International Journal of Psycho-Analysis* 31:42-47.

Reid, J. B., and Taplin, P. S. (1977). A social interactional approach to the treatment of abusive children. Unpublished manuscript.

Richman, N., and Graham, P. J. (1971). A behavioral screening questionnaire for use with three-year-old children: preliminary findings. *Journal of Child Psychology and Psychiatry* 12:5-33.

Riley, R. L., Landwirth, J., Kaplan, S. A., and Collipp, P. J. (1968). Failure to thrive: an analysis of 83 cases. *California Medicine* 108:32-38.

Rosenfeld, A. et al. (1977). Incest and sexual abuse of children. *Journal of the American Academy of Child Psychiatry* 16:32-339.

Rounsaville, B. J. (1978). Battered wives: barriers to identification and treatment. *American Journal of Orthopsychiatry* 48: 487-494.

Rubin, R. (1963). Maternal touch. *Nursing Outlook* 11:828-831.

Rutter, M. (1972). Maternal deprivation reconsidered. *Journal of Psychosomatic Research* 16:241-250.

Sabbeth, J. (1969). The suicidal adolescent. *Journal of the American Academy of Child Psychiatry* 8:272-286.

Sandgrund, A., Gaines, R., and Green, A. H. (1974). Child abuse and mental retardation: a problem of cause and effect. *American Journal of Mental Deficiency* 79:327-330.

Satten, J., Menninger, K., Rosen, I., and Mayman, M. (1960). Murder without apparent motive: a study in personality disorganization. *American Journal of Psychiatry* 117:48-53.

Schneider, C., Helfer, R., and Pollock, C. (1972). The predictive questionnaire: preliminary report. In *Helping the Battered Child and His Family*, ed. C. H. Kempe and R. E. Helfer. Philadelphia: Lippincott.

Scott, P. D. (1974). Battered wives. *British Journal of Psychiatry* 125:433-441.

———(1978). The psychiatrist's viewpoint. In *The Maltreatment of Children*, ed. S. M. Smith, pp. 175-204. Baltimore: University Park Press.

Scrimshaw, M. S., and Gordon, J. E. (1968). *Malnutrition, Learning, and Behavior*. Cambridge: M.I.T. Press.

Serrano, A. C., Zuelzer, M. B., Howe, D. D., and Reposa, R. E. (1979). Ecology of abusive and nonabusive families. *Journal of the American Academy of Child Psychiatry* 18:67-75.

Sgroi, S. (1977). Kids with clap: gonorrhea as an indicator of child sexual assault. *Victimology* 2:251-267.

Silver, L. (1968). The psychological aspects of the battered child and his parents. *Clinical Proceedings of The Children's Hospital in the District of Columbia* 24:355-364.

Silverman, F. N. (1953). The roentgen manifestations of unrecognized skeletal trauma in infants. *American Journal of Roentgenology* 69:413-427.

Simons, B., Downs, E., Hurster, M., and Archer, M. (1966). Child abuse. *New York State Journal of Medicine* 66:2783-2788.

Smith, C. A., and Hanson, R. (1974). 134 battered children: a medical and psychological study. *British Medical Journal* 14: 666-670.

Smith, S. M., Hanson, R., and Noble, S. (1973). Parents of battered babies: a controlled study. *British Medical Journal* 4: 388-391.

Spinetta, J., and Rigler, D. (1972). The child abusing parent: a psychological review. *Psychological Bulletin* 77:296-304.

Spitz, R. A. (1945). Hospitalism: an inquiry into the genesis of psychiatric conditions of early childhood. *Psychoanalytic Study of the Child* 1:53-74.

Starr, R. H., Ceresnie, S. J., and Steinlanf (1978). Social and psychological characteristics of abusive mothers. Paper presented at the annual meeting of the Eastern Psychological Association, Washington, D.C., May, 1978.

Steele, B. (1970). Parental abuse of infants and small children. In *Parenthood: Its Psychology and Psychopathology*, ed. E. Anthony and T. Benedek. Boston: Little, Brown.

———(1975). Working with abusive parents from a psychiatric point of view. DHEW Publication No. (OHD) 75-70. National Center on Child Abuse and Neglect.

Steele, B., and Pollock, C. A. (1968). A psychiatric study of parents who abuse infants and small children. In *The Battered Child*, ed. R. E. Helfer and C. H. Kempe. Chicago: University of Chicago Press.

Steinmetz, S. K. (1978). Wife beating: a critique and reformulation of existing theory. *Bulletin of the American Academy of Psychiatry and the Law* 6:322-334.

Summit, R., and Kryso, J. (1978). Sexual abuse of children: a clinical spectrum. *American Journal of Orthopsychiatry* 48: 237-251.

Swanson, D. W. (1968). Adult sexual abuse of children. *Diseases of the Nervous System* 29:677-683.

Talbot, N. B., Sobel, E. H., Burke, B. S., Lindemann, E., and Kaufman, S. B. (1947). Dwarfism in healthy children: its possible relation to emotional, nutritional and endocrine disturbances. *New England Journal of Medicine* 236:783-793.

Tanay, E., (1969). Psychiatric study of homicide. *American Journal of Psychiatry* 125:1252-1258.

Terman, L. M., and Merrill, M. A. (1937). *Measuring Intelligence: A Guide to the Administration of the New Revised Stanford-Binet Tests*. Boston: Houghton-Mifflin.

Terr, L. (1970). A family study of child abuse. *American Journal of Psychiatry* 127:665-671.

Wahl, C. (1960). The psychodynamics of consummated maternal incest. *Archives of General Psychiatry* 3:188-193.

Walker, L. E. (1977-1978). Battered women and learned helplessness. *Victimology* 2:525-534.

Weinberg, S. (1955). *Incest Behavior*. New York: Citadel.

Whitten, C. F., Pittit, M. G., and Fischoff, J. (1969). Evidence that growth failure from maternal deprivation is secondary to undereating. *Journal of the American Medical Association* 209: 1675-1682.

Wolff, G., and Money, J. (1973). Relationship between sleep and growth in patients with reversible somatotropin deficiency (psychosocial dwarfism). *Psychological Medicine* 3:18-27.

Wolock, I., and Horowitz, B. (1977). Factors relating to levels of child care among families receiving public assistance in New Jersey. First report. Grant No. 90-c-418, National Center on Child Abuse and Neglect, Office of Child Development, Department of Health, Education, and Welfare.

Wooley, P., and Evans, W. (1955). Significance of skeletal lesions in infants resembling those of traumatic origin. *Journal of the American Medical Association* 158:539-543.

Yorukoglu, A., and Kemph, J. P. (1966). Children not severely damaged by incest with a parent. *Journal of the American Academy of Child Psychiatry* 5:111-124.

Young, L. (1964). *Wednesday's Children: A Study of Child Neglect and Abuse*. New York: McGraw-Hill.

Zalba, S. (1966). The abused child I. *Social Work* 11:3-16.

Index